# Multihulls Offshore

*By the same author*
*OCEAN SAILING*

# Multihulls Offshore

# Rob James

Dodd, Mead & Company
New York

First published in the United States in 1984

Copyright © 1983 by Robert James
Line drawings by Ray Harvey B.Sc., C.Eng., MRINA

Published by Dodd, Mead & Company, Inc.
79 Madison Avenue, New York, N.Y. 10016

First Edition

Printed in Hong Kong

Library of Congress Catalog Card Number: 83-072344

ISBN: 0-396-08283-1

## Publisher's note

In the middle of March 1983, Rob and Naomi brought me the corrected proofs of the text of this book. Rob spent most of the day checking the accuracy of the line drawings: he made a few changes and added a new sail plan. Over lunch he talked of his plans for the next three years: the race from France round Bermuda and back, the two-handed race from England to southern Portugal, both of those in *Colt Cars GB*; then a major project to build a maxi ocean racer for the 1985–86 race around the world. meanwhile Naomi was expecting their first child in about three weeks.

Just five days later on Sunday 20th March, Rob slipped and fell into the water off the deck of *Colt Cars GB*, while stowing the mainsail. With four companions he had sailed the trimaran in moderate weather from Cowes to Salcombe for work to be done on the yacht. It was before dawn off Salcombe entrance when the accident happened. Efforts to recover him from the icy sea failed, despite the bravery of Jeffery Houlgrave, who jumped in and himself had to be treated for hypothermia. Rob was eventually picked up by helicopter, but it was too late.

The contents of this book are exactly as written and revised by Rob and I am thankful that we can pass them on to all sailing men and women.

One item he would have written later is a paragraph of acknowledgements. On his behalf I would like to thank all those people who supplied him with information that is here. They include the designers and builders of his various boats, the firm of *Colt Cars* and his previous sponsors, the photographers and the technical illustrator whose names are given below (but apologies to any that we have missed out in the circumstances), fellow crewmen and competitors and organizing clubs, especially the Royal Western Yacht Club of England. Special gratitude goes to members of his family and, of course, Naomi, who assisted at all stages of the book.

*Peter Johnson*

## Line drawings by Ray Harvey B.Sc; C.Eng; MRINA

## Photographic Credits

Gilbert le Cossec, 186, 189, 196, 223:  Dupes Colour Ltd, 119, 120, 232:  Peter Dunn, 157:  Eric Guillemot, 51:  Guy Gurney, 73:  Rob James, 208:  William Payne, 113:  J. H. Peterson, 91:  Patrick Roach, 109, 122, 123, 124, 125, 126, 127, 168, 172b, 190, 216, 241, 242, 265:  B. Rubinstein, 49:  Chris West, 100, 107, 108:  Yachting Monthly, 237, 279.

*Rob James*
He is holding the Val Trophy for beating three other Val trimarans in 1980 (see Chapter 3).

# Contents

# *Introduction*

The development of the modern multihull has been held back over the years by the extreme conservatism of boat builders and yachtsmen. The first multihull designer in the West was Sir William Petty. Like many contemporary multihull designers it was his hobby and obsession and, as such, despite several successful and fast voyages, it earned his catamarans only ridicule. The diary of Samuel Pepys records the following summary of Petty's 30-ton catamaran 'experiment' made by the Compe de Commings in 1664: 'It really is the most ridiculous and useless machine that the spirit of man could conceive; the doctor who invented it should return to his original profession and leave shipbuilding to those who are qualified'.

Over 300 years later the same comments are still made. The American yacht designer Nathanael Herreshoff must have come very close to becoming a multihull man in 1876 when he designed the first catamaran specifically for racing. His 24 footer easily won the New York Yacht Club's centennial regatta and was immediately banned – with all other multihull craft. This attitude effectively stifled multihull development for over 50 years.

The first transocean voyage by a multihull was the result of an accident. Eric de Bishop was wrecked on the coast of Hawaii in 1936 and as his monohulled vessel was a total loss he had to devise some means of getting back to Europe. Heavily influenced by the models of the old Polynesian double canoes, he built his 45ft junk-rigged catamaran, *Kaimilea*, in which he and a friend sailed from Hawaii to France in a little over a year – for the time a reasonably quick passage.

As there were no lightweight building materials available at that time all catamarans were heavy. This changed with World War II: the rapid development of marine plywood and waterproof glues provided a strong, light medium, ideal for multihull construction. The first catamaran to achieve a high sail power-to-weight ratio – what multihull sailing is all about – was *Manu Kai*, designed by a Mr Brown and built in 1946. She is reputed to have weighed only 3000lbs on a length of 40ft – thereby probably being the first of the multihulls whose designers persistently claim that their boats are lighter than they really are! However, *Manu Kai* was a great success; she was undoubtedly fast and soon began to influence the development of future catamarans.

Where, one may ask, were the trimarans up to this time? Well, up until World War II there were none. Victor Tchetchet, a Russian living in the USA, did not create the name until 1946. Tchetchet was building and sailing 24ft trimarans with great success but for some reason did not build anything bigger. It took a brave Frenchman to try the first ocean voyage in a trimaran, which was basically a monohull with small outriggers. In 1946 M. Sadrin became the first to attempt successfully a North Atlantic crossing in a multihull. By all accounts it was an uncomfortable vessel to sail and convinced Sadrin that the day of the ocean-going trimaran had not yet arrived. His attitude was obviously not universal: soon Arthur Piver began production of ocean-going trimarans which were reasonably fast and seaworthy.

Apart from the dinghy-sized range of craft, both catamarans and trimarans were developing as cruising yachts and in general were dangerously heavy. The English yachtsman Derek Kelsall should be given credit for changing this trend. In the 1964 Observer Single-handed Transatlantic Race (OSTAR) he sailed a Piver-designed trimaran called *Folatre*, completing the east–west crossing in 35 days. As a result he became a trimaran designer. His new concept included increasing the overall beam, increasing the size of the floats and discarding Piver's V-section hulls. Instead of the latter he went for the less drag U-section and relied on a large centreboard to combat leeway. The result was *Toria*, in which he won the 1966 Round Britain Race, completing the course in the very quick time of 11 days.

Meanwhile, in the USA, the designer Dick Newick was also breaking away from the Piver theme, building wider, lighter boats, and incorporating U-shaped hulls. Both Newick and Kelsall played significant roles in the staggeringly rapid development that was now taking place. This was fostered by the introduction of open racing. The Royal Ocean Racing Club had always maintained that it would never allow multihulls in its races – and indeed it never has. But the introduction of the OSTAR in 1960 (held every 4 years) and the two-handed Round Britain Race in 1966 provided excellent opportunities for designers to be as adventurous as they liked. Any boats were allowed to enter these races with no restrictions on size or type, provided they passed a safety scrutiny. In the 1964 OSTAR two cruising catamarans and one cruising trimaran completed the course successfully. Four years later a formidable array of multihulls was entered, with very mixed results. Extraordinarily, the most successful achieved third place – the Newick-designed proa (two-thirds of a trimaran) called *Cheers*, sailed by Tom Follett; she was the first of the very few successful transatlantic racing proas. The fastest yacht in the fleet was Eric Tabarly's 70ft all-out racing trimaran, *Pen Duick IV*. Unfortunately the Allegre-designed yacht was in collision shortly after the start of the race and Tabarly was forced to retire. The first catamaran finished in fifth place. Unhappily the race attracted a lot of amateur-designed, amateur-built and amateur-sailed multihulls, many of which foundered, causing unwanted and unwarranted adverse publicity of multihulls in general.

Multihull racing became more popular in the 1960s and early 70s when several inshore races were staged. None-the-less, it remained dependent on the marathon offshore events for further development. This stimulation was mainly due to sponsored entries being allowed in the much publicized OSTARs and round Britain races. 'Win at any cost' does wonders for development! The 1972 OSTAR was almost a clean sweep for multihulls. The winner was the four-year-old *Pen Duick IV*, sailed by Alain Colas, in a time of 20 days 13 hours. Three of the first five yachts were trimarans, all of them rigged as ketches. The multihull had come of age. Development was still advancing but in a less noticeable, more subtle way. Rigs continued to lag behind as the highly efficient windward sloop rigs were mistakenly believed to be too big to handle; the persevering attitude that 'a little bit of sailing free wouldn't hurt' (horrors!) didn't help either. Catamarans had been left behind, both on the drawing board and on the water, by their three-hulled cousins, mainly because of the immense difficulty in engineering a structure light enough and yet strong enough to support a mast stepped on thin air.

The 1974 Round Britain Race brought together an amazing collection of trimarans and one enormous catamaran. In an indirect way the results of this race influenced the direction of my own initiation into multihulls. Chay Blyth, for whom I was working, was planning a monster multihull for 1976 but was undecided on the tri/cat dilemma. When Mike McMullen finished the race in his 46ft trimaran *Three Cheers* only a very short distance behind Robin Knox-Johnston's 70ft cat, *British Oxygen*, Chay decided to go for a trimaran. His decision was vindicated when the cat broke up in 1976. (It was not until 1981 that ocean-racing catamarans came back into the prize list.)

And so as a result of sailing Chay's first trimaran, *Great Britain III*, I became very interested in, but not necessarily hooked on, the power and relatively effortless speeds of these great machines.

Part 1 of this book tells the stories of the multihulls I have raced, *Great Britain III* and *Great Britain IV* (with Chay), *Boatfile* (alone), *Brittany Ferries* (with Chay) and *Colt Cars GB* (with my wife, Naomi). It recounts the preparation, the hard sailing, the disappointments and, ultimately, the joy of achieving good race results.

Part 2 covers what I have learnt from the boats and the many miles I have sailed in them.

# PART I

# 1

## *Great Britain III*

Chay Blyth had an ambition to win the 1976 Observer Single-handed Transatlantic Race. As there were no restrictions as to size or type of yacht, and as multihulls had acquitted themselves so well in the 1972 OSTAR, the decision was made to go for more than one hull.

At the time, I was sailing Chay's yachts *British Steel* and *Great Britain II* (both large monohulls) on regular trips across the English Channel carrying charter guests – or 'supersailers' as we called them. The new vessel was to be built over the winter of 1974–5 to be ready for a newly announced 1975–6 Multihull Atlantic Race, and then for the OSTAR the following year. Jack Hayward, who had sponsored Chay with *Great Britain II* in the previous Whitbread Round the World Race, again put the money up for the new yacht, *Great Britain III*. The dilemma was, should she be a catamaran or a trimaran? Both types had been entered in the 1974 Round Britain Race so a close appraisal of the relative performances of each would, we hoped, answer the question.

The interesting catamaran to watch was Robin Knox-Johnston's 70ft *British Oxygen* designed by MacAlpine-Downie. This large creature had two symmetrical hulls measuring approximately 70ft LOA by 5ft beam connected by four aluminium cross beams that were nothing more than mast sections. The sloop rig was stepped on one of these beams and herin lay one of the difficulties of large catamarans at that stage of development. The crossbeams could not take the enormous compression loads of the mast without moving. To try and counteract this the cap-shrouds came down to the beam and did not make full use of the width of the boat (see Part 2, Chapter 10). Even so, *British Oxygen* was referred to as a flexible structure. Ranged against her were several trimarans (and monohulls), the two most notable being Alain Colas's *Pen Duick IV/Manureva*, and Mike McMullen's *Three Cheers*.

*Pen Duick IV* had won the 1972 OSTAR in the good time of 20 days, beating, among others, the 128ft monohull *Vendredi 13* and, significantly, the Newick-designed 46ft *Three Cheers* then sailed by Tom Follett. As a 'lap of honour' Colas sailed *Pen Duick IV*, renamed *Manureva*, single-handed round the world stopping only at Sydney – a remarkable voyage which proved that a racing trimaran could be made sufficiently seaworthy, admittedly in the right hands, to survive a voyage in the Roaring Forties. While Colas was attempting his circumnavigation the first round the world race for monohulls had got underway. It so happened that I, as one of the crew of *Second Life* (71ft), had the pleasure of listening to Colas on the HF radio regularly relaying the weather forecast to the rest of the fleet. He was cruising single-handed, we were racing fully crewed; each day from Sydney to Cape Horn his mileage was the same as ours and it was he who received the forecasts and had time to pass them on – a remarkable achievement for man and boat.

*Three Cheers* had finished fifth in the OSTAR '72, seven days behind Colas, which left Tom Follett feeling very unhappy about the amount of calm weather he had encountered. He felt his trimaran had much greater potential. Looking back, *Three Cheers* was certainly the most advanced multihull of her day with a displacement of only 7000lbs, a maximum sail area of 1420 sq ft and a good beam of 27ft. Mike McMullen also recognized the boat's potential: he brought it back to England for the Round Britain Race.

The Round Britain Race takes place in July every four years and has become one of the 'open' classic events. The course consists of five legs, and starts and finishes in Plymouth, with a compulsory 48-hour pit stop for each competitor in Crosshaven (Cork, Ireland), Barra (Outer Hebrides), Lerwick (Shetlands) and Lowestoft (East Anglia). *Manureva* proved to be disappointingly slow, possibly owing to the extra weight of her round-the-world refit, and *Three Cheers* was easily able to turn the tables on her. The race developed into a tussle between *Three Cheers* and *British Oxygen*. From an observer's point of view, the two boats appeared to be similar in speed. *B.O.* gained almost 12 hours over her rival on the penultimate leg by superior tactics, and possibly luck, and hence started the last leg with a large lead. *Three Cheers* almost closed the gap and was only a short distance behind at the finish. The decision was made: if a 46ft trimaran could almost beat a 70ft catamaran, then *Great Britain III* would be a tri.

Derek Kelsall was chosen as the designer. He drew a boat measuring 80ft LOA with a 38ft beam which weighed in at about 13 tons. She was to be massively sloop rigged with several innovative ideas – some of which were excellent, and some of which were not, as will be seen. Trident Marine at Porchester, Fareham, was chosen to build the main hull and fit the boat together, while Kelsall produced the crossbeams and the two floats. Construction, using Aerex foam core and conventional glass skins (see Part 2, Chapter 9), started in the autumn. As Chay wanted to retain my services as a yacht charter skipper for the next season, he put me in the yard as his representative. It would be wrong to claim that I contributed much to the project but I was at least able quietly to observe progress.

From the point of view of design there were several aspects worthy of note. The two crossbeams were box sections made up of extrusions of carbon fibre. These extrusions were long battens approximately ¼in by 1in cross section laid along the length of the beam and glassed in. This was the first use of carbon fibre in multihull crossbeam construction. When the beams were fitted to the boat their leading edges were faired in with a light glass structure which proved to be both the wrong shape (see Part 2, Chapter 6) and not strong enough. Consequently they had to be strengthened and made heavier. The centreboard was interesting insofar as it was exactly that – a pivoting centreboard, and not a daggerboard, offset to port of the centre-line adjacent to the mast. As it lifted it swung backwards and up into an internal box, the theory being that it would swing upwards if struck by an underwater object, such as the seabed. In fact, the severe turbulence in the centreboard box when the board was down caused such a problem that it was eventually replaced by a daggerboard. (Incidentally, as can be seen in Part 2, Chapter 6), a centreboard is wrong for a multihull. As it is being raised the centre of lateral resistance moves aft – ideal for monohulls and sailboards but not for multis. They need the centre of resistance to come forward as the board is raised in heavier winds or in reaching conditions in order to counteract the lee helm created by the boat's tendency to trip around the lee float.) The rudder was also pivoting on an upside down A-frame on the transom. A friction device held it down, but it developed the annoying trait of occasionally popping up at speeds when a rudder is most useful.

The boat was completed inside the shed at Trident Marine and launched by dismantling the end of the building, and sliding her out into Fareham Creek. Final fitting-out and rigging was done alongside Wicormarine's pier in the spring of 1975. In some ways the rig was ahead of its time. The twin spreader masthead rig was stayed down to the main hull in conventional monohull fashion and the standing rigging was made of Parafil. Parafil consists of filaments of Kevlar laid parallel inside a black plastic outer sheath. One of its advantages is lightness, therefore achieving a considerable reduction in the overall weight of the standing rigging. Another advantage was the ease with which the terminals could be fitted to the ends of the stays. Its strength is equivalent to stainless wire for a given diameter and the stretch is said to be similar, although to me it appeared more. Unfortunately, the only factor that made it impractical in the long term was its susceptibility to chafe.

No use was made of the beam of the boat when it came to spinnaker work (see Part 2, Chapter 12). Instead the rig was fitted with twin spinnaker poles and all the heavy hoists and other handling gear that this entails. The mainsail was fully battened and the headsails were of the jib top/staysail (cutter rig) configuration; jib attachment was by hanks; an hydraulic backstay did its best to tension the rigging; there was no vang and only a short main track, making mainsail control very awkward. Jib sheeting was done with the help of Lewmar coffee grinders.

In order to manoeuvre this floating double tennis court an ingenious system of hydraulic outdrives was conceived. A 120-horse-power diesel was fitted under the cockpit floor, which in turn would power hydraulic outdrives mounted on the aft side of the forward beam to port, and aft beam to starboard. The outdrives were to be controllable both in power and direction – an ambitious scheme which got no further than the fitting of the diesel. This made it necessary to sail in and out of harbours and anchorages or, if it was flat calm, to use an inflatable dinghy with a 25-horse-power outboard as a tug. The latter solution was surprisingly effective if the dinghy was lashed firmly to the main hull just behind the aft crossbeam. Owing to the flare in the topsides with a beam difference of 8 to 16ft from water-line to deck, *GB III* had plenty of space below. The saloon was fitted out with teak and boasted a large galley and nav area. With two heads and nine to ten berths she was a far cry from the spartan racing multihulls of today.

After an emotional naming ceremony performed by Dame Vera Lynn, Chay was able to start sailing trials. Unfortunately I missed these as I was away yet again on the charter circuit with *Great Britain II*, but news of some of the early voyages did reach my ears. By all accounts she was a very big boat to sail, with very high loads on all the gear and a fast turn of speed. The beam fairings cracked and were strengthened, and the centreboard gave trouble from the very beginning. As the board was buoyant it had to be winched down and, of course, very carefully controlled on raising. During one of the early sails a

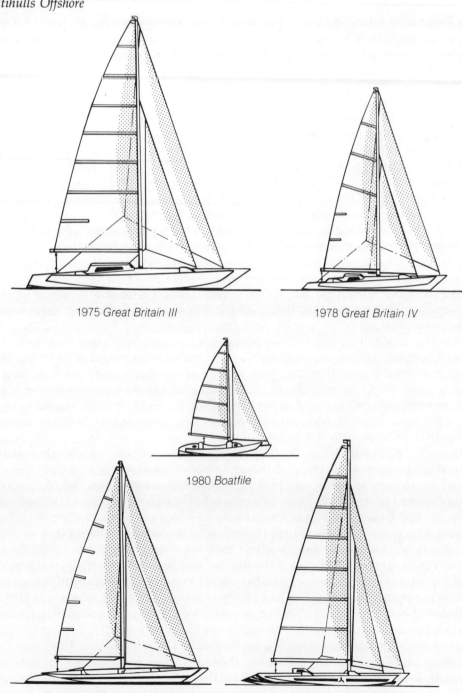

1975 *Great Britain III*    1978 *Great Britain IV*

1980 *Boatfile*

1981 *Brittany Ferries GB*    1982 *Colt Cars GB*

**Fig. 1** *The five multihulls most featured in these pages*

crewman let go the centreboard downhaul and the board shot up into its box, straight through the top of it and into the saloon! The top of the box then had to be heavily strengthened and bolted down every two inches (it formed the serving table between galley and saloon) and the offending downhaul line marked red. Even so the problem was not solved as the turbulence in the box when the board was down threatened to do more damage.

At some stage during these trials a charter group had booked a holiday on *GB III* and as Chay could not take them it was left to me. As I pointed out to Chay I had never sailed a multihull of any sort or size before and my first go was going to be on the largest one in the world! Not only that, my crew were charterers, I had no auxiliary power, and I was expected to take our guests to the Channel Islands. Chay calmly pointed out that if I treated the trimaran like any ordinary boat, all would be well.

We were towed to the entrance of Portsmouth harbour and let loose. The wind was a very light north-easterly and as we reached with full sail towards Cowes I was immediately impressed with how little fuss the boat made as she cut quietly through the water. There was not enough wind to depress the lee float. At Cowes we bore away on to a dead run for the Needles. I was delighted to find when I hoisted the light reacher that it set with the guy led out to the windward float and there was therefore no need for the pole. Towards late afternoon we were totally becalmed and had to anchor off Lymington to avoid being swept back by the tide (an interesting lesson – no matter how fast your yacht is, if there is *no* wind you can't sail, despite what some people might say).

The breeze came up from the south-west just before dark and we beat out to sea. There was absolutely no problem with tacking, provided not too much helm was used too quickly, and there was no need to back the jib. Once clear of the Needles the wind rose to force 4 which was fine for the yankee and staysail but necessitated a slab reef in the main – again no problem. It was interesting to discover that a fully battened main does not flog when the sheet is eased but instead moves quietly in an S-bend shape. Sailing close-hauled into the English Channel chop I discovered one of the less pleasant characteristics of multihulls – they pitch and jerk with a most violent motion. Although the pitching is much reduced in modern trimarans there is no hiding the fact that it is necessary to hold on tight at high speeds – more like being in a power boat than a yacht.

When I went down below to my amazement I found the saloon floor swimming in water. There was an almighty thumping coming from inside the centreboard box as the water swirled around in the empty cavity. The pressure building up was occasionally spurting the sea water out through the join at the top of the box and flooding the saloon. Until the centreboard was replaced some months later with a daggerboard the routine was to put on boots and foul weather gear when going below and remove them when on deck!

After what I then thought to be a most uncomfortable night we arrived in Guernsey and sailed in to anchor in Havlet Bay. Naturally I felt a sense of achievement in having completed my first multihull voyage without incident.

Leaving harbour was not so easy and my early attempts were somewhat clumsy. The difficulty in a confined space was to ensure that the bows fell off the right way when the anchor was weighed (by hand of course). On this particular occasion, with main hoisted, jib backed and anchor just off the bottom, the bows started to swing the wrong way and *GB III* accelerated towards the harbour wall. Disaster was averted with a push on the bow

Great Britain III *at 14 knots. Notice the sag in the rigging.*

*Great Britain III sailing on charter in company with British Steel.*

*Great Britain III's 80ft length is emphasized by the space in front of the forestay.*

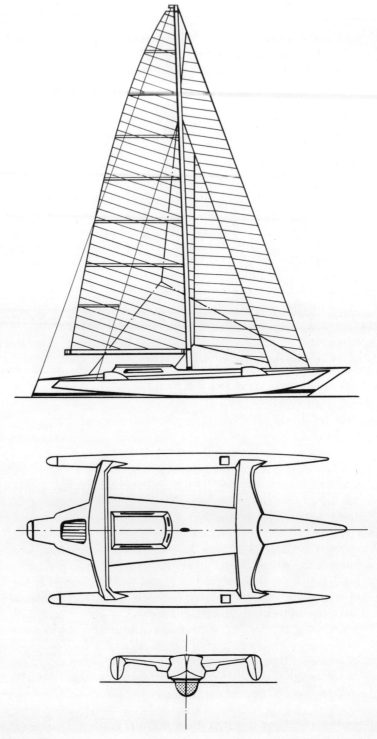

**Fig. 2** Great Britain III

14

from the dinghy and outboard – standing by for just this eventuality. Nerve-racking all the same. Once clear of the land we picked up speed extremely quickly and were soon reaching up through the Alderney Race *against* a spring tide and still making a good 7 knots.

The next obstacle was Portsmouth harbour. Ideally, *GB III* was to be sailed four miles inside the harbour entrance up a fairly narrow creek to Wicormarine. The first move was to have the anchor ready to drop and the dinghy launched well before entering confined waters. Then, nonchalantly sail into the harbour and up the creek, although taking a lot of care with each tack. The channel got narrower and narrower. The wind strength at 12 knots was perfect even if the direction, a beat, was wrong. As the jib was sheeted in after each tack we would accelerate to about 4 knots before it was time to tack again. The inevitable eventually happened, I missed a tack and had to yell for the anchor to be let go and the sails got down before we drifted into a moored boat at the edge of the creek. Having finally sorted out the mess of sheets and sails I managed to moor up alongside an old barge half a mile short of our destination. I was happy with that for a beginner!

A couple of months later (mid-summer 1975) *GB III* was again out on charter. In company this time with *British Steel*, I sailed her to St Malo. On the way we stopped at Guernsey for a day. No problems this time in the anchorage. The sail from St Peter Port to St Malo was interesting from a number of view points: *British Steel* left just before us and we soon overhauled her in a fresh westerly. Sailing with a reefed main and no. 2 yankee, we shot past her. On board, we were convinced we were taking the world apart with our bursts of speeds of 18 and 19 knots. Three hours after leaving we were at the south-west Minques buoy going great guns and shortly afterwards we were in St Malo. It was only later when I studied the charts that I realized our average speed had been 13 knots, not 16 or 17 as I had convinced myself. This taught me two more multihull facts of life: first, to achieve an average of 13 knots one must go a lot faster than that most of the time and, second, an average of 13 knots is fast!

Sailing around between St Malo and Dinard I thought I would moor up to a large metal 'big ship' buoy to wait for *British Steel*. We sent the dinghy away with a complete mooring line on board so that it could secure an end to the buoy and then drift downwind with the line fully extended. Meanwhile we positioned ourselves so that we were able to sail slowly up to the dinghy, take hold of the line, and there we were, moored with a 100ft warp to the buoy. This manoeuvre will not work if there is wind over tide; in such a case, anchoring is the only safe thing to do. *British Steel* duly arrived and, with her tied alongside one of our floats as our tug, we passed through the lock and tied up alongside the quay. The last multihull lesson of the day was that they attract crowds in direct proportion to their size – and an 80ft crowd in France is a big one.

I handed back Chay's monster after an uneventful return trip home to Dartmouth. I didn't sail *GB III* again and although I learnt a lot, and was impressed with her performance, it was not enough to convert me to multihulls. In fact, I sailed over 50,000 monohull miles including the 1975–6 Atlantic Triangle and the '77–8 Whitbread before I sailed a multihull again. It is interesting, though, to record *GB III*'s progress during this time.

Shortly after my second and last trip attempts were made to cure the tri's centreboard problems. A system with air bags was devised. The bags could be pumped up when the

*Preparing to hoist the mainsail on* Great Britain III.

Great Britain III (*above and below*).

Great Britain III. *Notice steps to help crew climb crossbeam.*

board was down and so they filled the empty box, displacing the water and preventing the heavy turbulence in the area. But the bags disintegrated under the pressure and that was the centreboard's last chance. After this failure it was cut out of the boat and replaced by a daggerboard that moved up and down in a parallel-sided box. This system has been used ever since on all racing multihulls.

The multihull Atlantic race was cancelled so, instead, Chay took *GB III* across the Atlantic. A stop was required in the Canaries to replace all the Parafil rigging with stainless steel wire sent out from England, as the former was losing the endless battle against chafe. A second stop in the Cape Verde Islands was made to strengthen the area round one of the capshroud chain plates which had split right through the hull. The final crossing from the Cape Verdes to the West Indies in just under ten days set up a record for the Atlantic. The trip back from New York was made in 13 days without once setting a spinnaker – a very quick time for the 1970s.

However *GB III*'s run of luck was over. While qualifying for the 1976 OSTAR on a February day Chay hit a coaster off Start Point. The collision severed one of the floats just forward of the forward crossbeam. In an attempt to make Salcombe, Chay had to sail with the damaged float to leeward – and capsized as a result (See Chapter 15). He was outside in the cockpit as the boat went over and had a hard time surviving in the freezing water until help arrived. *GB III* was towed, upside down, into Plymouth and was dismasted when the masthead, 100ft underwater, hit the bottom. The missing piece of float was

Great Britain III *anchored in Havlet Bay, Guernsey.*

subsequently dredged up in a fisherman's trawl and the whole vessel rebuilt. However, as a result of this accident, insurance for the OSTAR was unobtainable and Chay withdrew his entry. That was a great pity, for her chances had been rated well. As Tabarly said: 'If there is one boat in the fleet for the '76 OSTAR that I would prefer to sail it is *Great Britain III.*'

After this disappointment she was sold and converted to cruising. Even so, she did race once again on charter to Pierre Fehlman for the 1978 single-handed Route du Rhum race from St Malo to the West Indies. It was possible to watch her rise inch by inch out of the water during the week before the start as Fehlman removed all her cruising interior. Despite speeding off on the first day of the race her luck was still out. Self-steering problems forced Fehlman to retire after only a few days.

The last time I saw her was under strange circumstances. Cruising in company with the fleet on the Route du Rhum, one night I was on the foredeck of *Grand Louis*, a 60ft schooner, hoisting sail after a severe gale in the Bay of Biscay. Halfway through the operation I happened to glance into the total darkness and saw a glimmer of light ahead. Shouting to the helmsman to alter course we peered into the gloom and could just make out a large shadow directly in our path. Just clearing her stern by inches we looked down on the unmistakable form of *GB III*, lying ahull while her exhausted skipper rested after the gale before turning back for France.

*GB III* was not a successful racing trimaran, nevertheless we should be grateful for the invaluable lessons she taught the multihull world.

# 2

## *Great Britain IV*

*Great Britain IV* was designed and built by Derek Kelsall for the 1978 Round Britain Race. The trimaran was conceived by Chay Blyth as a smaller but faster replacement for the recently sold *Great Britain III*. Jack Hayward was again underwriting the project. 'As fast as possible with a bias to light airs performance within a maximum overall length of 56ft', was the brief to Kelsall. Although there was no size limitation for the Round Britain it made sense, as regards cost and handling considerations, to come down from *GB III*'s 80 ft. Also, by choosing 56ft the boat would come inside the newly imposed maximum LOA for the forthcoming OSTAR '80.

Kelsall very bravely went for the ultimate in weight-saving. As a result there were a few weaknesses in the structure. In the four years since she was built construction materials have improved so much that it is now possible to build a vessel of the same size and weight as *GB IV*, but one which is immensely strong. Nevertheless, in 1978, and indeed for several years afterwards, *GB IV* was probably the fastest sailing boat in the world in light airs (anything up to force 4, after which problems occurred). Her hull and floats were made from an Airex foam core with uni-directional glass-fibre skins. Carbon fibre was used to reinforce some of the panels in the hull and the crossbeams were also carbon fibres laid up in a box section and later faired with a light glass structure. The whole building programme was undertaken in a great rush and a number of the later hiccups can be attributed to this.

As I was to sail with Chay in the two-handed Round Britain and Ireland Race I spent some time in the spring of '78 at Sandwich in Kent watching parts of the building process. The three hulls and two crossbeams were put together on rough ground between Bayside Marine's shed and Sandwich Creek. I remember a few incidents about this time that resulted from the rush to qualify for the race before the deadline. On one occasion we were matching the floats to the beam ends by the simple expedient of several men holding a float by hand while Kelsall lined it up, in three directions, by eye. Having wedged it into place on oil drums it was glassed on. The same procedure was repeated with the other float. Although the result looked correct there was a general feeling that the boat went better on one tack than on the other. A few weeks later the lads from Spencer's Rigging arrived to rig the mast. With the rigging attached to the masthead and a crane holding the mast in place the men could measure each wire to the relevant chain plate, cut it, swage it (as all wire was 11mm or less this could be done by a portable machine on deck) and then attach it with a bottle screw. The last wire to be fixed was the backstay and it was only as the rigger stood on the afterdeck with the wire in his hand and a perplexed look on his face that we realized no provision at all had been made for a backstay!

Because *GB IV* was built so lightly it was possible to put only medium tension in the rig – any more and the structure would have bent. The rig was large and the genoa was masthead; this meant that the mast was stepped on the main hull between the two beams and as a result the athwartships staying suffered from flex in the floats and beams. Fore and aft the problem was the same with the hull bending upwards at each end under load. There was a permanent forestay sag which continually hindered the set of the jib. Initially the rig was designed with the foot of the inner forestay well forward near the forestay itself, so that only a staysail and mainsail would be used in a breeze (the staysail would, of-course, be bigger by putting its tack well forward). Unfortunately, in addition to interference between the two parts of the cutter rig, we found that when it became necessary to sail under staysail alone it gave too big a sail area. Therefore the inner forestay was moved aft to a more conventional position and the sail plan looked like this:

    no. 1 yankee (jib top)
    no. 2 yankee (jib top)
    staysail
    main (three reefs)
    2 spinnakers

*Assembling* Great Britain IV *on rough ground at Bayside Marine.*

. . . Not many sails but short-handed sailing was the order of the day and that precludes endless sail changing; weight-saving also was all important. We were soon to discover that any sort of sail handling was a nightmare as the foredeck was very narrow.

The first trial sail took place in Sandwich Bay on a spring Saturday. I couldn't be there as I was best man at a wedding but I learnt that all went very well with flat water and light airs. After driving all night I arrived on board at Ramsgate at 4 a.m. the next day. We set sail immediately with just over 24 hours to go until the Round Britain Race deadline for qualification. The crew consisted of Chay, myself, Derek Kelsall and John Shuttleworth who worked with Kelsall on the *GB IV* design project.

The trip was a particularly boring one, simply clocking up the miles. The wind initially was light and we were unable to learn much about the yacht's handling. After trying several sail combinations we were still not entirely convinced that we were getting anything like maximum performance out of her. Our priority was to get the miles in without damage so we weren't prepared to take any risks. As darkness fell the wind rose slightly and a nasty chop built up in the channel. We reached fairly fast backwards and forwards pounding with a very violent motion – at which stage I was more occupied with my hangover than with anything else. The mast was moving fore and aft in the middle most alarmingly and in general it was an unpleasant sail. Back in Ramsgate with an hour to spare it seemed to me that if the qualifying trip had taught us nothing about sailing the boat, it certainly showed us that the rig needed more adequate staying.

Before the Round Britain we decided to enter two other races, the Round the Island (Wight) and the Crystal Trophy. Racing with a crew of four we anticipated learning a lot from these short sprints, as indeed we did. After the initial trials the mast had been beefed up with two jumper struts and the inner forestay position moved aft as mentioned. Although we were still not happy with the sails we thought we would leave them alone for a while in order to learn more about how they could be improved.

There were over 700 entries in the Round the Island Race and the multihulls started last. Our main rival for this event – and for the Round Britain – was Phil Weld and his 65ft Newick-designed *Rogue Wave*. Weld had come over from the USA to compete in the two previous Round Britain Races and had come third each time. In 1970 he sailed the early Kelsall-designed *Trumpeter* and in 1974 the Newick-designed *Gulf Streamer*. Weld capsized *Gulf Streamer* in mid-Atlantic in 1976. His preparation for just such an event being as it was, he and his crew were able to live in the upside down hull for four days before being rescued. He named his new trimaran after the wave that destroyed the old. She certainly looked strong and fast – though was under rigged by *GB IV*'s standards.

The Round the Island Race started with a spinnaker run west from Cowes. As we picked our way through the smaller end of the fleet we were glad to see that *Rogue Wave*, with her specialist reaching sail, was going a little slower than we were with our conventional spinnaker. Chay was sailing brilliantly, carving a 38ft-wide path through a solid sea of yachts. Within one and a quarter hours we were by the Needles having overtaken all 700 boats. On the close reach down towards St Catherine's Point we were making 15 knots and holding *Rogue Wave* a quarter of a mile behind. We reefed and still kept up speed – morale was mountain high.

From St Catherine's we had a dead beat up to Bembridge into a very nasty sea. Things started to go badly wrong. First we were pitching horribly and if we pointed at all high the speed dropped back to under 8 knots. Reaching off proved to be of no use as velocity made good to windward dropped immediately. We soon learnt that we had to keep the speed down to 8 knots while on the wind – higher speeds meant we were simply not pointing. The wind increased and we decided to change from the no. 1 to the no. 2 jib. We were losing ground to *Rogue Wave* so it was essential to keep sailing with the staysail while we made the change. Once the jib was lowered it took ages to unhank and get under control. With the narrow foredeck pitching so much it was necessary to hold on with one hand at all times. Chay got so annoyed with our slow sail changing that he started to politely suggest we get a move on. I suggested just as politely that he leave the wheel and give it a try up the pointed end himself. He came forward and hurriedly agreed that the motion was very bad. We finally got sailing again properly but 20 minutes without a headsail had let *Rogue Wave* through. We pitched on to windward with waves crashing alarmingly into the forward crossbeam fairing which appeared to be angled to catch each lump of spray full on. It was a reach back from Bembridge to Cowes. Despite a nice beam wind we could not get the speed up above 17 knots. At one point we felt overpowered and dropped the jib (in error for the staysail) and the speed still remained at 17 knots. Jib back up and no change, as though that speed was an impenetrable barrier. *Rogue Wave* disappeared ahead of us.

Back in the Solent the wind went to the quarter and became quite variable in strength, though still strong. Steering was very difficult in the puffs and the hydraulic linkage was particularly tricky to 'feel'. At one point when I was steering I watched how we were being pressed on to the lee float. As this happened our bows tended to go down rather than to rise. There was too much buoyancy at the back of the float and the flat transom was dragging through the water with great turbulence and commotion. Suddenly we shot up to 18 or 19 knots as a puff hit us, at which moment the lee helm became uncontrollable and we tripped round to leeward. We were on a dead run before the helm came free and I was able to steer again. Each time we reached the tendency to bear away was there. We finished the race second, with a lot to think about.

Chay's first move was to order a furling jib system and new sails. A furler jib, even reefed and misshapen would be better than trying to change sail. The new staysail had a higher aspect and was smaller. Chay discarded the fully battened mainsail to make way for a new conventional one. (In my view the old mainsail with full battens was OK, but the battens were too stiff and they upset it.) These changes made an enormous improvement. The next thing to go was the hydraulic steering, to be replaced by a much better system of wires. The shape, position and angle of the floats received no attention as we could not identify the problem and, anyway, that was a *fait accompli*. But we did know that we had a fast, light airs boat.

The next outing was the Crystal Trophy Race, the annual UK championship for multihulls. The course is from Cowes to a buoy off Cherbourg, then to Wolf Rock off Land's End and back to the finish in Plymouth. All shapes of catamarans and trimarans were entered which, with the exception of *GB IV* and *Rogue Wave*, were either cruising or older racing multihulls. At the pre-race briefing a westerly gale was forecast and I can't say that our intrepid crew approached the line with much enthusiasm. The start was a reach eastwards and by the time we had passed Bembridge Ledge Buoy and had come close-hauled heading south across channel, *Rogue Wave* was already half a mile ahead of

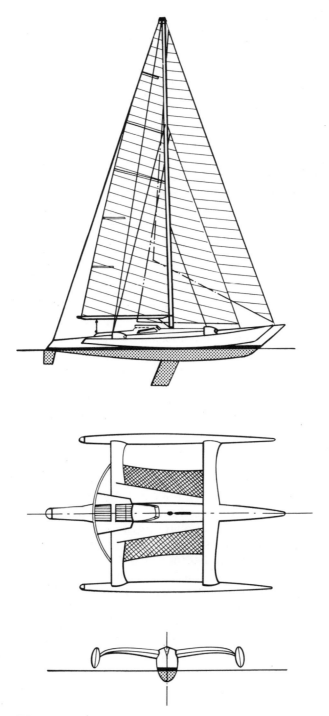

**Fig. 3** Great Britain IV

us. Our problem seemed to be a lack of speed in all directions when the wind was over force 4. Off the wind the boat was difficult to steer and on the wind we pitched and slammed in amost undesirable fashion. The night developed into a pretty miserable beat after CH 1 buoy had been located and rounded off the French coast; it was then a dead beat westwards. While Chay and I were relatively unaffected both the other two crew were chronically seasick – a situation not helped by the violent motion and lack of comfortable, indeed any, bunks below.

Early next morning we detected a hole in the underside of the beam fairing, no doubt caused by the slamming. We decided to retire from the race and make for our home port of Dartmouth where we were faced with a daunting workload, and a naming ceremony, before the start of the Round Britain in two weeks time.

The repairs were done, the fairings strengthened and the yacht spruced up for her christening. The new furler forestay arrived along with the new sails and we began to feel a bit happier when we saw how good the new set-up looked. On the Monday before the race we presented ourselves in Plymouth for scrutiny, a standard check made of all entries to ensure that they meet the race rules on all matters of construction and safety. In Milbay dock we eyed up our competitors to decide which of them, besides *Rogue Wave*, would be most formidable. There was Nick Keig with *Three Legs of Mann II*, a near sister ship (but slightly heavier) to *GB IV*. This was the first time I'd met Nick, quite a humourist and a great supporter of multihull racing, then on his third home-built multihull. As I dashed to and fro on vital errands I couldn't help noticing the apparent calm and total preparation on *Three Legs*, and paused to ask Keig if he really was as ready as he looked. 'No', he replied, 'tell Chay I've got a really serious problem. I can't seem to get rid of the flutter in the port stereo loud speaker.'

Wally Green, who had sailed a 31ft Dick Newick Val class trimaran in the 1976 OSTAR, was back with *A Cappella*, a similar looking boat to the Val but 3ft bigger and designed and built by himself. He was sailing with his wife Joan. There was a Val 31 in the race as well, *Jan of Santa Cruz*, sailed by Nigel Irens and a crew man who looked far too big for the tiny trimaran.

The other leading contenders were monohulls, the more noticeable being *GB II* and *Tielsa II*. *GB II* was of course the same 77ft monohull that I had just raced, with a crew of 16, round the world. It is quite feasible to sail a 77 footer short-handed, even if it's laid out for fully crewed racing, as *GB II* was, but Robin Knox-Johnston and Billy King-Harman were to find it virtually impossible to race such a huge yacht effectively over the short distances of the Round Britain Race, simply because of the slowness implicit in handling such massive sails with none of the traditional short-handed systems to aid them. Consequently, it was felt that Dirk Nauta, sailing *Tielsa II* (ex *Bestevaer*, designed by Jerry Dikstra for the 1976 OSTAR), would be the strongest monohull contender.

Having passed the scrutiny we sailed back to Dartmouth and discovered, in our first downwind sail with waves, another of *GB IV*'s vices. As the speed built up on a surf she would fail to respond to the helm. The steering would become completely light and no amount of winding would make any difference until we reached the trough between the waves, at which point she would, seemingly unpredictably, sheer off violently either to port or starboard. It was very confusing. To try and see what was going wrong I went out on the float to watch. As a wave approached from aft the stern lifted high and the rudder came completely clear of the water. Before the wave could pass, *GB IV* would shoot off down its face and sail the rudder back into the wave top. Now the problem was obvious. As the rudder came clear the helmsman would attempt to correct the course and the rudder would still be turned hard over or part over, as it dug back into the water thus causing the violent alteration of course. We soon discovered that the secret was to centre the wheel when the helm went light, ensuring perfect control when the rudder shot back into its element! Moving a lot of the gear into the stern helped a bit – but not enough, as she remained bow down.

The naming ceremony was duly performed by HRH the Duchess of Kent and after the festivities it was time to sail to Plymouth again. On the way round yet another problem showed up. I had just reefed and was sheeting the main in when I noticed that the main track was lifting; investigation showed that it was not just the main-sheet track but rather the whole cockpit box that was lifting off the afterdeck. We came about and returned once more to Dartmouth, to ask the long suffering Dartmouth Yacht Services team if they would perform one last rush job. The afterdeck, it transpired, had been painted before the cockpit box was glassed on and the join at the back of the cockpit overlapped the painted area: in the rush the paint had not been ground back before bonding was begun.

At last – and finally – a day before the race, we were ready to start.

## The 1978 race

Saturday 8 July dawned clear and fine with a force 4 to 5 westerly – more than we'd hoped for but not too bad. The start outside the breakwater was a reach across the line towards the Eddystone lighthouse. The first leg of the course finished at Cork harbour, leaving all land to starboard, a distance of 230 miles.

I remember feeling very tired from hoisting the mainsail as we approached the line. However, with our furler jib stowed and the staysail pulling we could manoeuvre with fair control as Chay somehow found a gap in the 100 starting yachts and we were away. We were delighted to find ourselves pulling ahead of all the competition, including Phil Weld and Nick Keig and by the Eddystone Rock we were a quarter of a mile in front. Looking back we could see *Tielsa II* sailing very high up the course as she and *GB II* vainly chased the leading bunch of four or five trimarans. (It was interesting to read a yachting report later that said that *Tielsa II*'s pointing ability after the start was so much better than the multihulls that she was sure to win. The correspondent hadn't noticed that the course was a close reach and no-one, except *Tielsa*, was interested in pointing.)

We eventually came on the wind to beat to the Lizard and the Scillies. Once again we started to pitch and pound and *Rogue Wave* came up from astern, sailing faster and higher than us. She was soon past and, having firmly demoralized us, she tacked off inshore. We went about later on and as evening fell we were lying close to the Lizard. It seemed like a good idea to remain inshore to keep to the flatter water for as long as possible. Eventually, with a reef and partly furled jib, we tacked out and back, then bore away slightly around Bishop Rock directly on course for Cork. We were going a cracking pace through the overfalls and had every hope of catching the leader.

I was on watch at 4 a.m. and as I steered I could see the shadow of the leeward float cutting through the water. It appeared to be submerging a lot and it crossed my mind that with a wind strength of 20 knots and full sail we should be well pressed but not overpowered. Fearing the worst I called Chay and we hove-to to investigate. Chay went out onto the float and undid the inspection cap and pump access to each of the watertight sections in turn. As he took the forward one off the water actually bubbled out of the float. The forward third was completely full to the brim. Chay remained where he was while I climbed down the afterhatch to pull out the hand bilge pump. Only a few seconds after I disappeared I heard a shout and the sound of rushing water. I dived back on deck and found *GB IV* moving flat out through the water. Having been knocked around from hove-to by a wave she had started sailing again on her own. Chay had lost his hand hold, there was not much to grab anyway, and had been washed down the float coming to a halt where I could see him clinging to a cap-shroud. He was furious because his boots got wet! When we finally got all the water pumped out we started sailing only to find the float full again within two minutes. Hove-to once more, we investigated the problem further and this time found the cause of the leak. The starboard beam fairing was smashed and water was pouring in through a 2ft-wide hole. This should not have affected the watertight integrity of the whole float but a crack where the fairing met the float was obviously bridging the bulkheads.

After a quick council of war we decided to make an attempt to stay in the race if at all possible. With just a staysail and reefed main we set off for Cork, with the partly flooded float to leeward looking quite alarming. We saw *A Cappella* pass us during the day and knew she would not be the only one. Towards evening we picked up the Kinsale Gas Field and crossed the line in Cork harbour at 23.00. Not knowing the area, we sailed a short way towards Crosshaven and anchored for the night. At 06.00 I got up and found the harbour calm; I reflected what a sorry sight we must have made anchored with our starboard for'd corner half submerged. We got a tow into Crosshaven and discovered we were nine hours behind the leader, *Rogue Wave*, with *Three Legs*, *GB II*, *A Cappella*, and *Tielsa* ahead of us, an almost impossible margin to make up.

The race rules allow for a 48-hour pit stop between each leg of the race. Competitors time themselves in and out and meanwhile have to survive considerable revelry as well as get repairs done. As soon as we could we beached *GB IV* in front of the Crosshaven Boatyard and work was started. The starboard fairing was ground down and reglassed, in the rain, and an ugly but effective repair achieved. We also had the fairing considerably strengthened where it met the float.

The second leg of the race was to the Isle of Barra in the Outer Hebrides, a distance of 400 miles. When Phil Weld departed at 2 p.m. the westerly winds of the previous few days had given way to strong north-easterlies – perfect for the reach down the south coast of Ireland to the Fastnet Rock. Meanwhile, we had just finished the repairs to *GB IV* and were trying to get some rest before our own departure. At dinner that evening an American yachting journalist covering the race arrived back at the Royal Cork Yacht Club (the host club in Crosshaven) to tell us he had timed *Rogue Wave* round the Old Head of Kinsale. He reckoned she'd averaged 17 knots and was then going even faster. This piece of information depressed us enormously – even when we worked out the journalist's timings and it appeared he'd added 4 or 5 knots to psyche us up.

Throughout the afternoon and evening the leaders left and eventually it was our turn to make for the starting line followed closely by the tiny *Jan of Santa Cruz*, who had finished the first leg just two minutes behind us. The wind was still north-easterly and we shot away from Cork harbour with full jib, staysail and main in hot pursuit of the leaders. We settled down straight away to the watch-keeping system that suited us best – one hour on, one hour off. As none of our self-steering gears were functioning we were obliged to steer all the time. An hour seems to be the longest anyone can effectively concentrate when steering a lively multihull; it was also about the longest we could stand the weather, as we moved further north and it got colder. Off watch you slept when you could between navigating, reefing or sail changing and cooking. One lesson this race taught us was the absolute necessity of a good self-steering system: it is imperative for maximum speed and efficiency when short-handed. However, we made good progress during the night, during which time we must have overtaken *GB II* and *Tielsa II*. At dawn the wind had died to a light easterly so we set our light spinnaker for the first time. The spi-squeezer system for hoisting and setting worked very well, so did the arrangement of three sheets on each side, using the beam of the tri to obtain a perfect setting. We had discovered that the windward clew tended to droop in very light airs so we'd brought along a light pole to hold it up. The system has since been improved (see Part 2, Chapter 12) but at the time it still gave us a good spinnaker set.

During the morning we sailed slowly past the Fastnet Rock in perfectly calm summer weather, overhauling *A Cappella* which brought our position up to third place. Chay and I celebrated the occasion with a bottle of champagne – mostly on account of seeing the rock for the first time. I'd rounded it a few times during the Fastnet Race but it had always been in the dead of night. For Chay it was the first time round, although he and I had tried to make it several times during our heavy-weather charter holidays in January and February of 1975. For seven consecutive long weekends we'd set off for the Fastnet Rock in order to give our guests a taste of heavy-weather going; each time gales made the thought of Falmouth or the Channel Islands much more attractive to their weakening stomachs and I can't say we ever tried very hard to dissuade them.

Once clear of the south-west corner of Ireland we turned north, still in light airs which were perfect for *GB IV*. Twenty-two hours out of Crosshaven we spotted a yacht ahead which we took to be *Three Legs of Man*, but it was too dark to be sure. We overhauled her during the night which just left *Rogue Wave* way out in front. *GB IV* was lighter (and smaller) than *Rogue Wave* but carried more sail so it was safe to assume that she would have a better light airs performance. But what were their relative speeds?

Next morning we were spinnaker reaching in fog and light airs. Navigation was a combination of radio direction finding, dead reckoning, sun sights and guesswork – the only aids allowed in the race rules. Having just completed a bit of after breakfast navigation I was dozing off on the saloon seat when I was startled awake by a frenzied shout of 'Rob!' from on deck. I leapt up the companionway expecting to find Chay in all sorts of trouble. Instead he was jumping up and down by the wheel with the binoculars glued to his eyes. I looked ahead and to my total amazement there, just visible 200 yards away in the mist, was *Rogue Wave*, the 'unbeatable', the 'fastest ocean going yacht in the world' and we'd taken nine hours out of her in 36 hours sailing! The effect it had on Chay and I was extraordinary. We had been so depressed by the time lost in the first leg that we really thought all chance of winning was lost, and if we ever did manage to catch up it would take the whole race – 12 days or so. Yet here we were back in the lead in 36 hours. It was the ultimate shot in the arm, and just what we needed. I remember seeing David Cooksey (Phil Weld's crew) running about on deck getting their spinnaker set to catch the freeing breeze that we'd brought up with us, and Chay and I shouting across the water, 'It's too late – you've had it now!' Rash words of course, but we were not thinking of the wind and trouble tomorrow might bring. For that moment, at least, we were on top of the world.

Later that day the wind veered to a northerly and we had to beat up the coast of Ireland. Fortunately the wind strength didn't rise enough to slow us down and we felt, providing we didn't make any mistakes, we could hold on to the lead. From the north-west corner of Ireland we took a long starboard tack out into the Atlantic to pick up the expected wind shift from north to north-west. When we tacked back many hours later the wind did in fact shift to such an extent that we were able to ease sheets slightly for the fetch back to Barra. As it turned out we'd over-stood and wasted some valuable time. Late that night we approached Castle Bay and raced across the finishing line – a nerve-wracking procedure in the pitch dark. We continued into the Bay as far as our limited vision would allow and dropped anchor at 3 a.m. Tired though we were we couldn't go to sleep; over near the beach we could see the shadow of an anchored yacht. Was it *Rogue Wave*? Had she passed us on the long beat north by staying further east or just by better boat speed? For nearly two hours I sat on deck staring across the anchorage trying to recognize some feature of the other vessel that would positively identify her as *not* being in our race. Eventually, it got light enough for us to see it was not a boat we knew. We were the only race boat there and none other was visible out towards the entrance of the bay. We were definitely in the lead.

Our stop in Barra was a high spot of the race. It was four hours before Phil Weld arrived followed by *Three Legs*, *A Cappella* and *Jan of Santa Cruz*. We had no repairs to make to *GB IV* at all. The aluminium head-foil extrusion which takes the luff of the jib up the forestay was bent into a 360 degree spiral, caused by the tremendous twisting force put in by the furler device. However, there was no way of fixing it and as it still furled and unfurled we decided to leave it alone.

Two days later off we went for the third leg out into the Atlantic around St Kilda, then north to the tip of the Shetlands and around to Lerwick on their east side. The whole leg was uneventful and frustrating. We only made 20 miles in our four-hour lead as the wind was so light; this did not matter so long as the wind stayed very light and didn't fill in from *Rogue Wave*'s direction first. It got colder and colder as we sailed north. At least the weather was clear and navigating by sunsight was easy enough even though we had to stretch a point in the sight reduction tables as we sailed up as far as 61 degrees north and the tables only went to 60 degrees. As we rounded Muckle Flugga at the top of the Shetlands and turned the corner an icy north-easterly wind came up to blow us home. This was the last thing we wanted; if the wind had stayed light our lead would have been four or even six hours, instead it was reduced to only two. With the wind came fog and a dicy reach down to Lerwick. *GB IV* was up to her old tricks of burying the bow of the lee float and tripping round to leeward every now and then. Even when we were under control the turbulence from the submerged transom of the float was horrific. Of course the lesson here was obvious: if the floats are mainly underwater when the boat is being driven hard they should be designed as underwater shapes, not flat and cut off.

A few miles from Lerwick the visibility closed right in and the wind allowed us to set a spinnaker. The approach to the harbour from the north is tricky as it means having to pick up the towering cliffs of Bressay Island and follow them round a turn of almost 180 degrees up towards the port entrance. If we were to over-shoot the cliff headland in the bad visibility it would be quite safe but considerable time would be wasted feeling our way back from the south. With this in mind I set a course from our previous fix (some rocks several miles back) to pass within half a mile of the point. Chay was steering and being as aware as I was of the danger of sailing straight past the harbour without seeing it he kept edging the course slightly to starboard towards the land to be sure of hitting it – with the result that we nearly did! The cliffs appeared dead ahead which gave us only about 400 yards grace to get the spinnaker down and head up to clear them. (In fact, if we'd stayed on the course I'd set we may not have seen the land, so bad was the visibility.) With the squeezer pulled down over the spinnaker we unfurled the jib, reached away from the cliff till we were clear enough to bear away again and reset the spinnaker. Less than a mile later we gybed around the tip of Bressay, lowered the spinnaker and came hard on the wind for the three miles to the finishing line off the town. As we hardened up we were nervous enough to keep the mainsheet in hand, mindful of an accident in this very spot in almost identical conditions that occured in the previous Round Britain.

Brian Cooke on *Triple Arrow*, a Simpson Wild-design 49 footer with moderate sail area and lightly constructed (7300lb, GRP foam sandwich), was lying fourth and had had a spinnaker run down from Muckle Flugga in a north-north-easterly force 5 wind. After rounding Bressay they came hard on the wind towards Lerwick. They did not consider themselves over-canvased as the no. 2 genoa had been set in anticipation of the beat up Lerwick harbour. The main was set full. *Triple Arrow* was very close under the land – less than half a mile – experiencing alternately complete calms and fairly strong gusts. Cooke and his crew, Jenson, were in the cockpit ready to let go the sheets if any of the gusts proved too severe for the sail area. Without warning a heavy gust hit the yacht and before they could ease the sheets she had capsized. The gust came down off the hills and caught the yacht lying with no way on and the sheets pinned in tight. Added to this was the fact that her floats were of less than 100 per cent buoyancy or were semi-submersible (i.e. they would press under water before the main hull would lift clear). The circumstances were certainly freakish but Chay and I knew that the three leaders had all experienced similar problems in the same place that year. Both *Three Cheers* and *Gulf Streamer* had had to let their genoa and main sheets run to avoid a capsize and *British Oxygen* had damaged her main track. Needless to say, we reefed down and gave the cliffs a reasonably wide berth. We crossed the line safely.

The finishing order was again *GB IV*, *Rogue Wave*, *Three Legs*, *A Cappella* and *Jan of Santa Cruz*. During our two-day stop-over in Lerwick the wind swung inexorably to the south and blew up to a force 5 – exactly the conditions that *GB IV* hated and *Rogue Wave* loved. So we set off on a 400-mile beat down the North Sea to Lowestoft, with a partly furled jib, staysail and reefed main; it was cold, very wet and slow, with *GB IV* pitching and pounding into the seas and taking a tremendous bashing on the for'd beam fairings. We didn't alter our sails for two days. As we'd feared all along, our fragile vessel began to fall apart: the starboard cap-shroud chain plate was the first to go, it was simply not man enough for the job. We tacked very quickly before the mast went and hove-to to work out a way of securing it. The only spare eye strong enough to take a shroud was back on the float where it joined the aft crossbeam. This eye was an alternative running backstay position which we'd never used. To make the shroud long enough to reach the eye we sawed off 20 links from the anchor chain. The result was an effective repair but it meant we couldn't ease the boom to starboard beyond the 45 degree position. The next breakage was the port for'd beam fairing which had cracked (although we didn't discover it at the time) during the beat south; fortunately, the water that got into the fairing didn't get into the float so it didn't slow us down. This was followed by the collapse of the main jumper strut which allowed the rig to bend alarmingly fore and aft as we punched the waves. We had no option but to let it bend and hope it wouldn't come down. The last thing to worry us, fortunately when the wind was dropping, was the jib furler. We needed more sail out but the furler refused to unwind. Again we hove-to to unroll the sail by hand – an almost impossible job. We couldn't reach the clew to take the sheets off so it meant handing both sheets and a flapping jib round and round the forestay a dozen or so times – an effort that cost us another hour of progress. Eventually, we got sailing again only to be totally becalmed among the oil rigs 100 miles north-east of Lowestoft. This did, however, ease our navigation problems as I could read the names of the rigs as we drifted past and find out their positions on the charts – it was just as well as we were pretty tired by then and needed all our energy just to keep the boat moving.

We knew *Rogue Wave* would have sped past but we were in some measure saved by the calms of the last few miles. In the event Phil Weld got in four hours ahead of us and we just maintained our second place over Nick Keig. Not too depressing, considering the problems we'd had.

Another 48 hours for repairs before the dash through the Dover Straights and down the Channel back to Plymouth. It began to look as though the race would be decided on the weather – strong winds for Weld, light for us. The wind, when *Rogue Wave* left, was a southerly 3 to 4, which it remained until our departure. We decided to stand out on a starboard south-easterly tack to clear the land and the Thames Estuary before making for the Dover Straights. Of course, the wind veered and far from tacking for the Straights, we were slowly lifted round until we were pointing, still close-hauled, towards Calais, having sailed in a big circle round the south-east corner of England. If we'd tacked earlier into the Thames Estuary we'd have been much better placed on the inside of the wind bend when it veered. Imagining now that *Rogue Wave* would have increased her lead enormously, we had no option but to push on. This was not easy; the wind slowly died again and we found ourselves short tacking up the beach just east of Calais against a strengthening tide. Finally, progress became nil and we had to anchor.

Less than 200 yards from the shore Chay and I sat down in the cockpit and had, for the first time, a meal together. It was almost relaxing – except for the thought of the rest of the fleet sailing in a good breeze over the other side of the straight. After two hours a light wind sprang up from the south and by the time the anchor had barely cleared the bottom we were sailing at 6 knots with Chay struggling to get the ground tackle back on board. We shot down Channel, slowly sheeting in until the wind went round to the west and we were beating again. East of the Isle of Wight we tacked out to clear St Catherine's, then back, and so on for 24 hours. Luckily, the wind never rose above force 4 so we were not slowed down. At Start Point, with 30 miles to the finish, we were totally becalmed again.

Sailing in a light airs boat is extraordinary because, while one hates to be becalmed, you know that it helps you in relation to the other boats; it is pleasantly surprising to discover that while you were worried sick about the wind dropping, the rest of the fleet were going even slower.

It was the middle of the night when the wind died, and when the lightest of zephers ghosted in from astern some time later we were almost too tired to hoist the spinnaker. The only way we could rouse ourselves was to say 'If this was the first hour of the race and the same thing happened, would we put up the spinaker?' The answer was yes, of course, so up it went. Ten lifeless minutes later we took it down again. And so on till, at dawn, we were off Prawle Point with 20 miles to go. We tuned into the local BBC radio station in Plymouth expecting, with dread, to hear an interview with the winner, Phil Weld. Instead, we heard the secretary of the race committee saying, '*GB IV* has been sighted 20 miles from the finish making slow progress in a light north-easterly. No news has been heard of the previous leader, Weld, but he may be approaching from an offshore direction and could still beat *GB IV* into Plymouth'.

We could hardly believe our ears. Surely, if *Rogue Wave* was between us and the finish, Phil Weld would have made contact by VHF. We began to feel we had the race won! Meanwhile, we weren't making much headway. The wind was very light and on the nose. We found by sailing at a 30 degree angle to the apparent wind we were making about 3 knots through the water – but tacking through almost 180 degrees. *GB IV* was making nearly all the apparent wind herself. In order to tack through anything like 90 degrees we had to pinch up to 20 degrees apparent. There is no doubt of the necessity to pinch up and sheet hard in very light airs: there is so little resistance to forward motion that the tight sheeting angle still provides enough drive – and sailing at $1\frac{1}{2}$ knots tacking through 90 degrees is better than doing 3 knots and tacking through 180 degrees.

Plymouth was almost in sight when we heard the next BBC news bulletin. 'Early this morning the winner of the Round Britain Race crossed the finishing line at Plymouth.' That was it. No names, or anything. There was immediate panic on board, even though we felt sure it was a mistake. Half an hour later we were glued to the radio for the next newscast. Sure enough it was a mistake, we were in the lead. Shortly afterwards a small fleet of motor boats including TV and press launches appeared about us. A quick scan of the horizon to make sure there were no other race boats in sight – there weren't. At the Plymouth breakwater the light breeze swung to the stern. With the spinnaker up for the last half mile, we soon crossed the line and heard the winners gun.

*GB IV* had been designed as a light-weather boat, and indeed, that is what she was. A lot of weaknesses showed up in her build during the race, especially chain plate problems, but whatever the critics said, she won the race she was designed for. Having said that, I personally don't think it was very clever to go to that extreme when the materials didn't allow sufficient strength for the weight. She was quite an unseaworthy boat.

Back at sea, Nick Keig had overtaken Phil Weld and they finished close together 13 hours behind us. It transpired that *Rogue Wave* had lost many hours drifting backwards in deep water off Dover. If the weather had been tougher she would undoubtedly have won. *A Cappella* was fourth and *Jan of Santa Cruz* fifth – a very good result for a boat of her size. The full results are given in Table 1.

As a result of *GB IV*'s structural weaknesses (another chain plate pulled out of the deck

**TABLE 1**

## 1978 – RWYC – OBSERVER ROUND BRITAIN RACE
## OVERALL FINAL RESULTS

| Position Scratch | Class | Class | Race no. | Yacht | Elapsed Time D | H | M |
|---|---|---|---|---|---|---|---|
| 1 | 1 | 3 | 58 | Great Britain IV | 13 | 1 | 24 |
| 2 | 2 | 3 | 114 | Three Legs of Mann II | 13 | 13 | 59 |
| 3 | 3 | 3 | 12 | Rogue Wave | 13 | 15 | 5 |
| 4 | 1 | 4 | 53 | A Cappella | 14 | 13 | 14 |
| 5 | 2 | 4 | 118 | Jan of Santa Cruz | 14 | 23 | 47 |
| 6 | 1 | 1 | 18 | Tielsa II | 15 | 1 | 4 |
| | | | | Includes time penalty of 03h 15m for late arrival Plymouth | | | |
| 7 | 3 | 4 | 28 | R.F.D. | 15 | 4 | 14 |
| 8 | 2 | 1 | 95 | Slithy Tove | 15 | 7 | 56 |
| 9 | 4 | 4 | 59 | Day Tripper | 15 | 9 | 21 |
| 10 | 5 | 4 | 29 | Whisky Jack | 15 | 11 | 11 |
| 11 | 1 | 2 | 54 | Petit Suisse | 15 | 11 | 37 |
| 12 | 3 | 1 | 43 | Great Britain II | 15 | 12 | 15 |
| 13 | 2 | 2 | 4 | Cherry Valley Duck | 15 | 12 | 52 |
| 14 | 4 | 3 | 17 | Johnwillie | 15 | 14 | 3 |
| 15 | 4 | 1 | 65 | Norvantes | 15 | 16 | 5 |
| 16 | 5 | 1 | 103 | N.S. 44 | 15 | 22 | 38 |
| | | | | Includes time penalty of 08h 00m for late arrival Plymouth | | | |
| 17 | 6 | 4 | 16 | Gazelle | 16 | 5 | 32 |
| 18 | 3 | 2 | 77 | Kurrewa | 16 | 7 | 17 |
| 19 | 7 | 4 | 66 | Comanche | 16 | 10 | 45 |
| 20 | 4 | 2 | 98 | Yamaha D'Ieteren | 16 | 11 | 45 |
| | | | | Includes time penalty of 00h 11m for late arrival Plymouth | | | |
| 21 | 8 | 4 | 100 | Run Around | 16 | 13 | 57 |
| | | | | Includes time penalty of 08h 00m for late arrival Plymouth | | | |
| 22 | 5 | 2 | 10 | Mezzanine | 16 | 14 | 12 |
| | | | | Includes time penalty of 02h 32m for late arrival Plymouth | | | |
| 23 | 6 | 2 | 5 | Attila | 17 | 0 | 34 |
| 24 | 7 | 2 | 94 | Jaws | 17 | 1 | 7 |
| 25 | 9 | 4 | 32 | Lydia Cardell | 17 | 18 | 0 |
| 26 | 6 | 1 | 8 | Bollemaat IV | 18 | 2 | 18 |
| 27 | 7 | 1 | 36 | Sherpa Bill | 18 | 19 | 8 |
| 28 | 8 | 2 | 27 | Assent | 18 | 21 | 57 |
| 29 | 8 | 1 | 88 | Ultima Thule | 20 | 17 | 37 |
| 30 | 9 | 1 | 38 | Lone Rival | 20 | 17 | 54 |
| 31 | 10 | 1 | 7 | Robertson's Golly | 20 | 20 | 45 |
| 32 | 11 | 1 | 48 | Gipsy Moth V | 20 | 21 | 13 |
| 33 | 10 | 4 | 92 | Telstar | 21 | 1 | 23 |
| 34 | 9 | 2 | 61 | Checkmate | 21 | 3 | 5 |
| 35 | 12 | 1 | 45 | Lydney Maid | 21 | 3 | 59 |
| 36 | 10 | 2 | 79 | Tsunami | 21 | 8 | 59 |
| 37 | 11 | 2 | 72 | Slightly | 21 | 11 | 37 |
| 38 | 12 | 2 | 82 | Kass-a-Nova | 21 | 16 | 14 |
| 39 | 13 | 1 | 25 | Haigri | 21 | 17 | 39 |
| 40 | 13 | 2 | 39 | Ocean Beetle | 21 | 21 | 0 |
| 41 | 14 | 2 | 89 | Pyledriver | 21 | 21 | 18 |

| Position | | | Race | | Elapsed Time | | |
|---|---|---|---|---|---|---|---|
| Scratch | Class | Class | no. | Yacht | D | H | M |
| 42 | 15 | 2 | 41 | Skol II | 21 | 23 | 3 |
| 43 | 16 | 2 | 85 | Ella | 22 | 5 | 8 |
| 44 | 14 | 1 | 44 | Elena | 22 | 6 | 0 |
| 45 | 5 | 3 | 35 | Lara of Bosham | 22 | 6 | 32 |
| 46 | 17 | 2 | 34 | Wild Rival | 22 | 6 | 48 |
| 47 | 18 | 2 | 14 | Tarnimara | 22 | 7 | 0 |
| 48 | 11 | 4 | 11 | Areoi | 22 | 7 | 33 |
| 49 | 19 | 2 | 69 | Sagitta | 22 | 7 | 36 |
| 50 | 20 | 2 | 81 | Hajji Baba | 22 | 7 | 55 |
| 51 | 21 | 2 | 99 | Contagious | 22 | 14 | 38 |
| | | | | Includes time penalty of 14h 15m for late arrival Plymouth | | | |
| 52 | 12 | 4 | 83 | B.P. Catcracker | 22 | 18 | 32 |
| 53 | 22 | 2 | 46 | Melodikum III | 22 | 18 | 33 |
| 54 | 15 | 1 | 87 | Ron Glas | 22 | 19 | 35 |
| 55 | 23 | 2 | 101 | Yacht & Boat Owner | 23 | 1 | 10 |
| 56 | 24 | 2 | 31 | West Wind | 23 | 4 | 29 |
| 57 | 25 | 2 | 75 | Christian Saul | 23 | 8 | 39 |

The following yachts failed to finish within the time limit for the race; they are included in the handicap results.

| | | | | | | | |
|---|---|---|---|---|---|---|---|
| 58 | 16 | 1 | 47 | Melmore | 23 | 21 | 20 |
| 59 | 26 | 2 | 2 | Supper Achilles | 23 | 22 | 30 |
| 60 | 17 | 1 | 50 | Galway Blazer | 23 | 23 | 12 |
| 61 | 27 | 2 | 9 | Bird | 24 | 2 | 25 |
| 62 | 28 | 2 | 51 | M. M. Microwave | 24 | 11 | 30 |
| Ret | Ret | 2 | 52 | Dytiscus III | | | |
| Ret | Ret | 4 | 23 | Heretic | | | |
| Ret | Ret | 4 | 104 | Anglia Pipedream | | | |
| Ret | Ret | 2 | 42 | Freemerle | | | |
| Ret | Ret | 2 | 74 | Hindostan | | | |
| Ret | Ret | 2 | 96 | Wily Bird | | | |
| Ret | Ret | 2 | 3 | Cutler Hammer Europa | | | |
| Ret | Ret | 2 | 70 | BBC Radio Birmingham | | | |
| Ret | Ret | 3 | 116 | Frygga of Cymru | | | |
| Ret | Ret | 1 | 71 | Nikonos III | | | |
| Ret | Ret | 2 | 33 | Demon | | | |
| Ret | Ret | 2 | 68 | Nimonic | | | |

on the return trip to Dartmouth) it was decided to strengthen her substantially. Herein, however, lay a problem. Because a trimaran's main hull is very narrow, it is very sensitive to changes in trim when the displacement is altered. For instance, *GB IV* was designed to weigh only four tons. She may have been slightly overweight when built. By adding half a ton of strengthening the boat would sink nearly 3ins, which plays havoc with the designed water-line. Not only are the crossbeams nearer the water, but the two floats are *in* the water – not just kissing the surface as intended. There is a further problem: the floats of *GB IV* were designed at 120 per cent buoyancy – each float displaces 120 per cent of the total weight of the boat. However, by the time the total weight has been increased, this figure would be approaching 100 per cent or less. This in turn would mean that when the boat was driven hard the lee float would be on the point of total immersion, with all the attendant problems of drag from the beam ends and the beam/float joints.

Because of these limitations it was impossible simply to add strength (and weight) to make *CB IV* bullet proof. There is no doubt that, had she been made strong enough to go well to windward in a breeze, she would have been so low in the water that the slamming of the forward crossbeams would have slowed her down even more. Also, her performance in light airs would have suffered. These problems contributed to her rather chequered career after the Round Britain Race and she never turned in another successful performance.

# 3

## *Boatfile*

Having looked fairly carefully at the relative performances of the Newick-designed *Rogue Wave* and the Kelsall-designed *GB IV* in the 1978 Round Britain Race I had started to think about taking a Newick trimaran in the 1980 OSTAR. Even though *Rogue Wave* had not won the race I'd been very impressed by her speed and reliability in moderate and heavy winds. The OSTAR – especially if it resembled the 1976 race – would be sailed with lots of wind on the nose, if not a gale or two. Unfortunately, I was in no position to either buy or commission a new boat so I had to bide my time and await developments. However as my wife Naomi was to do the race in her 53ft monohull *Kriter Lady*, I was determined to find a way of beating her.

Shortly after the Round Britain Race (July 1978) there was a rematch of the first four boats in that race. Organized by the French and called the Route du Rhum it was a single-handed event from St Malo to Pointe-a-Pitre, in the West Indies. The course was interesting as it involved beating out of the Channel and across the Bay of Biscay against winter gales before reaching better weather further south. Two possible routes presented themselves: to go south past Madeira and down the trade winds or the much shorter course past the Azores and through their associated calms. The entry list was formidable. As well as Phil Weld in *Rogue Wave* and Chay Blyth in *GB IV* there was Nick Keig's *Three Legs of Man III*, renamed *Seiko* and sailed by Alain Glicksman, and Wally Green's *A Cappella* sailed by Mike Birch. Birch had made a name for himself by finishing third in the stormy 1976 OSTAR in a Newick-designed Val 31. For this race he was delivering Green's *A Cappella* back to the USA. (She had to be lengthened to 35ft on the water-line to comply with the race rules for the Route du Rhum.) There were also a lot of other interesting boats. The old *GB III* had been brought out of retirement by Pierre Fehlman who hoped to be able to handle this 80 footer single-handed. Eugene Riguidel had a near sistership of *GB IV*, called *V.S.D.*. Olivier de Kersauson was sailing a 70ft trimaran called *Kriter IV* – interesting as it was designed (against the current trend) with floats of less than 100 per cent buoyancy, similar to Colas's old *Manureva*, another partnership in the race. Against the trimaran fleet there was a monster catamaran called *Paul Ricard*, sailed by Mark Pajot and designed as a cruiser–racer by Spronk. The leading monohull challenger was *Kriter V*, a slim, lightweight 70 footer with a modern fractional rig and Michel Malinovsky at the helm. Altogether, plenty of material for a dramatic race – as indeed it was.

Having helped my former skipper prepare *GB IV* I joined, along with my wife, the crew of the French *Grand Louis*, the 65ft cruising schooner accompanying the fleet as the radio relay vessel. We hoped this would give us a good chance to keep an 'eye' on the fleet and analyse relative performances.

The drama began very soon after the start. On the first day, despite relative calms, there were several incidents. Pajot ran over a small spectator yacht nearly sinking it and possibly damaging his own catamaran; *Disque d'or* (ex *GB III*) returned to St Malo with self-steering problems, likewise *GB IV*; and *V.S.D.* hit the spectator ferry and was forced to return to port for repairs. However, they were all soon back in the race and making good time out into the Atlantic.

On the second or third day a real humdinger of a gale blew up. The seas were bad and on *Grand Louis* we hove-to for a few hours at one point. How, we wondered, were the single-handers coping. Blyth had retired with more self-steering problems; Pajot had to abandon his catamaran when one of the floats flooded; Fehlman had stopped sailing, exhausted with no self-steering and enormous sails to cope with; Weld had trouble with a mainsail over the side. Malinovsky (*Kriter V*), Birch (*Olympus Photo*) and De Kersauson (*Kriter IV*) survived the storm unscathed.

Before we could hear any more news our radio broke down leaving us, the radio relay vessel, incommunicado. We stopped at the Azores for two days while an electrical engineer flown out from France succeeded in making the total radio failure an intermittent one. For the rest of the trip, therefore, we picked up only small bits of information from the fleet and it was not until we were less than 100 miles from Guadaloupe that we heard of the dramatic battle for the lead. Two wildly different boats were vying with each other for the front place over the last 60 miles of the course which included a compulsory circuit of Guadaloupe Island. They were Mike Birch in his little trimaran *Olympus Photo* and Malinovsky in his large monohull. There was no news of Weld, De Kersauson, Riguidel, Colas or any other of the race favourites as all ears were glued to the live commentary of the last few hours of the race as reported by Guadaloupe Radio. With 60 miles to go Birch was five miles ahead, having taken the southerly trade wind route, while Malinovsky had come straight past the Azores. Together they beat southwards down the west coast of the island with the monohull taking a small lead. Round the southern tip of the island and still close-hauled *Kriter V* held the advantage, and at the point where the course freed to a close reach for the last six miles, she had a one mile lead. The commentators voice came clearly and excitedly into the saloon on *Grand Louis* where the whole crew huddled eagerly round the radio. The atmosphere was electric.

'Malinovsky has 10 kilometres to sail and his lead is up to more than one kilometre, he will surely win for France', said the commentator.

'Wait till they ease sheets for the finish', I replied optimistically.

'Malinovsky's beautiful yacht is powering to the finishing line and although Birch is now gaining, it is too late', continued the commentator. Then a few minutes later he was very excited:

'Malinovsky has 2 kilometres to go and Birch is 500 metres behind and is catching up – maybe he will run Malino close'.

'Come on Mike!' I shouted at the radio, much to the amusement of our French crewmates, and aside to Naomi, 'If Mike wins let's try and buy his old Val 31 – if he can do it

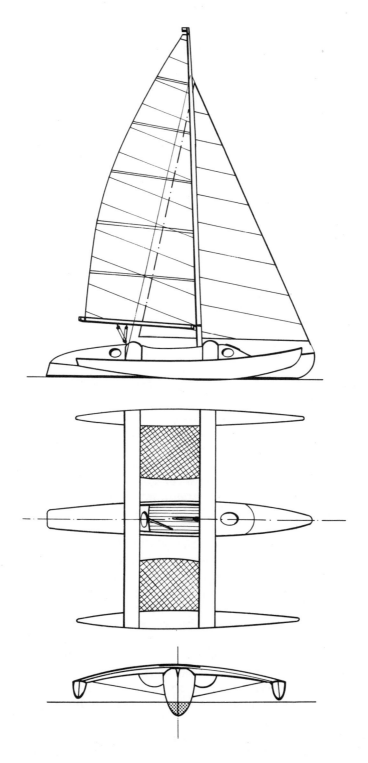

**Fig. 4** Boatfile

with *Olympus Photo* I'll have a go at the next OSTAR with *Jan.*' Rash words! Again the commentator:

'It's a race to the finish, one and a half kilometres to go and Birch is 200 metres behind . . . he's going very fast . . . one kilometre to go and Birch is 100 metres behind . . . now 50, now ten, and he's sailing straight past! . . . It's unbelievable, Birch is going to win . . .'

He crossed the line and Malinovsky crossed 90 seconds after him.

Over the next few days the rest of the fleet came in and the picture of the race became clearer. Phil Weld, who had taken the southerly route, came third, followed by De Kersauson, way below the best performance potential of his trimaran. Riguidel put *V.S.D.* on a reef north of Guadaloupe. Colas was never seen again; it was presumed he had been run down by a ship or had sunk. Glicksman brought ex *Three Legs* in way down the fleet having retired from the race and picked up crew in the Azores. And so those who had come first, second, third and fourth in the Round Britain came retired, retired, third and first, and I bought a 31ft trimaran for the 1980 OSTAR.

Back in England I picked up *Jan of Santa Cruz* and laid her up in Fareham Creek, Portsmouth, for a year before sailing her to Crosshaven in Southern Ireland for the winter of '79–'80 where I would be able to prepare her for the race in the summer.

Working on a 31 footer is very easy compared to the larger vessels I had been used to. *Jan* was renamed *Boatfile* and hauled up on the beach for her refit. Her equipment was exactly as it had been for the Round Britain Race in 1978 and as such needed considerable improvement before I could undertake to sail this 'day sailer' to windward across the North Atlantic. The rig and sails were in good order; none-the-less after sailing her I felt there was a gap in her wardrobe. As well as the mainsail, fully battened, and spinnaker, there were three jibs: genoa, no. 2 and storm. I added a no. 3 to fill the gap below the no. 2 (see fig. 5). The Old Autohelm I changed for a new one and fitted solar panels to provide battery charging. Down below the cabin was so small – about 10ft by 2ft 6ins by 4ft high – that there was no scope for improvement. I just hoped that there would be enough room to fit my gear, food, water, radio equipment, myself etc (see fig. 6).

Although I'd only sailed *Boatfile* for a short time at that stage, it had been enough to learn certain tricks. Firstly, handling the boat: control was, in general, good and tacking was easy provided one was not too heavy on the tiller – an initial angle of 10 degrees gradually increased as the tri slowed down was enough to execute a perfect tack. Backing the jib was a mistake as it stopped the boat – a last resort only if all way was already lost. Reefing I could do while continuing to sail – steering with one foot – but jib changing was best accomplished by stopping the boat completely, quickly doing the sail change and then starting again. This system – using hanks – was so rapid, because of the small sails, that I didn't consider it necessary to use a furling jib.

I also came across one or two drawbacks: when the wind blew hard and the sail was reduced the trimaran suffered from bad lee-helm. This was not helped by the position of the centreboard, aft of the mast and too far back, and also the storm jib which was set right forward rather than close to the mast as would have been the case had she had an inner forestay. However, there was nothing I could do within my budget to improve the situation, so I accepted it as it was. (See Part 2, Chapter 6.)

To qualify for the OSTAR each competitor was required to sail 500 miles single-handed

**Fig. 5** Boatfile *sail plan*

and non-stop. I elected to do this without any form of self-steering, so that I could test my reaction to no sleep and/or force myself to get the trimaran to steer herself. It proved to be an informative first single-handed voyage. I chose a route – the English Channel to southern Ireland – which turned out to be on the wind all the way. *Boatfile* would *not* steer herself – it is not a trait of multihulls, I discovered – so I steered all the first day and night, all the second day and night and on the third morning I had perfected a system of steering while asleep. Of course, I'd wake up with the sails aback or sailing free and fast in the wrong direction. The most time I could get to eat, sleep or navigate was ten or 15 minutes while she almost took care of herself. On the third day I stopped for four hours in mid-ocean and slept. I finished the voyage very tired and hungry; I had a lot to learn about single-handed sailing.

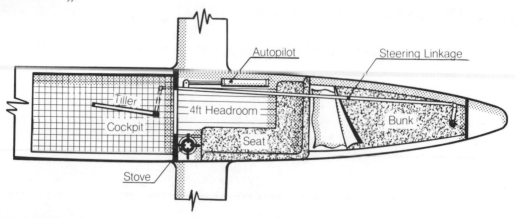

**Fig. 6** Boatfile *accommodation*

A 100 per cent reliable autopilot is essential for short-handed multihull sailing – let there be no doubt of that. I eventually took four, although I used only one. Other than that immediate modification I was pretty happy with the yacht. I knew it would be diabolically wet in mid-Atlantic, but then, with a small yacht – especially one with a low free-board and a forward facing companionway – that was to be expected.

Two weeks before the OSTAR my wife Naomi and I took *Boatfile* in the Crystal Trophy. This event, specifically for multihulls, follows a course of 360 miles around the English Channel and is considered the UK Multihull Championship. I had the boat prepared for the OSTAR and hence met all the safety rules for that event. But such was the mess that the safety rules were in, they required me to add several items of safety gear, including a bigger anchor and a massive pulpit, just for a weekend race! The weather was mainly light, which suited us, and I remember learning two things. First, it is essential to fly a spinnaker whenever possible. We were sailing alongside another, larger, trimaran in the night and we were both carrying spinnakers on a close reach when our guy came undone. As the apparent wind was on the beam I thought we would be just as well off with the genoa. Not so, we discovered; although our speed felt the same our competitor drew slowly ahead. Second, I learnt again that if there is *no* wind, then *no one* moves! However fast a multihull is, it still needs some wind. We finished the race behind the larger trimaran.

In late May 1980 I took *Boatfile* to Plymouth for the final week before the OSTAR. It was the time for final adjustments and much studying of the rest of the fleet.

The rules for previous OSTAR's had specified no upper size limit but had included classes for smaller yachts. The smallest class was for yachts under 32ft and it is probable that Dick Newick had this in mind when he designed the Val 31. However, for the 1980 OSTAR there were several changes. The upper size limit was set at 56ft to keep the monsters of past races at bay. This change meant there was almost no chance of a monohull winner as no 56ft monohull could hope to beat the vast armada of multihulls. There was also a water-line length limitation introduced to discourage entries with blunt bow and stern (thus trying to maximize water-line length within the overall class lengths).

*Boatfile on the beach in Currabinny, Cork during preparations for OSTAR 1980.*

Therefore, the smallest – or Jester class – limit was set at 32ft overall with a 26ft water-line. *Boatfile*, at 31ft overall but with a 28ft water-line, was therefore moved up a class. I was not too upset about this as I'd known it was going to happen and anyway, although I thought I wouldn't do well in class 2 (the Gipsy Moth class), it still left me the challenge of trying to beat all the Jester class.

The entry list included a number of trimarans near the 56ft limit. Eric Tabarly had entered his hydrofoil trimaran *Paul Ricard* although, alas, an old skiing injury forced him to retire from the race at the last minute and to be replaced by Mark Pajot. As a result the

Boatfile—*Notice the small centre cockpit.*

yacht became an 'unofficial entry' – which in no way diminished the interest in this strange looking craft. The foils were fixed to the low-volume float and were designed solely to provide lift to the lee float, and hence stability. The whole was an interesting design but potentially dangerous as the floats in themselves were short and small; in other words, sailing fast in a gale *Paul Ricard* would be a very stable vessel but lying ahull in a gale she could easily be capsized by wind and wave action.

In the absence of *Great Britain IV* (she'd been withdrawn), the designs of Derek Kelsall and, indeed, the hopes of an English victory, depended on Nick Keig with *Three Legs of Mann III*, a similar design to *The Legs of Mann II* from the Round Britain Race. A new *V.S.D.* similar to the old one which had ended up on the rocks in the Route du Rhum was entered by Eugene Riguidel. She was a more racy and lighter version of *Three Legs* with no concession to cruising comforts.

Phil Weld was back with a Newick trimaran, designed especially for the race. (His old *Rogue Wave* was outside the size limit). *Moxie* was rigged fairly conservatively with not only a roller headsail (now standard practice on all multihulls except the very smallest for short-handed sailing) but a furler mainsail as well – easy to handle but how efficient? Also by Newick were Mike Birch's new *Olympus Photo* (46ft) with lines typical of her designer, incorporating a solid 'wing' rather than two crossbeams, and Tom Grossman's radical *Kriter VII*. She was strong and light with an interior wire and strut space frame and a fairly

Boatfile—*The lifting skeg and rudder are visible.*

sophisticated composite skin. Her appearance made her favourite with the bookies but probably not with the other competitors; her very low crossbeams looked as though they would be hit hard by the flying wave tops, producing the same slowing down effect that had marred *GB IV*'s strong wind performance.

Walter Green had designed and built a group of trimarans for Eric Loiseau (*Gauloise IV*), Phil Steggall (*Jeans Foster*) and himself (*Chaussettes Olympia*) which were all around the 40ft mark and similar in design to his *A Cappella/Olympus Photo* (fourth in the 1978 Round Britain, first in the 1978 Route du Rhum). They were all large enough to win overall.

Up against this bunch of trimarans there was one proa (which capsized), no fast catamarans and a lot of monohulls, none of which finished higher than sixth. 1980 was still the age of the trimaran.

The weather for the start was almost perfect and my thoughts as I was towed out to the line (by Naomi on *Kriter Lady*, her old 53ft *Express Crusader*) were devoted entirely to guessing what the next three weeks would bring. *Boatfile* at 31ft would probably be beaten by some of the larger monohulls, but I was sure a trimaran would win. Of the dozen or so top runners at least a few of them must get through unscathed, but I was equally sure that some would fall.

The first to drop out of the running was *Kriter VII*; Grossman was sailing around in the area of the start a few minutes before the gun when he suddenly dived below to get his stop-watch and sailed slap into the 48ft sloop *Garuda*, damaging his starboard float in the process. Although he started again 24 hours later, he was not in contention, finishing in tenth place three days behind the leader.

*My wife Naomi, on* Kriter Lady, *tows me out to the OSTAR start.*

At last, after a nerve-wracking last few minutes jockeying for a position on a crowded start line the gun went and 88 yachts and their skippers started beating westwards towards Lands End, the Atlantic and the USA.

What happened to me in the race is best told by quoting my brief, cryptic and sometimes emotional log entries. These, along with a daily explanation taken from memory give an interesting insight, not only into small multihull sailing but also into the effect on the sailer of bad conditions, apprehensiveness about single-handed sailing, and various other factors.

*Day 0*

| | | | |
|---|---|---|---|
| 11.30 Towed out of Milbay | Wind W | 12 knots | Course 245 |
| 19.40 Abeam Lizard 3 miles | Wind NW | 10 knots | " 255 |
| Track wheel broke | | | |

Not a lot of information or navigational details in the first 24 hours. In fact, I found soon after the start that my course made good on the starboard tack was almost 45 degrees to the course required for the Lizard Point miles ahead, so I tacked back in towards the shore.

*One minute to go to the OSTAR start. I drive* Boatfile *down the line looking for a gap.*

This payed me enormously as, first, it got me clear of the turbulent air and water from the other competitors and hundreds of spectator boats and, second, it put me, when I tacked back, on the right side of the course as the wind swung from west to north-west. Approaching the Lizard I could see *Moxie, Paul Ricard* and *V.S.D.* ahead and I appeared to be fourth. I knew it couldn't last but I hoped, at that stage, to maintain a place in the top ten.

The damage to the track was to one of the four wheels on the mainsheet traveller which meant that I could only alter the boom position when there was no weight on the sheet. Annoying but not crippling.

During the first night I stayed on deck and steered from sunset till daybreak. I didn't dare sleep with other competitors around and I kept the use of the self-steering gear to a minimum to conserve battery power. Fortunately, the weather was OK.

*Day 1*

| | | | | |
|---|---|---|---|---|
| 03.00 | 15 miles south Bishop Rock | Wind NW | 10 knots | Course 255 |
| 05.30 | Self-steering 5 hours to date | Wind W | 8 knots | " |
| 10.00 | Tacked to 310 | | | |
| 12.00 | Noon fix 49° 20' N 08° 20' W Run 180 miles in 20 hours | | | |
| 18.00 | Rough – reefed | Wind SW | 25 knots | Course 280 |

In general a good day and my morale was obviously fairly high. I'd got a good fix at noon and progress was satisfactory. By the evening I was laying the desired course – west – close reaching on port tack. Since the start I'd been sailing with the no. 2 jib and full main. Towards evening I put in a reef, working by the mast and steering with a foot.

*Two hours after the start. The Argos automatic position transmitted can be seen on the afterdeck.*

Boatfile *showing the sail hatch forward, the centre cockpit and the aft accommodation.*

I notice that I recorded (or estimated as I had no instruments) the wind speed as 25 knots and the sea rough. Everything is relative: in a small boat with such a low free-board the sea starts feeling pretty rough when the wind touches 20 knots. I wrote very little at this stage, especially concerning navigation. There were two reasons for this: first, I was not too worried about accurate navigation as a position error ten or 20 miles north or south

Boatfile *after the OSTAR start.*

would not alter the course I wanted to steer; and second, I was totally busy with eating and sleeping (a total of five hours in 24). Actually, I had already found the routine I liked best: I steered all day with the exception of meal or navigation breaks, during which time the autopilot would take over; slept for two hours before sunset; then steered all night without a break till daylight, when I slept for another two hours before starting the day again. Occasionally I slept for an hour in mid-afternoon.

*Day 2* 9 June
Rough

Not very informative and not a lot of navigation going on. I think there must have been a small depression centre over the fleet as I experienced 30 knots of wind swinging from ahead to astern and then settling in the north.

   During the night I changed jib for the first time and found it only took a few minutes if I prepared for it properly. Before sailing I had fixed a line to the eye on the end of the jib halyard. This line then led through a block at the base of the forestay and back to the cockpit; when the jib was set the line lay up the luff of the sail. To change sail I could let go the halyard and pull on the line to bring the sail down to the foredeck while still steering in the cockpit. As *Boatfile* slowed down I'd clip the tiller amidships and the boat would lie head to wind, weathercocked by the mainsail. In this position her motion was easy and it was a quick job to nip up, unhank the jib and replace it with another. Of course, my line on the halyard meant that I could unsnap it from the jib and just leave it without having to

*My main rival – Naomi on* Kriter Lady, *a Gallant 53ft sloop.*

hook it to any point on deck. With the new jib on and the sheets changed I'd go back to the cockpit, unclip the tiller, hoist the sail, back it to get the bow off the wind, and I'd be underway again.

*Day 3* 10 June
Good talk to Naomi
Noon 49° 18′ N 16° 55′ W                  Wind N   15 knots   Course 285
Late N   wind Heavy

'Good talk' indicated my only successful attempt at radio communication. Naomi had good radio equipment on board her big monohull while all I had space for was a good radio direction finder and a portable emergency radio employing the recognized frequency 2182. In theory, Naomi would listen to all the race broadcasts, including a weather forecast and the other yachts, positions and, at a prearranged time each day, I would raise her on my small set and she would relay all the news. The system was fraught with complications. To meet a fixed radio time each day is difficult when racing single-handed as one is invariably doing something vital – such as sleeping – at the appointed hour. Also, my set required a telescopic aerial to be raised above decks and an earth wire to be trailed in the water (this I could do by dropping a small lead sinker down the centreboard box with the earth wire attached – fine until the sinker caught on the centreboard and the wire broke). Not least of the problems was that my battery power may be needed for an emergency so I could only transmit quick acknowlegments to Naomi's longer messages. On this occasion we had a long chat, I heard the forecast, the only one I received in the race, and I learnt to my great astonishment that I was lying sixth. The race organizers were receiving the position of each yacht using the Argos system (see Part 2, Chapter 16). Altogether, it was a great boost to the morale.

Later that evening the wind rose to 30 knots, but fortunately still from the north, so I could steer west. I found, though, that the wave angle directly on the beam was giving *Boatfile* an almighty hammering. In larger multihulls driving hard on the wind presses the lee float down and the windward one is held well clear of the approaching waves. This is not so on a small tri as the windward float is still near the water and is regularly clouted. Another interesting experience was the way in which a wave peak would pass under the main hull, lifting the boat high in the air, then under the lee float, lifting it and hence making the trimaran heel to windward causing the windward float to slam down on to the back of the wave. I could have avoided this by keeping more sail up, but I thought that would be too big a risk.

*Day 4* 11 June Altered clocks to GMT.
N'ly   force 8   Very rough
3 reefs   no jib
Steering 240–270
? forecast any worse
? what does the weather map look like
? your tactics
? when will it end
Est Noon   48° N 20° W -about

A pretty miserable damp day. Sailing with the storm jib and two reefs was just possible but when I put the third reef in (for the first time ever) I found that the severe lee helm made *Boatfile* impossible to control. (The problem is explained in the chapter on multihull design Chapter 14.) At any rate, I couldn't improve the situation without a way of bringing the sail area aft (i.e. staysail instead of jib) or the centreboard forward. All I could do was lower the jib and sail with just the mainsail, depressed at the thought of the miles I was losing. My list of questions were ready to be asked if radio contact could be established. I couldn't understand why the wind remained northerly and rose to gale force; I was keen to get a description of the weather map so that I could work out my own forecast. My efforts only resulted in getting the radio wet. Still no navigation – it was too wet to use a sextant unless absolutely necessary. Neither did I have an accurate DR as I didn't possess the instruments to record the relevant details.

The autopilot worked perfectly and always seemed to steer a better course than I did when the wind was constant in direction. The unit itself was mounted below with its drive arm fixed directly to the rod connecting the tiller in the centre cockpit with the rudder. This rod passed through the tiny aft cabin along the side of the bunk, which arrangement allowed me to alter the compass heading on the autopilot both from my bunk and on deck. Lying in my bunk I could, then, be faced with two possibilities: if I was getting the desired course free of the wind, any alteration in wind direction would be felt by the sails flapping or stalling and I'd have to go on deck to adjust them; or, if I was close-hauled and not making the course, any change in wind direction would be felt by the boat luffing or tearing off at a breakneck speed. The latter I could correct simply by resetting the compass on the pilot a few degrees free or closer to the new wind angle. I was often woken from a nap by the change in the boat's movement but I got used to reaching out and resetting the pilot without getting out of my sleeping bag. Occasionally I would not be wakened by the tell-tale signs and so the autopilot would happily continue to steer a constant course into a wind that was slowly but surely heading me, until *Boatfile* ended up aback. By then it would be too late and I'd have to crawl out and do something. I soon discovered it was easiest, in this situation, to steer the boat round in a complete circle and back on course rather than tacking the jib, getting going again and tacking back.

*Day 5* 12 June
Wind N'ly force 6   storm jib and 2 reefs
Becoming lighter   changed to no. 2 and full main
Estimated noon   46° 30' N 23° W
Fix at noon   46° 53'N   25° 25'W   possibly less
Course W mag
Limits required W mag to 300 mag
Changed clothes

A much lighter wind on this day afforded a chance to navigate and dry out. I was surprised to get a fix from the sun which put me further west than my DR. I was quite happy to accept the extra distance as it made no difference to my course and there was no land for 1000 miles, so I didn't bother to check for errors.

I recorded my course limits as 270 degrees magnetic to 300 degrees magnetic. My tactics were, each day, to calculate (or measure) the rhumb line and great circle courses and choose the heading that gave me the best speed within these limits. Beating, I'd choose the tack nearest to either heading.

*Day 6* Friday 13th!
Altered clocks to GMT −1                     Wind N'ly
03.00 Headed slowly
04.30 On to autopilot tacked to 330°          Wind W'ly
05.30 All's well
07.30 Woke to find wind freed reset
Autopilot to 285°                             Wind S'ly   Boat speed 8 knots
To noon   150 miles on about 15° south of W true
Back beam creaking at joint; tightened bolts
Heard you on the radio
? I'm 6th
? 4 people rescued
Wind rising from SW all night   Making 300° till mid-night
Retied all battens   Sewed up gloves

I didn't bother to calculate a sight on day 6 but, perhaps put out by the discrepancy between the DR and the fix the day before I at least estimated a day's run and direction.

My mainsail had full length battens, supporting a high roach, and I'd noticed they were coming untied. I lowered the mainsail, checked it carefully for signs of chafe, retied all the battens and rehoisted it. This took about 20 minutes and was well worth the sailing time wasted compared to the possible loss of sail shape if I'd lost a batten or two.

That night the wind showed all the signs of getting up to a westerly gale.

*Day 7* 14 June
Wind gale force
Down to storm jib and 2 reefs till 05.00 then stopped
Main only going north on port tack 1 knot
Up at 09.00 tacked to 255° mag   Lashed helm amidships   Making 2–3 knots
Spent morning in bed
Est. noon 46° N 31° W   Must aim for 42° N at 47° W
19.00 Tried sailing   Wind still NW 7 to 8   No good – need a smaller jib – going too fast and hitting waves. Jib down fore-reaching under main again
What are you doing?
Heard you talking to a Dutch yacht but could only make out the odd word
'lowest I've seen' depression I suppose
'Azores' – who?
21.00–24.00 sailing again on 255° but no good   Bad waves   Stopped again

A letter to Naomi followed in the log which pointed out, in general, how stupid we were to be single-handed sailing in mid-atlantic. It ended with a few resolutions:
  1. Buy a house.
  2. Settle down.
  3. Never sail a trimaran single-handed.
  4. Always carry a good radio so that communication is possible.

This letter only goes to show how much a bad, rough, wet day can depress one into rash promises! I did find, though, that the more depressing the weather the more determined I became to race hard, on the basis that at least a good result would justify the misery.

When there was too much wind to sail I found I could put a very deep third reef in the mainsail (albeit with difficulty as it required standing way aft to reach the boom end to re-lead the second reefing line), lower the storm jib and then, by lashing the helm amidships, get *Boatfile* to steer herself. Set up like this I was able to make two to three knots 60 degrees to the course – to windward – without wasting self-steering power. It was safer than lying ahull as the boat had the speed to climb waves at a fine angle rather than lay at their mercy. Meanwhile I could sleep properly and solidly for the first time. On the debit side, having a way of slowing down and handling bad weather in relative safety may have made me overcautious or even lazy, yet it turned out to have been the more prudent policy to adopt as my two sister ships suffered sufficient damage to hold them back, allowing me to stay ahead.

*Day 8* 15 June
Estimated course noon to noon

$$64 \text{ miles on } 240°$$
$$7 \quad '' \quad \text{on } 330°$$
$$7 \quad '' \quad \text{on } 215°$$

09.00 wind force 9    Bad bit
Is Naomi sailing while I'm stopped here?
Noon 45° N 33° W
Present position is 1200 miles to Plymouth co. 090°

$$420 \quad '' \quad \text{to Horta (Azores) co. } 175°$$
$$1700 \quad '' \quad \text{to finish} \qquad \text{co. } 270° \text{ to } 290°$$

6 p.m. heard you call up and caught a few words: 'all is well . . . 45° N . . . any problems . . . call tomorrow'
18.30 started sailing at last          Wind W and N
Wind dropping   One reef out

By the time the worst of the storm had passed I had been stationary for 34 and a half hours in the previous two days. During this period, I later discovered, I'd dropped from sixth or seventh place to sixteenth. I'd been very concerned over the safety of my little boat (and myself) and working out the distances to the nearest port in case some calamity overtook me was the best way I had of assuring that nothing would go wrong. One pleasant aspect as a result of the storm was how much fitter I felt from all that sleep.

My attempts at radio communication were pretty futile. In fact, Naomi was level with me at that stage, only 300 miles further north on the great circle route. She continued to transmit at the appointed hour every day but, at those distances, it was not surprising I had trouble hearing her.

*Day 9* 16 June
05.00 Tacked to 320°                    Storm jib 2 reefs
07.00 Tacked to 245°                    No.3 jib 1 reef
Noon tacked to 320° Wind going S of W   No.2 jib

Noon pos 43° 40' N 33° 20' W
Hove-to to pump out starboard float
Repaired canvas cockpit sides
Been sitting here drinking tea waiting for the schedule to listen for you on the radio and all the time the clock had stopped. When I checked it with the Chronometer it was 10 minutes too late – blast. Chin up.
Steered 300° till midnight. Wind and sea rising.

While I'd managed to get a few repairs done, I was still concerned about the movement where the aft crossbeam was bolted to the main hull. I managed to rebolt it using some stainless plates as large washers, which helped a bit but it continued to move more as a result of upward pull from the mainsheet than from structural weakness. The canvas cockpit sides had ripped during the storm but were easily repaired. Water was getting into the starboard float; I'd stopped to check both floats as a precaution and found inches of water in one. I had to pump it dry daily from then on. If it was to windward I'd climb out with the portable pump and do the job while still sailing under autopilot. If it was to leeward I'd have to put the boat about, pump out and then have to complete a circle to get sailing again.

Needless to say, I was pretty bored with steering by this time. I had several positions to steer from; sitting on the cockpit floor, sitting on the cockpit rim, standing leaning against the canvas dodger and netting wire or sitting on same. I'd used a deckchair while practising before the race which fitted nicely in the cockpit but it was no use in deep sea because it kept capsizing when the boat pitched. I'd also brought along a small padded cushion and eventually found that standing leaning against some support with the cushion wedged in between – not very comfortable and therefore good for staying awake – was the best way to endure the endless hours on the helm.

Each day I forced myself to do some filming. I had a small 16mm camera, a tape recorder and a lot of film. The equipment had to live crammed under the bunk along with all the other boat equipment and despite getting pretty damp it always worked. The TV company had fixed a bracket on the cockpit to which I could mount the camera while I 'performed' in front of it. Instead, I found it was easier to ignore the bracket and simply wedge the camera in a coil of rope or a sail and hope for the best. More self-discipline is required to film on a boat when you're tired than to do *any* other activity. It seemed so unproductive but, having said I'd do it, I forced myself to use up a two-minute reel each day, and not a minute more. The results were unspectacular but some of it did come out OK.

*Day 10*
Steered 300° till 02.00 then wind at gale force
Main only making 2 knots on 315° Wind W'ly
09.00 woke after 4 hours sleep to find a large container ship almost parked along side. He disappeared when he saw me on deck. Started sailing again course 310°
Speed 7 knots Wind going SW
Fog reflector up

A further seven hours lost through being unwilling to sail into gale force seas. Looking back it seems over cautious but at the time it felt as though I either had to stop, or the boat would fall apart.

In those bad conditions, when sailing was possible, life would have been transformed if I could have used the autopilot all the time – or at least more than the eight hours I allowed. I had on board one 60-amp-hour battery, charged by two solar panels which produced 2½ amps in full sunlight. This meant I had, say, 10 amp hours a day to play with, of which I allowed four (½ amp for eight hours) to the autohelm and 6 for all other needs, i.e. lighting. I could keep consumption down by steering each day and every night which meant the compass light was the only one in continual use. With more solar panels I could have used the Autohelm all the time, but then, whatever one is prepared to give for an extra pair of hands at sea, one is very reluctant to justify the enormous cost of solar panels when gently rocking in a marina.

*Day 11* 18 June
00.00 Co. 315°      Boat speed 5 knots      Storm and 2 reefs
06.00 Co. 330°        ''        ''    7 knots        No.2 1 reef
Course to St Johns Newfoundland 305° 600 miles
        to Newport R.I. on rhumb line 280°
        to avoid gulf stream more than 265° required
06.15 turned in with wind going astern
08.00 reef out no.1 genoa/reacher goosewinged wind E'ly dead astern
Noon 45° 23′ N 38° 20′ W
Half way in 10 days!
14.00 wind ESE light making 3–6 knots
16.00 wind S              ''      7 knots
19.00 wind SW close-hauled again Wind 20 knots rising

Although I carried a spinnaker I didn't use it at that stage; the seas were too rough with a leftover swell and the wind was not steady enough either in strength or direction to set it safely. Given the same situation again I would risk it.

My position lay almost exactly along the course I thought would be ideal. Passing through the position 46 degrees north and 40 degrees west was far enough north to ensure good winds and was, in distance, only slightly longer than the great circle course which gave other yachts far worse weather.

*Day 12* 19 June
Altered clocks to GMT – 2
00.00 – 05.00 sailing 6 knots into SW 6      Storm jib 2 reefs
05.00 – 08.00 Autohelm Co. 280°    speed 5 knots
08.00 steering   wind now gale force
12.00 Cold wet very tired   STOPPED SAILING jogging under main only
Noon pos. 45 N 41° 40′ W      DR 1300 miles to go
I am totally exhausted. Too weak   Lunch of marmite sandwich and 2 eggs, 1 hour's sleep then a struggle to go on deck again to tack. Still jogging
20.00 sailing again on 235° 6 knots      wind WNW 6 and dying

I also wrote: 'I'm very tired of this trip. The trimaran is too small. I don't like multis. I don't like single-handed sailing – especially not both at the same time'.

I think most depressing was that I had only just got dried out from one gale when along came the next one, and what really got to me was that these force 7s and 8s forced me to stop but wouldn't stop the bigger boats. Altogether, I spent two days and one and a half hours making little or no progress. One good reason one only finds grumpy comments in a log book is because, when the weather is good, navigating, eating, repairing and sleeping are the priorities – not writing. Having said that, next day I actually qualified the previous entry by adding that single-handed sailing would be all right providing one had

1. A large boat;
2. A good autopilot; and
3. Reliable electrics and communications.

*Day 13* 20 June
Light wind all night    Course variable but predominantly W Speed 2 knots
Noon fix 44° 55′ N 43° 08′ W
1255 miles left
Target 11 days at 114 miles made good each day
Fog wind SSW

Only 45 miles made good towards the finishing line. The wind was rising again from the west-south-west, which meant being close-hauled by evening.

My target for 11 days meant an optimum time for the whole voyage of 24 days, the time Mike Birch had taken four years previously for the same class of trimaran and doing the same course; as far as I could gather it was the record for a vessel of 31ft or less. 114 miles a day were required to break it – well within my grasp, provided the expected calms towards America were not too extensive.

Fog gradually became a regular feature of the voyage and, initially, I was quite frightened by the thought of hitting a ship in the bad visibility. However, I soon changed my views and actually came to like the complete white out. From my own experience as a merchant navy deck officer I knew that a much better lookout was kept in the fog as the radar, which in good visibility was never switched on, would be carefully monitored. Therefore there was a greater chance of being run down when the visibility was good. I also reasoned that avoiding a ship while doing 8 knots or so in very thick fog would be impossible, anyway, so one might as well relax and not bother to look out at all. Of course, the seamanlike thing to do would be to slow down enough to take avoiding action and watch constantly – but that is not racing.

*Day 14* 21 June
Wind force 3–5
Steered all night – cold and thick fog
Sea getting rougher all morning
13.00 fog cleared    noon sight 43° 49′ N    DR 47° W
To go 1105 miles   110 miles per day
I HATE ROUGH SEAS
Steered 280° in the evening wind strong SW fog back

*Day 15* 22 June
05.00 reduced speed to 6 knots because of rough seas
08.00 7 knots again
10.00 Force 7 reduced to mainsail only 3 reefs making 4 knots on course
Noon DR 43° 17′ N 50° 30′ W
To go 950 miles target 105 miles per day
Fog

At noon on the 22nd I was just on the tip of the Great Bank of Newfoundland. My DR put me just south of the tip but it was obviously wrong as I passed several large buoys and poles which I assumed were attached to fishermens' pots – 250 miles from land?! If I'd had news of the other competitors during such uneventful, but frustrating, days I may have sailed harder. The greatest difficulty in single-handed racing is keeping the drive going, there's no one to pace and no one to keep you at it. The following two days gave me a break in the line of depressions and strong winds from behind drove me well ahead of my target.

*Day 16* 23 June
Wind SSW and fog all morning
12.00 fog cleared wind NE'ly
Noon sight   42° 50′ N 54° 20′ W   60 miles more than DR. THAT'S BETTER!!!
18.00 wind ENE   (dead astern) force 7 making 9–11 knots
18.00 to 24.00 good surfing fast speeds
MIDNIGHT FLOODS

*Day 17* 24 June
All morning surfing
Noon RDF from Sable Island (range 100 miles NW)
Pos. 43° 15′ N 50° W   run 230 miles! 560 miles to go
New target 22 days (5 days at 112 a day)
Everything wet
19.00 wind NW'ly
22.00 wind to SW tacked
24.00 wind died Fog again

*Boatfile* went tremendously well in those strong following winds; she was dead easy to handle and due to the rocker in her hulls she showed no tendency to dig in her bows. The only problem was the major flood. At some stage in the night I left the Autohelm to handle the downwind slide and went below. I found 6ins of water above the floor boards and quite a few items of equipment floating about. I pumped out and then moved all the gear from under the cockpit floor so that I could investigate the most likely place that could have split open – the join between centreboard box and hull. There was no hole and no sign of any water coming in. Mysterious. I went on deck again to steer through the night. A short while later *Boatfile* was picked up by a wave and surfed forward into the pitch dark at terrifying speed. I heard the sound of rushing water and looked into the cabin – sure enough, in the torch light I could see water sloshing about over the floor again. Once more under autopilot I sat below hunched on the small seat between the hatch and the bunk to think about the situation. On the next surf the answer revealed itself. The Val class has a steering rod which goes through the cabin to the rudder stock, as I mentioned previously. The head of the rudder is in a tube, the top of which is *inside* the transom, at the foot of the bunk (the bunk takes up all that end of the cabin). As we surfed a jet of water shot up the tube with such force that it hit the deck head and then rushed forward over my bunk. Whatever seal there had been at the head of the rudder stock was no longer there. The only things in the boat which were not soaked were the navigation equipment and a bundle of dry clothes which were high up on a shelf.

Having covered a rag in grease I jammed it in the top of the rudder tube and it made a reasonable seal. I was very tempted to get into my only set of dry clothes but had to concede that it was pointless; as soon as I got into oilskins or my saturated sleeping bag, or even sat on the bunk, they'd get wet. There was no alternative but to remain wet and hope the cold didn't get too severe.

Despite these troubles I was overjoyed at a day's run of 230 miles. The fog returned as soon as the wind went southerly, the result of the warm air from the Gulf Stream crossing over the cold but favourable Labrador current.

*Day 18* 25 June
00.00 Light N W'ly's Fog cleared Making 3 knots
06.00            Course 270° 6 knots
Compass error check by moon 2° E i.e. *nil*
03.00–08.30            285°
08.30–noon            270° slow progress *Sunny*
Noon 42° 50′ N 60° 32′ W        490 miles to go
16.00 DR as chart
20.00      "        wind light W'ly

Noticeably more attention to navigation now as the US coastline gets closer.

*Day 19* 26 June
Slow progress
04.30 sailed within ¼ mile of an anchored boat!
05.30 Tacked to sail off fishing grounds
Several sunsights
Noon 42° 44′ N 63° 00′ W        390 miles to go
Full sail into 20 knots of wind

After steering all that night I was very tired and went below just before it got light. To kill time till daybreak, when I felt I could 'safely' sleep, I made a cup of coffee and climbed into my sleeping bag to get warm. The wind was only 10 knots and everything was quiet. Just before dozing off I thought I should take one last look on deck, and was confronted by a wall of steel 400 yards dead ahead. It was an anchored factory ship or enormous trawler – I'm not sure which. I would have sailed straight into it if I'd stayed below. I got smartly out of its way and continued to steer till 09.00, passing seven ships in the fog, until I felt it was clear enough to turn in for some sleep.

*Day 20* 27 June
| | | | |
|---|---|---|---|
| 00.00 Pos as/chart | Wind freed | Co. 255° | 6 knots |
| 09.00 Wind dropping | Set genoa | 285° | 4 knots |
| 11.00 Light | | 250° | 3   " |
| 12.00 DR 43° 30′ N 65° 00′ W | no horizon for sight | | |
| 13.00–17.00 becalmed | | | |
| 18.00 Light WNW | | | |
| 20.00 NW 10 knots, fog, large swell but flat sea | | | |
| 24.00 | | Co. 230° | 6 knots |

It was hard work trying to maintain progress that day. During the evening the visibility closed in; there was an enormous swell with no waves, smooth mountains of water rolling out of the mist – very eerie. I was in a position 75′ south-east of Sable Island on the edge of Brown's Bank, and it was time to work south-west down towards George's Shoal and Nantucket. I had decided to cut across the Nantucket shoals as much as the visibility would allow. 360 miles to the finish.

I was suffering from the cold at this stage as I couldn't get any of my gear dry. I felt all right while working but I could never get warm in my wet sleeping bag and thought nervously about hyperthermia. Five minutes after getting into the soggy, unpleasant mess that was my sleeping quarters I'd have to decide if I'd warmed up at all; if so, I'd allow myself to go to sleep; if not, I'd get up again and do something to improve my circulation. No wonder I used to write odd comments in the log about the sort of boat I'd like next time – if there was to be a next time.

*Day 21* 28 June
All night wind NW'ly making 6–7 knots
Sunny day good horizon
Noon fix   41° 23′ N 67° 37′ W   To go 200 miles
14.00 calm
14.00–1800      12 miles made on 255°
19.00–2400      no miles on 315°

For once the weather was good to me and I was able to take accurate sights several times during the morning, obtaining an excellent fix for the approach to Newport. I didn't want to have to steer south in order to pick up the RDF beacon on the Nantucket Light Vessel, it would be quicker to stay nearer the shoals.

The above was my last log entry and from that point on I wrote all my positions and data on the chart.

Day 22 took me across Nantucket Shoals. The visibility was not very good so I edged clear of the very shallow parts. I picked up a buoy at one stage which confirmed my position. The wind was variable and for a time I had the spinnaker up – the only time. I stayed up all that day and the following night and at dawn on day 23 I was beating up towards the finishing line. I was relieved to see the Brenton Reef Tower at one end of the line – I'd been confused by the lights I'd seen during the night and had found the RDF beacons difficult to pick up accurately. I crossed the line at 08.00 and was met by *Great*

*Britain II*, the 77ft maxi yacht which I'd skippered in the '77–'78 Round the World Race – she made an excellent launch to tow me into the marina.

The first question I asked was: 'What position am I?' Then , 'Who won?' And then, 'Any news of my wife?'

I had finished sixteenth in a time of 22 days 23 hours. Although sixteenth place was no great shakes (and I thought if only I hadn't lost two days virtually stopped in the gales I might have been seventh), at least I had made it with no damage and three days ahead of the next yacht of my size – another Val 31. If I had been allowed in the class for yachts of under 32ft that is the margin I would have won by.

The overall winner was Phil Weld in *Moxie* – a great performance, helped by the utter reliability of the trimaran, the correct choice of route (the same as I had followed by chance) and his own determination. Nick Keig on *Three Legs of Mann III* was second seven hours behind the leader and third, 40 minutes later, was Phil Steggall on his much smaller (38ft) *Jeans Foster*. In fact, but for a damaged centreboard, Steggall may well have won. Mike Birch was fourth, another 30 minutes behind, having lost time when a wave punched a hole in the underside of his solid wing crossbeam. Walter Green was fifth, thus making a clean sweep for trimarans.

The other big multis that may have made the honours were all slowed down by varying degrees of damage; *V.S.D.* lost her centreboard and finished nineteenth; Tom Grossman finished tenth on *Kriter VII* having made up good time after his delayed start; Eric Loiseau retired *Gauloise IV* with a damaged crossbeam; Pajot managed a fifth place, with jib furler problems, on his unofficial entry *Paul Ricard*. His foil stabilization had worked well at high speed but in light winds, not only were they a drag, they didn't provide enough lateral resistance. This latter problem was the greater of the two as, as that time, *Paul Ricard* had no centreboard. The foiler's reputation, however, was made on the return trip to England when she broke the transatlantic record.

Naomi arrived in twenty-fourth place in a time of 25 days 19 hours – good enough for the women's record. It transpired that she had been level with *Boatfile* at the halfway point but then lost ground when she had a day of strong head winds while I had strong following winds; then her forestay furler broke and for the last 1000 miles she had to sail with loose luffed genoas and jibs.

The results (see Table 2) showed that the speed differential between big and small trimarans – and other multis – while significant, is not as marked as in similar ranges of monohulls. The differential is further reduced when the vessels are sailed single-handed.

**TABLE 2**

## ROYAL WESTERN OBSERVER SINGLEHANDED TRANSATLANTIC RACE 1980 RESULTS

**Race start 1300 G.M.T. 7th June**

| Overall Position | Yacht | Skipper | Race No | Elapsed Time (+ Penalty) | | | | Type M T C | Class P G J | Pos in Class |
|---|---|---|---|---|---|---|---|---|---|---|
| | | | | D | H | M | | | | |
| 1 | Moxie | Philip Weld | 12 | 17 | 23 | 12 | | T | P | 1 |
| 2 | Three Legs of Mann III | Nick Keig | 11 | 18 | 06 | 04 | | T | P | 2 |
| 3 | Jeans Foster | Philip Steggall | 89 | 18 | 06 | 45 | | T | G | 1 |
| 4 | Olympus Photo | Mike Birch | 66 | 18 | 07 | 15 | | T | P | 3 |
| 5 | Chassettes Olympia | Walter Green | 35 | 18 | 17 | 29 | | T | C | 2 |
| 6 | Spaniel II | Kazimierz Jaworski | 111 | 19 | 13 | 25 | | M | P | 4 |
| 7 | Chica BOBA | Edoardo Austoni | 46 | 20 | 02 | 30 | | M | P | 5 |
| 8 | Brittany Ferries I | Daniel Gilard | 37 | 21 | 00 | 09 | 40m | M | G | 3 |
| 9 | Nike II | Richard Konkolski | 17 | 21 | 06 | 21 | | M | G | 4 |
| 10 | Kriter VII | Tom Grossman | 6 | 21 | 08 | 01 | 7hr 50m | T | P | 6 |
| 11 | Stadt Krefeld | Wolfgang Wanders | 97 | 21 | 14 | 22 | | M | G | 5 |
| 12 | Tyfoon VI | Gustaf Versluys | 117 | 21 | 15 | 01 | | M | G | 6 |
| 13 | Hydrofolie | Alain Labbe | 16 | 21 | 15 | 51 | | T | G | 7 |
| 14 | Kriter IV | Olivier de Kersauson | 18 | 21 | 20 | 30 | 10hr 00m | M | P | 7 |
| 15 | Gulia Fila | Pierre Sicouri | 123 | 22 | 02 | 34 | | M | P | 8 |
| 16 | Boatfile | Robert James | 118 | 22 | 22 | 55 | | T | G | 8 |
| 17 | France Loisirs | Dennis Gliksmann | 77 | 23 | 10 | 00 | | M | G | 9 |
| 18 | Voortrekker | Bertie Reed | 100 | 23 | 12 | 42 | | M | P | 9 |
| 19 | V.S.D. | Eugene Riguidel | 32 | 24 | 01 | 27 | 20m | T | P | 10 |
| 20 | Haute-Nendaz | Philippe Fournier | 38 | 24 | 03 | 05 | | M | G | 10 |
| 21 | Open Space | Jean-Pierre Millet | 36 | 25 | 01 | 05 | | M | P | 11 |
| 22 | Garuda | Victor Sagi | 69 | 25 | 08 | 23 | | M | P | 12 |
| 23 | Moonshine | Francis Stokes | 91 | 25 | 14 | 07 | | M | G | 11 |
| 24 | Kriter Lady | Naomi James | 112 | 25 | 19 | 12 | | M | P | 13 |
| 25 | Third Turtle | William Homewood | 52 | 25 | 20 | 13 | | T | G | 12 |
| 26 | Ambergris | Robert Bocinsky | 122 | 26 | 00 | 39 | | M | G | 13 |
| 27 | Les Menuires | vJean-Jacques Jaouen | 76 | 26 | 15 | 21 | | M | G | 14 |
| 28 | Spaniel | Jerzy Rakowicz | 61 | 26 | 19 | 29 | | M | G | 15 |
| 29 | Free Newspapers | John Chaundy | 87 | 28 | 00 | 56 | | M | J | 1 |
| 30 | Edith | William Doelger | 71 | 28 | 04 | 10 | | T | G | 16 |
| 31 | Yoldia | Uno Hylen | 57 | 28 | 05 | 48 | | M | G | 17 |
| 32 | Wild Rival | Desmond Hampton | 34 | 28 | 13 | 44 | | M | G | 16 |
| 33 | Atlantic Harp | John Charnley | 43 | 29 | 06 | 21 | | M | G | 19 |
| 34 | Jabulisiwe | Ian Radford | 19 | 30 | 14 | 38 | | M | J | 2 |
| 35 | Moonshadow Basildon | John Oswald | 73 | 30 | 15 | 30 | | M | G | 20 |
| 36 | Crumpy Nut | Oscar Debra | 93 | 30 | 16 | 32 | | M | G | 21 |
| 37 | Warrior Shamaal | Richard Clifford | 3 | 30 | 16 | 45 | | M | G | 22 |
| 38 | Victoria | Henk Jukkema | 82 | 30 | 18 | 02 | | M | J | 3 |
| 39 | Sadler Bluejacket | Chris Smith | 125 | 30 | 19 | 20 | | M | J | 4 |
| 40 | Achillea | Chris Butler | 84 | 30 | 20 | 49 | | M | J | 5 |
| 41 | Hollemaat IV | Kees Roemers | 8 | 30 | 21 | 24 | | M | G | 23 |

# Multihulls Offshore

| Overall Position | Yacht | Skipper | Race No | Elapsed Time (+ Penalty) | | | Type M T C | Class P G J | Pos in Class |
|---|---|---|---|---|---|---|---|---|---|
| | | | | D | H | M | | | |
| 42 | Demon of Hamble | Angus Primrose | 33 | 30 | 23 | 08 | | M | G | 24 |
| 43 | Parisien Libere | Roger Forkert | 39 | 31 | 10 | 45 | | T | G | 25 |
| 44 | Ratso II | Guy Bernadin | 79 | 31 | 11 | 45 | | M | G | 26 |
| 45 | Dream Weaver | James Kyle | 9 | 31 | 23 | 05 | | M | J | 6 |
| 46 | Cat Marine | Alain Veyron | 124 | 32 | 02 | 50 | | T | J | 7 |
| 47 | Abacus | Don Clark | 42 | 32 | 07 | 17 | | M | G | 27 |
| 48 | Mistral | Thomas Gochberg | 45 | 32 | 18 | 35 | | M | G | 28 |
| 49 | Egret | Luis Tonizzo | 47 | 33 | 05 | 25 | | M | J | 8 |
| 50 | Tangra | Nikolay Djambazov | 53 | 34 | 10 | 53 | | M | G | 29 |
| 51 | Black Pearl | Wytze Van Der Zee | 99 | 35 | 11 | 20 | | M | G | 30 |
| 52 | North Wind | Jose Ugarte | 141 | 36 | 06 | 43 | | M | G | 31 |
| 53 | Tjisje | Hank Van de Weg | 94 | 36 | 22 | 22 | | M | J | 9 |
| 54 | Christian Saul | Paul Rodgers | 30 | 37 | 03 | 11 | | T | G | 32 |
| 55 | Jeantex | Wolfgang Quix | 90 | 38 | 03 | 02 | | M | J | 10 |
| 56 | Cecco | Giampaola Venturin | 70 | 38 | 08 | 55 | | M | J | 11 |
| 57 | Crisan | Jean Guiu | 15 | 38 | 13 | 43 | | M | G | 33 |
| 58 | Seagull II | J. R. Verwoerd | 92 | 38 | 17 | 00 | | M | J | 12 |
| 59 | Olympius Sailing | Bob Lush | 5 | 39 | 01 | 46 | | M | J | 13 |
| 60 | One Hand Clapping | Tony Lush | 29 | 39 | 06 | 56 | | M | J | 14 |
| 61 | La Peligrosa | Andre de Jong | 40 | 39 | 16 | 55 | | M | J | 19 |
| 62 | Prodigal | Bob Lengyel | 68 | 40 | 06 | 09 | | M | J | 16 |
| 63 | Peggy | Tom Ruan | 44 | 40 | 20 | 16 16hr 20m | T | G | 34 |
| 64 | Elbe | Ernest Sonne | 83 | 41 | 10 | 45 | | M | G | 35 |
| 65 | Crystal Catfish | John Hunt | 49 | 41 | 13 | 18 | | M | J | 17 |
| 66 | Miscin | John Beharrell | 20 | 42 | 10 | 00 | | M | G | 36 |
| 67 | Mulat | Beppe Panada | 74 | 42 | 18 | 20 12hr 30m | M | P | 14 |
| 68 | Mare | Per Mustelin | 78 | 43 | 03 | 34 | | M | J | 18 |
| 69 | Novia | William Wallace | 102 | 44 | 10 | 42 | | M | J | 19 |
| 70 | Casper | Martin Wills | 21 | 46 | 13 | 52 35hr 00m | M | J | 20 |
| 71 | Pytheas II | Burg Veenemans | 131 | 49 | 08 | 16 3hr 40m | M | P | 15 |

**Penalties for Late Arrival Plymouth** (20 minutes for each hour late)

| | H. | M. |
|---|---|---|
| Brittany Ferries I | | 40 |
| Kriter VII | 7 | 50 |
| MV Lat | 12 | 30 |
| Pitheas | 3 | 40 |
| V.S.D. | | 20 |
| Peggy | 16 | 20 |
| Casper | 35 | 00 |
| Old Navy Lights | 76 | 50 |

**Early Across the Start Line** (30 mins. per second)

Kriter VI   Returned to recross but failed to do so – estimated effective time over the line 20 seconds = 10 hours penalty

**Disqualified** (Rule 21)

Le First   Jerry Cartwright

# 4

## *Brittany Ferries GB*

The 1981 Observer/Europe 1 Transatlantic race was announced by the Royal Western Yacht Club when it became apparent, in 1979, that the 1980 OSTAR was heavily oversubscribed. Rather than increase the entry limit, which had been set at a safety-conscious 100 yachts, it was decided to hold another event over the same course – Plymouth to Newport, Rhode Island – in the following year. The differences between the races were the number of crew (two for the new race) and a size difference: the LOA top limit for the OSTAR was 56ft, for the 1981 race it was increased to 85ft. The increase in crew was a sensible decision from the seamanship point of view and popular with the competitors as it improved the true racing aspect of the crossing. To distinguish the race from its OSTAR origins it became unofficially known as the TwoSTAR.

Naomi and I were entered in the race from the outset as it was part of Naomi's contract with her sponsors, Matthew Clark and Sons (Kriter). I had agreed to go with her and we thought we'd do well as a team. My only reservation was with our boat; fine though she was, she could not compete with the number of larger multihulls in contention for the top prizes. A monohull of 53ft, even if she had been of the most modern design, was in my view no longer capable of winning the race.

Eighteen months before the start Chay Blyth phoned to tell me he had sponsorship for a 65ft trimaran and would I like to crew for him. Needless to say, the idea of repeating our performance in the Round Britain was too tempting to refuse and I said yes. I had no idea who his sponsor was or what the boat would be like, yet I had the highest confidence in Chay's ability to get a project together. After the lessons Chay had learnt with *GB IV* I felt the new boat must be a good one. Meanwhile I left Naomi without a crew but it was not long before she had signed up Laurel Holland, an American, an experienced sailor and a friend. Laurel was married to the yacht designer Ron Holland, who was keen on her doing the race – albeit in a boat he had not designed.

After completing the OSTAR I left my Val 31 in the USA, optimistically believing I'd sold it, while Naomi, Laurel, myself and three recruits brought *Kriter Lady* back to England. It was a pleasant, leisurely trip, during which Naomi typed the last two chapters of her book and Laurel did a lot of sailing. Back in England the two girls dropped the rest of us off and sailed to Ireland in order to qualify for the next summer's race, and I went to see Chay and his new trimaran.

The sponsor was reflected in the boat's name, *Brittany Ferries GB*, and John Shuttleworth had been chosen as the designer. It was John's first independent design, as he had been employed by Derek Kelsall for the previous few years. It was apparent from *Brittany Ferries'* general appearance that she was a development of *GB IV*, but closer inspection showed the two boats to be quite different, especially in the areas of the crossbeams and floats. *GB IV*'s floats had turbulence-inducing transoms whereas *BF*'s tapered out to create a perfect underwater shape – where they always end up when the boat is pressed. At the same time her floats were of high buoyancy and their centre of buoyancy was well forward. The fore and aft trim of the float was also an improvement on the bow high aspect seen on *GB IV* (see Part 2, Chapter 6). The mast-step crossbeam geometry was well resolved, too. It had become generally accepted that a much stiffer trimaran could be developed if the mast were stepped on, or near, a crossbeam and the cap-shrouds taken out to the end of that beam; that is if the rig is fractional the mast may be stepped by the for'd of the two-beam configuration, but if the rig is masthead a third, central beam is needed to support it. *Brittany Ferries* adopted the latter solution.

For sail handling we had a furler jib which could be rolled up progressively or changed to a smaller jib top or a larger light genoa if conditions, and our strength, were up to it. The deck layout was conventional with winches on the mast for halyards and all other controls led back to the cockpit. In fact, the rig was fairly conservative compared to the flat-out racing monohulls, and indeed multihulls of the day; on the other hand it was ultimately strong and reliable.

The hull construction was Airex foam with skins of glass and Kevlar. Carbon fibre was used in the crossbeams and also for stiffening within the hull. The lifting daggerboard was aluminium and the rudder, which incorporated a brilliant trim tab self-steering arrangement (details later), was hung on a skeg right aft. Launching was not due until the Spring of '81 and there was nothing for me to do till then.

Meanwhile, I had been approached by a company in England, Fairways Marine, which manufactured three ranges of glass-fibre cruising boats, including the unstayed-rigged Freedoms (25, 30 and 40 footers). Their idea was to build a much larger Freedom as a prototype fast cruiser which I would take in the next Whitbread race and Naomi in the TwoSTAR. The story of the design and building of the Freedom 70 are outside the scope of this book; of relevance only is the agreement by Naomi's sponsors that she should take the new boat in the TwoSTAR instead of her old one and it was subsequently named *Kriter Lady II*. Everyone was pleased with the arrangement, especially Naomi who now had a much better chance of doing well in the race.

*Brittany Ferries GB* was launched on time and sailed by Chay and a crew out to Santander in Northern Spain. I took a ferry out and joined him to sail back to the UK for our qualifying trip. As soon as I sailed on the new trimaran I realized we had a very different beast from *GB IV*. For a start she easily took off to speeds her predecessor would never achieve, and, not only that, one could actually control her at those speeds. If she had any weakness it seemed to be in very light airs but my initial impression was that she was a great all rounder. Chay was similarly impressed and realized very early on, as he put it, 'If we don't win with this boat we'll never win'. The sail-handling systems worked well and the spinnaker seemed ridiculously easy to use (see Part 2, Chapter 12).

We were close-hauled nearly all the way home but still put up an average speed of 9

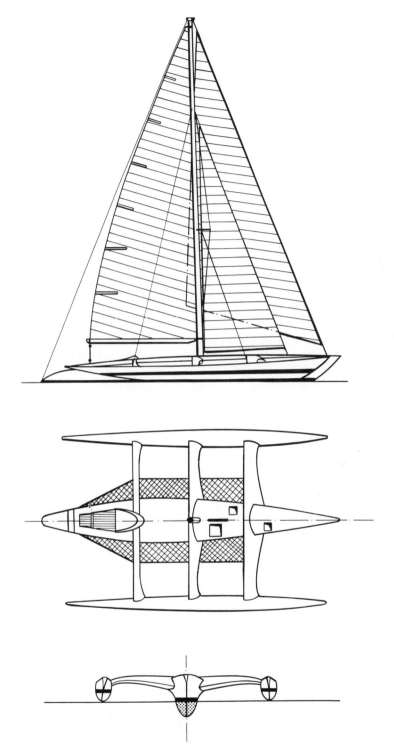

**Fig. 7** Brittany Ferries GB

*Naomi (at the wheel) and Laurel Holland qualified the Freedom 70* Kriter Lady II *for the 1981 two-handed transatlantic race.*

knots through the water. It was difficult to judge our pointing angle without another boat nearby but it felt all right. It could have been better with shorter spreaders and a narrower shroud base but we were content.

After a few minor modifications on our return to England we sailed up the ever-narrowing Thames estuary for the naming ceremony in London. We were delighted with the manoeuvrablility and ease of handling of the tri.

As in the previous year the fleet gathered in Plymouth for a final week of preparation before the race. Studying the opposition, it was immediately apparent that enormous advances in multihull design had been made in the preceding 12 months. To begin with, after an absence from competition for several years, two new racing catamarans were putting in an appearance, each quite different from the other but both potential winners. Here is a description, in order of size, of the most interesting multihulls in the race:

*Jacques Ribourel*, Olivier de Kersauson and Gerard Dijkstra (France).
An 80ft trimaran designed by Allegre and following the theme of *Pen Duick IV/Manureva* and *Kriter IV* – that is, low buoyancy floats and what can only be described as an 'old-fashioned look' with her ketch rig.

*Sea Falcon*, Robin Knox-Johnston and Billy King-Harman (GB).
A 70ft catamaran designed by MacAlpine-Downie and identical in hull shape to the

ill-fated *British Oxygen/Kriter III*. The crossbeams (the weak part in the earlier design) were, however, quite different and looked massively strong. Her sloop rig was stayed with such a wide shroud base and with spreaders of such a length as to make it impossible for her to point. Nevertheless, freed off in a breeze she would be fast.

*Elf Aquitaine*, Marc Pajot and Paul Ayasse (France).
A 63ft catamaran designed by Langevrin and quite different to *Sea Falcon*. The two hulls were narrower with less freeboard; steering was by tiller from either cockpits in the aft end of each float (*Sea Falcon* was steered by wheel from a centre pod); she sported a modern, low drag, fractional rig which looked large and very efficient.

*Royale*, Loic Caradec and Philippe Facque (France).
A 60ft trimaran lightly built from composite materials with a modern fractional rig. Compared to *Brittany Ferries GB* she had a very low freeboard which brought her crossbeams very close to the water. However, she had proved to be as fast as *Elf Aquitaine* in her first race (La Boule – Dakar) and had since been fitted with a retractable hydrofoil on each float. These foils, which were hydraulically damped, provided lift to the lee float and hence stability.

*Sudinox*, Guy Delage and *Eterna Royal Quartz*, Jean-Marine Vidal (France).
Two 55ft proas, neither of which survived more than five days (a third proa in this race was lost on the way to the start). The advantages of sailing with two-thirds of a trimaran are considerable and the undoubted speed of the proa will ensure its continuation. As reliability improves they may yet become a threat to cats and tris.

*Tele-7-Jours*, Mike Birch and Walter Green (Canada).
A 53ft trimaran designed and built by Walter Green along the lines of his successful yachts of the previous year. An obvious threat to us – particularly in view of the sailing capabilities of the crew.

*Star Point*, Paolo Martinoni (Italy).
A sister ship to *Tele-7-Jours*

*Paul Ricard*, Eric Tabarly and Patric Tabarly (France).
The same hydrofoil-stabilized trimaran as that sailed by Marc Pajot in the 1980 OSTAR. She now had the addition of two asymmetric centreboards to help light airs performance and an experimental 'padded' aerodynamic mainsail. Extraordinarily enough, last year's progressive boat looked almost old fashioned among this year's fleet.

*Lesieur Tournesol*, Eugene Riguidel and Jean-François Coste (France).
This 52ft Derek Kelsall design was the old *V.S.D.* which won the Transat en Double, a two-handed race from Lorient round Bermuda and back to Lorient, beating *Paul Ricard* by five minutes. However, she looked pretty tired by the time she reached Plymouth.

*Gautier II*, Jean-Yves Terlain and Christian Fevrier (France).
A very interesting trimaran, 45ft long, with inverted Y foils under each float to provide high stability and low drag. These foils also allowed the trimaran to track straight and steady to windward with little or no pitching. In light airs, though, she would be slowed down by the drag from the fixed foils.

*Bonifacio,* Philip Steggall and Tom Wiggins (USA).
A 45ft Dick Newick design for the man who came very close to winning the 1980 OSTAR. Although a potent combination it was generally felt that 45ft was too small to win in this calibre fleet.

*Gauloises IV,* Eric Loiseau and Halvard Mabire (France).
A Newick 44 footer which retired from the 1980 OSTAR with structural damage – also considered too small to be a threat.

*Brittany Ferries FR,* Daniel Gilard and Lionel Pean (France).
Mike Birch's old 44ft *Olympus Photo* in which he finished fourth in the 1980 OSTAR despite suffering structural damage.

*Mark One Tool Hire,* Mark Gatehouse and Michael Holmes (GB).
The smallest multihull in the fleet, a trimaran of only 30ft, designed by Derek Kelsall and modified by Mark Gatehouse. After sailing trials the centre deck of the main hull, crossbeams, and hence floats, were all lifted up 7ins to give more wave clearance. I was interested to see how their time would compare with mine the previous year on *Boatfile* – almost the same sized boat.

Against the multihulls were a few monohulls which might have had a chance of getting through in the unlikely event of *all* the big multis being forced to slow down by the weather. Two, *Kriter VIII* and *Monsieur Meuble* (ex *Kriter V*), were long (75ft and 69ft), narrow, deep-keeled, and designed specifically for short-handed racing; two other possible leaders, *Faramserenissima* and *Charles Heidsick*, both 65 footers, were designed under the IOR rule and were eventually intended for the fully crewed Whitbread Round the World Race. According to general feeling, even if one of the monohulls could outsail the multis early on, as soon as the lighter, freer winds on the other side were reached, it would be overtaken.

Both *Brittany Ferries* and *Kriter Lady II* were virtually ready when they arrived in Plymouth seven days before the race. They were moored alongside each other in a corner of Millbay Dock and, with help from some of my crew for the next Whitbread race, were well organized and under complete control – until the Tuesday before the start. On that day Naomi had confirmation that she had an ovarian cyst and very sadly went into hospital the next morning for an operation. Suddenly, the last four days became very busy; as well as helping to prepare our trimaran I had to see that Naomi was all right and find, and brief, a new skipper for the Freedom 70. Fortunately we had great support from Fairways Marine, the owners, and Matthew Clark and Sons, Naomi's sponsors, and everything was resolved. John Oakeley, ex skipper of the 12-metre *Lionheart*, stepped into Naomi's place, Naomi's operation was successful and I was very glad to be able to get on with the race.

The forecast for the start was west-south-westerly gales. The thought of beating down the Channel against strong winds was quite horrible. I secretly hoped the start might be postponed, but it wasn't. On the morning of 6 June we were towed out of Millbay Dock and out into a very windy Plymouth Sound. As we intended making a film of the race we had a BBC film crew on board at this stage, getting under our feet as we hoisted the main with two reefs and the staysail. We reached back and forth in the Sound and put our nose outside the breakwater on one occasion – it was rough and so didn't impress any of us.

With two hours to go we dropped the film crew into a waiting launch and had a cup of tea, paying close attention, meanwhile, to our competitors sailing out to the line two miles offshore. We'd decided to use our no.2 furler genoa rather than the no.1, on the basis that we may be able to use it fully unfurled, and although we knew we'd probably have to change sail later on we felt it would pay us to be as efficient as possible for the start. With the no.2 hoisted, furled but ready to break out, we continued to reach at breakneck speed around the starting line with just the main and staysail set.

An hour before the start we had another cup of tea. We did not expect the line to be too crowded as it was fairly long and had been sensibly divided so that the monohulls started at the starboard end and the multis at the port end. With ten minutes to go we approached the line; with 2 minutes to go we were held sailing *away* from the line by a monohull during its last manoeuvres. By the time we'd sailed out of its way, unfurled the genoa and headed back for the line, the gun had gone and we were racing.

*Day 0* 6 June 1981

It took us a while to get sheeted in and settled down. We were flying to windward at 10 to 11 knots and literally taking off over the short steep waves. We were on a starboard tack

*Brittany Ferries GB at the start of the TwoSTAR. Chay and I have set the main with two reefs, the number two yankee, and a staysail.*

*Two hours after the start of the TwoSTAR. Brittany Ferries GB takes the lead. The jib is now partly furled.*

Brittany Ferries GB *in flight.*

heading out into the Channel and couldn't see what was happening at the other end of the line but we could see *Royale*, sailing higher and just as fast, going away from us. It was a depressing sight and we could only console ourselves with the thought that it was a long way across the Atlantic. Eventually we tacked on to port to head down the Channel underneath *Royale*'s stern. The visibility was very bad so we couldn't see where any of the other competitors were. We tried sailing with more main (only one reef) and with 75 per cent of the genoa, and found our pointing ability much better. Straight away we started our watch keeping system – one hour on, one hour off. It was very wet.

During the afternoon we overtook the leading monohulls that had got away at the start and after a few short tacks off the south coast of Cornwall we cleared the Lizard and set a course due west – close-hauled on a port tack. In the gathering gloom of nightfall we could make out *Sea Falcon* and *Ribourel* nearby both on a course north of west which was faster but not, in my view, in the right direction. We hoped we were the three leaders but were concerned at not having seen *Paul Ricard, Elf Aquitaine* or *Royale* again.

*Day 1* 7 June
Noon position 49° 55′ N 09° 50′ W   Run 230 miles

With a strong south-westerly wind we continued close-hauled on a port tack. There was a great temptation to free off slightly and sail 2 or 3 knots faster on a course north of west. We considered this option very carefully but decided to stick to our plan of following the

Rhumb line as closely as possible (see fig. 8). It was a difficult choice to make. Although the Rhumb line had been the favoured course in 1980 the conditions obviously had been different. That year during the first few days of the race there had been northerlies so to sail on the Great Circle had meant heading up. Now the wind direction favoured the Great Circle but would it pay in the long run? We thought not.

During the afternoon we shook out the reefs in the mainsail. No sooner had we done so and sheeted in then the slide holding down the clew pulled out. The clew shot up until it was restrained by the outhaul wire, by which time it was 6ins above the boom and the foot of the sail had ripped clear of the foot slides for a length of about 6ft (see fig. 9). We managed to get a lashing through the clew eye and round the boom. The broken fitting had been far too weak for the job – the loads exerted by the leech tension from a big mainsail are enormous, more so on a multihull than on a monohull, as a multi doesn't heel when a puff hits it, and is thereby unable to let the pressure off the mainsail. My reaction to this minor mishap was to become convinced that the race would be won by the multihull that suffered the least damage and not necessarily by the fastest.

*Day 2* 8 June
Noon position 50° 20′ N 15° 40′ W    Run 230 miles

The weather conditions remained much the same all day. Still we stayed on a port tack although now making a course slightly south of west. As the wind dropped to less than 20 knots we replaced the no.2 genoa with the no.1. The time wasted in the change, and the

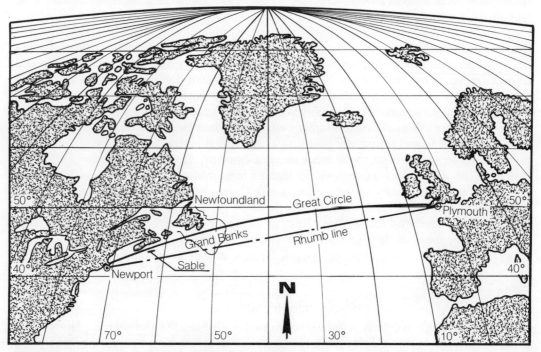

**Fig. 8** *Great circle and rhumb line. Plymouth to Newport*

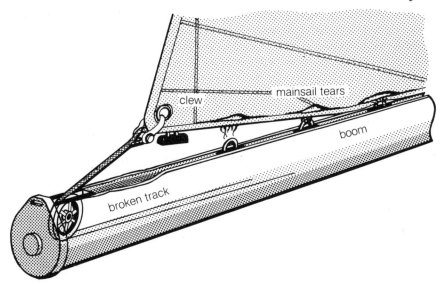

**Fig. 9** *Mainsail damage. Day 2 OSTAR*

effort required, was considerable and as a result we stuck to the no.1 from then on, furling it to storm jib size when necessary. This genoa was cut with a very high clew (more a jib top/yankee than a genoa) which meant we could leave the sheet lead in the same place fore and aft as we furled in and out. *Brittany Ferries'* system had the advantage of not needing a track for the genoa sheet, just a fixed eye, which saved weight and required less effort to furl in and out. However, it had the big disadvantage of always having to be sailed with a cutter rig (jib top and staysail). I believe it's better to have a proper genoa and accept the bother and extra weight of a movable sheet lead. In fact, we found that we *did* have to move the lead inside the shrouds as we passed the half furled position.

At this stage we were both working too hard to consider listening to the radio for news of the other boats or to bother calling ashore on the RT. Instead, we steered to windward hour after hour, cooked (usually Chay), navigated (usually me) and slept. We'd settled into a steady routine and it was a question of carrying on automatically until the next 'event', such as gear failure, caused a break in the cycle.

*Day 3* 9 June
Noon 48° 00' N 20° 00' W   Run 215 miles

At last we were able to lay a reasonable course with sheets slightly eased. For the first time we set the autopilot – an Autohelm 2000 – to steer the boat. Again I marvelled at how well it held a compass course, only wavering 5 degrees either side if we were hit by a wave. It could manage this sort of performance on any point of sailing and at any speed, and the only reason we steered ourselves close-hauled was because the Autohelm steers a compass course and cannot react to the slight differences in wind direction. Also it can't see the waves.

The Autohelm 2000 worked on a trim tab system – it would have been too much to expect it to steer 65ft of trimaran directly. Instead, the push–pull rod was linked to a trim tab at the aft end of the rudder. When the tab was angled to port the rudder was forced to starboard by the water flow over the trim tab. The beauty of the system was in the way the tab acted as a servo thus the pilot needed very little electric power to operate the gear. Another advantage was that all the autopilot needed to work on was a free swinging rudder; the steering linkage to the wheel was driven back to front while under autopilot. In other words, if a steering wire had broken the autopilot could still function (see fig. 10).

Once comfortably under autopilot control we had a little more time to sort ourselves out. One of the priorities was to try and get some news of the race. Chay had an amazing old transistor receiver that has been with him on all his voyages and I must say his faith in it was based more on loyalty than technical evaluation. At any rate, we tuned in at the appointed hour to the twice-daily race reports from the BBC World Service. Through the crackle we made out,

'The two British yachtsmen Chay Blyth and Robin Knox-Johnston sailing *Brittany Ferries* and *Sea Falcon* are joint leaders of the Observer / Europe One Transatlantic Race'.

Needless to say we were somewhat surprised that *Sea Falcon* was so well up, after

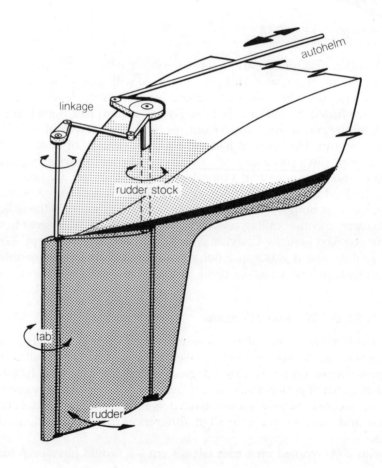

**Fig 10**

having written her off as a poor windward performer. The explanation was soon given in a radio report which gave Knox-Johnston's position as 200 miles north of ours. Robin had been sailing freer and considerably faster taking the Great Circle course – how long would it pay him, we wondered. The answer to the question, 'Where was *Royale*?' was also given – she had been dismasted within an hour of the start. Unbelievably, the one boat we had *seen* to be faster than us was out of the running so soon. No news of *Elf Aquitaine* or *Paul Ricard* except that their positions were fourth or lower. Third place was held by *Jacques Ribourel*, also further north than us. We weren't too worried by De Kersauson's tri because although she was in third place, she hadn't looked as if she had the light airs potential to do well in the later stages of the race. Interestingly enough, the leading monohull was back in eleventh place – who said multihulls can't go to windward?

Despite being under autopilot we kept our watches going to maintain a good standard of sail trim and to keep a lookout. The one on watch could furl the jib without calling the man off watch but we were both needed to reef or unreef the main; even so, that night we nearly wrote off the mainsail. We'd been sailing with two slab reefs and had lashed the reefed part of the sail up to the boom with sail ties through the rows of reefing eyes. Although this was not essential for the set of the sail it was necessary to keep the flapping cloth out of our line of vision. When we came to take the reef out I missed one of the lashings and as I let the reefing leech line go the whole weight of the sail came on the sail tie. It held but the sail ripped. Fortunately it didn't go far and as it was a reinforced part of the sail it didn't even need repairing, but it served me a timely reminder of how close the line between care and disaster can be.

*Day 4* 10 June
Noon 48° 00′ N 26° 30′ W   Run 260 miles

By midday we'd sailed 936 miles in four days, an average speed of 9¾ knots made good to Newport. As we were sailing basically to windward in near gale-force conditions we thought progress was remarkable. There was one thing in our favour, though: the wind was gale force because the depressions were fairly far south this year, i.e. just to the north of us. This meant that our course took us near to the depression centres, which meant we were sailing west in a south-westerly or even a southerly and when the low passed a quick wind shift to north-west allowed us to lay the course on the other tack. It was rough but it was certainly fast.

On this day the first of the bad depressions was rapidly approaching. The wind actually went to the south-east during the evening, indicating that we may even pass north of the low centre. This disturbed us as it would give any yachts north of us a big advantage. Just before dusk we set a spinnaker. We hoisted it in its spinnaker-squeezer (see Part 2, Chapter 12), rolled up the jib and I then pulled on the endless line to raise the squeezer tube. At this point, the endless line jammed, the wind filled the sail automatically and the squeezer tube and bell shot up to the head. The sail set perfectly but by this time the downhaul rope – essential to re-squeeze the sail – had pulled out of my hand and was out of reach. In effect, we had no easy way of lowering the spinnaker, dark was approaching and the wind was rising. For two hours we tore along, regularly touching 20 knots until the situation began to feel a bit hairy and we had to consider getting the sail down. There was nothing for it but to lower and gather the 3000 sq ft spinnaker in the conventional way. To help us we took the lazy guy on the leeward side and led it to a snatch block at the base of the mast and then to a winch so that before snapping the windward clew the leeward clew was already winched in securely to the deck. The sail came down and in without too much trouble.

What had occurred was something we had been told could 'never happen'. The endless line had become tangled with the sail in the tube. Before we'd set off, in order to comply with the race rules, we had asked a sailmaker to remove or disguise the Brittany Ferries logo on the spinnaker. After the sail was returned to us there was too much wind to hoist it in the harbour for a check. So we left it as it was, assuming all was well. Doubly annoying was the fact that we'd been aware of the potential trouble in that quarter but had not been meticulous enough in our preparations to avoid it.

With the jib, staysail and full main we powered on into the night, occasionally touching 25 knots. It couldn't last though; the wind headed to the south, then south-west and we finished the night close-hauled, deep-reefed and slower.

*Day 5* 11 June
Noon 47° 20′ N 30° 35′ W   Run 170 made good (230 through the water)

Before 01.00 we were headed to a north-west course as the storm raged from the west. Down to storm staysail and deep-reefed main we were still making good ground to windward even though the seas were building up to an enormous size. At daybreak we could see how bad the weather was – the wind was over 50 knots with steep waves up to 30ft. To steer in these conditions one had to try to luff up into the waves and bear away rapidly on their peaks in order to slide sideways down the back face. The danger arose when the trimaran got knocked off the wind and suddenly accelerated from a comfortable 7 or 8 knots to 15 or more. At this speed one could do a lot of damage taking off over the top of a wave. The secret was to stay slightly free, hitting the waves fast but at a wider angle, until a gap to windward presented itself. Then a sharp luff back to close-hauled would bring the situation under control again. It was nerve-wracking and the slamming over the waves, despite careful helming, was enough to send the off-watch crewman off his bunk and into the cabin roof.

Not long after dawn the reefing leech line broke; the only way to reeve a new one was to lower the mainsail. With it down we lay ahull reasonably comfortably and actually chickened out of getting under way again. Two hours later the wind shifted to north of west and we wore around to lie ahull on the other tack. Suddenly, a large breaking wave approached and started to lift the windward float. We had raised the centreboard so the boat slid sideways as intended but not before she'd been lifted to a 45 degree angle. This was pretty frightening and stupid; we immediately realized that with way on we would have climbed the wave instead of being nearly rolled over by it. We instantly started sailing again.

No sooner were we under way than it struck us what a mistake it had been to stop at all. The broken leech line had put us into a position which we were too lethargic to reverse. The only good aspect was swearing to each other that we would never stop again – whatever the weather. *Brittany Ferries* seemed to be standing up to the punishment very

78

well – no structural damage or movement whatsoever, so it would be easier in future to force ourselves to push on.

By evening the wind and sea were down and we could relax a little. A radio report gave us a 50-mile lead over *Sea Falcon* who was still 240 miles further north. It was good to hear that Robin Knox-Johnston, although well north of us, had not managed to get around the depression; if he had, with gale-force following winds he'd have been away to a good lead. We resolved to try a link call to shore the next day to find out a bit more about our competitors' positions. The whole fleet were carrying Argos automatic beacons which transmitted a signal, via satellite, to a computer back in France. From this signal the computer could calculate the exact position of every yacht, and relay them to race control every six hours. Any call to a third party at home should secure us these positions.

*Day 6* 12 June
Noon 47° 15′ N 30° 35′ W   Run 250 miles

Fast sailing in a north-westerly breeze changing rapidly to southerly in the afternoon. We had an HF radio transmitter receiver on board more by chance than planning. The way it came about was indicative of the tremendous media interest in the race in France. The Thomson organization, in conjunction with Europe One, had set up a press office in France. To be sure of getting more than just the Argos position reports from the yachts they lent 20 HF radios to key competitors, fitted and tested them in the week before the race *and* lent portable generators or solar panels to provide battery charging. They fitted each radio with only those frequencies required to communicate with the secondary range of channels at St Lys radio (the French equivalent of Portishead radio in the UK or Ocean Gate in the USA). This channel at St Lys was then reserved exclusively for the yachts in the race so that no waiting for, or competing with, high-powered ships was necessary before establishing contact. It was a perfect service. The operator at St Lys would give free link-calls to anyone, provided the calls were restricted to five minutes. They also read a fully detailed weather forecast once a day. In return we, the yacht, were expected to give any interesting news to the press office. The arrangement worked unbelievably well.

So on this, our sixth day of racing, I called St Lys. To my amazement they replied immediately and put me through to the press office who were desperate for items of interest from us – the leaders. They confirmed our lead, which was up to 90 miles, with *Sea Falcon* and *Tele-7-Jours* (Mike Birch) second and third. Then I spoke to Naomi who was convalescing at my parents' home. Knowing the severe limitations on transmitting power on a yacht, Naomi and I lost no time with personal talk; instead we got straight down to business. I asked her to call race control every morning and get the latitude and longitude of the leading six yachts. Then when I called her in the afternoon she could relay the positions to us and we could plot them and work out any necessary tactics to cover. On this occasion Naomi gave me the order as:

1. *Brittany Ferries GB*
2. *Tele-7-Jours*
3. *Sea Falcon*
4. *Starpoint*
5. *Elf Aquitaine*

6. *Jacques Ribourel*
7. *Kriter VIII* (first monohull)

We learnt, also, that *Gautier II* had lost her rudder, *Jacques Ribourel* had had to slow down on account of a bent mizzen, *Paul Ricard* had retired with a leaking main hull and *Bonifacio* had capsized. Of these snippets of news Phil Steggall's capsize was the most astonishing as he was one of the best multihull sailors around. (He told us after the race that a wave had thrown them over while he was below and his crew was sailing quite happily to windward.) We were feeling very optimistic about our own position as we expected to gain the advantage over the fleet in the lighter airs towards the end of the race and yet here we were already doing well in the heavy weather.

Later on that day we picked up a weather forecast from St Lys which foretold of a depression of 960 millibars approaching from the west. It was predicted to move due east along our latitude. In fact, we had picked up the depression on our own weather facsimile recorder the previous day and were trying to track its progress as it moved towards us. Tracking it correctly was vital; if it stayed on our latitude we would need to steer north of west during its approach, thereby benefiting from the strong easterly winds above the low centre. If it went north-east we should stay where we were. Unfortunately, our weather facs' chose this moment to break down (we never got it going again) so we had to fall back on intuition and guess work. My view was that the depression would soon track north-east, not east, and hence go way north of us. On balance we decided it would be a waste of time to head north. Instead, we adhered to our plan and stuck to the Rhumb line. Even so, we were very nervous about Robin Knox-Johnston a long way north of us, hoping to get around the top of the low.

The mainsail foot outhaul wire broke that afternoon. It was taking more strain than it should, as it was required to help hold the clew down to the boom. We reefed down and replaced the whole of the clew attachment with a solid lashing of several turns of 10mm rope. From then on it was not exactly adjustable but at least we knew it would not be going anywhere.

*Day 7* 13 June
Noon 46° 45′ N 39° 15′ W   Run 100 miles made good (from 170 sailed)

The night of 12–13 June was one of the most unpleasant that I ever spent at sea. The forecast depression arrived and it blew with a vengeance. Initially the wind was a south-easterly which gave us some tremendously fast reaching but all too soon it headed west-south-west and we pounded into enormous waves and 60 knots of wind. Trying to steer facing forward was impossible as the fine spray, head high, felt like a fire-hose full bore. The only way to steer was facing to leeward, attempting to glimpse out of the corner of one eye the waves and the sea ahead. Total misery. After an hour I'd rush to get into a bunk and what seemed like only a minute later would be called on deck again. On with wet oilskins, determined to manage a two-hour watch so that one could claim a two-hour sleep afterwards. After ten minutes of the fire-hose treatment, I'd be struggling to survive even the hour. After 12 hours of this our steering was somewhat less than 100 per cent efficient so we tried the autopilot. We were still going to windward but we set the black box a compass course. Great was the relief to find the Autohelm managing to control the boat and sailing better than we had close-hauled. For the remainder of the gale the man on watch stood below next to the autopilot control but with one eye on the boat speed and one on the windex at the masthead. If the boat speed went to more than 8 knots a quick glance at the wind direction would confirm that we were too free. The remedy was to adjust the autopilot compass course a few degrees to windward. Conversely, if the speed fell the opposite action was required. In effect, we steered from below using regular incremental adjustments to the pilot. And so we hammered on, hitting an occasional wave with an almighty crash but always making good speed towards America.

As expected, the wind shifted to north of west during the storm and we tacked to head south-west again. After the wind shift the wave directions were very confused, resulting in high breaking peaks. On one occasion Chay handed me the watch saying, 'We were within an inch of going over just now so don't hook your harness on. You must be free to dive below if she goes over'. He then added, 'If you feel a near one coming, leap down the hatch straight away'.

As it was daylight and the wind not so strong (although the waves were worse), I was steering from the cockpit again. I never quite felt the need to dive for the hatch but I must say I looked forward to calmer weather.

Like all storms, this one finally passed by and, although it remained windy, we were able to get a meal inside ourselves and listen to the weather forecast from St Lys. This forecast was read in French and then in English, giving a general synopsis and then a detailed forecast for sea areas A to H. This was no earthly good to us. Somewhere along the line the information, or map, specifying where the areas were had not arrived on board with the radio. It was ridiculous that we were probably the only yacht to which these forecasts meant nothing. I amused myself trying to identify the latitude and longitude of the areas from the observed weather and the synopsis, but was not very successful. It was interesting, afterwards, to see the map and note where the areas were – and interesting to wonder if, had I had that information to hand, I might have tried to talk Chay into some 'clever' tactics.

The press office gave us a reduced lead of 55 miles, which showed that other entries were made of sterner stuff when it came to gales on the nose. *Tele-7-Jours* was behind us, then *Starpoint*. The leading monohull had come up to fourth place. All the large monos had gained places (not miles) as some of the multis slowed right up or stopped. *Sea Falcon*, forced to come south in the gale, had dropped from third to eleventh place; this was good news for us, as it showed she'd not managed to reach the top of the depression. Another favourite out of the running was *Jacques Ribourel* which had lost its mainmast.

By noon, seven days after leaving Plymouth, we had covered 1500 miles and were half way across. With a good lead and some of our main competitors retired, we felt, 'So far, so good'.

*Day 8* 14 June
Noon 45° 20′ N 41° 20′ W   Run 160 miles

A good day to do some maintenance on the boat. It was the first time the deck had been dry in eight days. While the autopilot steered we brought the generator up on deck and for 18 hours charged up our four batteries which had got very low. Solar panels would have been a better system but we'd had no time to fit them.

One problem we could do nothing about was the centreboard. Being buoyant, it required winching down, but needed no weight on the uphaul line to be hoisted. Suddenly it was the other way round, indicative of a lot of water in the board. Obviously, the alloy plates had sprung a leak; all we could do was to remove the inspection cap on the head of the board so that water would be encouraged to run *out* of the leak when the board was hoisted for off-wind sailing.

We attempted some filming that day. Unfortunately, the most suitable of our cameras for good sailing pictures, the one with the wide-angle lens, was on the blink, so we could only shoot each other working on certain areas of deck.

Our lead over Mike Birch was up to 80 miles but we considered *Elf Aquitaine* (lying ninth after the storm) to be the bigger danger. She was not far behind *Tele-7-Jours* and could pose a problem later on in the light airs with her massive sail area.

There were two minor crises in the galley that afternoon. We had started with 15 gallons of fresh water in three containers. When we dug out the second one from its stowage we found it split and empty. This meant only five gallons of water for a crew of two in mid-Atlantic. Actually it was not as bad as all that because at our rate of progress we could expect to be ashore within six days – so we wouldn't even go short. The other problem was sugar. In order to keep weight down to a minimum Chay had only supplied the boat with two bags of sugar, with the view that he would give it up for the voyage. This he didn't do and as our meagre stock dwindled rapidly I started to complain. 'OK', said Chay. 'When one bag is empty I'll give up and you can use the second bag.' And so, at some stage during the storm, I had made Chay a cup of sugarless tea and without comment passed it up to him on deck. He looked so miserable and sad drinking it and I felt so mean, that I couldn't enforce the bargain we'd made, and in any case Chay would have overruled it. Consequently we were running out of sugar.

*Day 9* 15 June
Noon 44° 12′ N 48° 50′ W   Run 320 miles

A great day with some glorious sailing. Lots of spinnaker reaching with the autopilot in full control. By noon we'd covered 320 miles in 24 hours – a very high average of over 13 knots. At times we were managing greater bursts of speed but it is extraordinary how much higher a boat's top speeds are than its daily average.

Our regular contact with St Lys radio and the Thomson press office were now the high spot of our day. I usually spoke to them while Chay steered and having noted down our progress relative to the other competitors I'd report to him. Chay reckoned he knew exactly what my report would be as he could read into my tone of voice on the radio the extent of the increase or decrease of our lead. On this day it had gone up by 50 miles to 130 – a large margin with only 1000 miles to go. Contrarily enough, the larger our lead became the more I worried about losing it through some stupid error or gear failure. *Tele-7-Jours* and *Elf Aquitaine* continued to be our closest pursuers but it was interesting to learn that Eric Loiseau had brought the 44ft *Gauloise IV* up to seventh place by following a much more southerly route than the other pace-setters.

*Day 10* 16 June
Noon 44° 00′ N 54° 00′ W   Run 230 miles

Another glorious day of spinnaker running. The weather was surprisingly clear considering that we were cutting across the Grand Bank of Newfoundland – generally known for its high percentage of foggy days. We had a north-easterly which was blowing cold air over cold water; if the wind turned to a warm southerly we could expect the Newfoundland fog.

Again our lead was up, this time to 150 miles. *Tele-7-Jours* was behind us, then *Elf Aquitaine* and *Gauloise*– all rapidly gaining places. *Sea Falcon* was gaining ground again too, now in eighth place. That afternoon an incident occurred which wiped out nearly a quarter of our lead. We were running at 12 to 15 knots with the medium spinnaker, keeping the apparent wind about 30 degrees aft of the beam in order to maintain the best possible speed made good downwind. Without warning the head of the spinnaker parted company from its halyard and the sail, plus squeezer and all associated ropes, guys and sheets, fell into the water over the leeward bow. The windward clew was held very near the bow of the main hull (but under it), the leeward clew was at the aft end of the lee float; both these corners were held by their three sheets, the foot of the sail was stretched over the top of the lee float, while the body of the sail was underneath the trimaran embracing the centreboard and rudder. The first priority was to stop the boat as the bow of the lee float was trying to pierce the bottom panel of the spinnaker. With the mainsail down the tri lay beam on to the wind, drifting sideways at half a knot. We cleared the cloth from the bow and paused to think about the best way to recover the sail intact. The first move was to release the sheets and guys from the lee corner. This done, the sail drifted under the boat – or the other way round I should say – and, miraculously clearing itself from the centreboard and rudder, floated to weather of the main hull, held just by one corner. At this stage the spi-squeezer bell began hitting the side of the hull so we thought we'd better start there. I managed to get hold of one of the squeezer control lines but with the squeezer sock full of water and unbelievably heavy our combined efforts couldn't get it on board. We applied some winch power via the spare spinnaker halyard and the line pulled straight through the edge of the fibreglass bell. Back to square one. Next, we attacked the clew of the sail still attached to the boat. Transferring the sheet to a halyard we winched away, which was fine, until the corner of the sail was a few feet in the air at which point it threatened to blow into the mast and wrap around the rigging. We tied another halyard around the body of the sail, hoisted it, released the first halyard and retied it lower down, and so on, until finally we could get at the squeezer tube from its closed end and work on that. As soon as half the sail was on board there was no more trapped water and the rest came aboard easily.

Before attempting to tidy up we hoisted the mainsail and got moving. Hoisting the second spinnaker took time as we'd had to cut some of the sheets: the whole operation took over two hours – with 30 miles lost. Amazingly, there was no damage and after a further two hours of fiddling we had the damp sail back in its squeezer and the bell repaired with tape.

The failure, it appeared, had not been due to the halyard breaking but due to the snap-shackle coming undone. It was useless to remind myself that ages ago I'd learnt of the necessity on long voyages of tying the spinnaker halyard to the head of the sail with a bowline, *not* via a snap-shackle. Ideally, a swivel should be fixed to the head of the sail and the halyard made fast to that but this is not necessary if care is taken with packing the sail.

For some reason *Brittany Ferries* had been rigged with snap-shackles and I had omitted to chop them off.

*Day 11* 17 June
Noon 43° 45′ N 57° 45′ W   Run 160 made good from 190

A day of interesting tactical decisions. The wind was fairly light and for most of the 24 hours we could lay the course and hence had to choose which route to take. From our noon position the Rhumb line was slightly south of west for a distance of 800 miles to Newport. Our original plan had been to cross the Newfoundland Bank near its southern tip and then take the first of the following two options:

1. Sail west, staying north of the Rhumb line, pass just south of Sable Island, stay on the edge of the shallow water off Nova Scotia, head south-west over the George's Bank during the last 200 miles to the Nantucket Shoals and then in to Newport. The route stays in the favourable Labrador current and out of the adverse Gulf Stream. Disadvantages: fog and the danger of prevailing south-westerly winds just when one wants to come south-west.

2. Sail south of the Rhumb line, thus approaching the Nantucket Shoals sailing west or even slightly north of west. Advantages: one gets upwind, should the south-westerly set in. Disadvantages: there is a risk of hitting the adverse Gulf Stream (see fig. 11).

The choice was made harder for us as it became apparent, when we radioed home, that our lead had indeed been reduced to 130 miles, more worrying still was *Tele-7-Jours* in second place 120 miles south of us, *Elf Aquitaine* 80 miles south and *Gauloise* 120 miles south. Despite this I felt sure that the first option was the correct one and we took it, though not to quite such an extreme as we may have done, had we had no competitors to cover. The expert commentators on Europe One considered, in a broadcast on that day, that our route would allow the French to gain on us.

*Day 12* 18 June
Noon 42° 30′ N 60° 55′ W   150 miles made good from 225 sailed

A miserable day of dead head winds, though fortunately not too strong. As neither tack was favoured we made four legs of six hours each so as not to stray too far from our intended route. Our constant concern over our competitors reaching along right on course to the south of us proved unfounded; instead, they must have been nearly becalmed as our lead pulled out to 190 miles by noon. The order behind us was unchanged so we allowed ourselves a little more confidence in the hope that the race was ours, barring damage. No sooner thought, than the jumper strut promptly broke, followed by the backstay linkage (see fig. 12). In fact, as we'd been suspicious of the jumper strut's ability to stop the bottom panel of the mast from moving forward we had doubled up the running backstay. Probably the jumper broke as it was 'moving' and not under load. The bottle screw joining the lower backstay to the link plate broke a few hours later. I went up the mast to secure the flogging strut and after the second incident we simply treated the two parts of the runner separately – the only drawback being the loss of the use of two winches on the starboard side. (The problems of fore and aft staying on a multihull are discussed in Part 2, Chapter 10.)

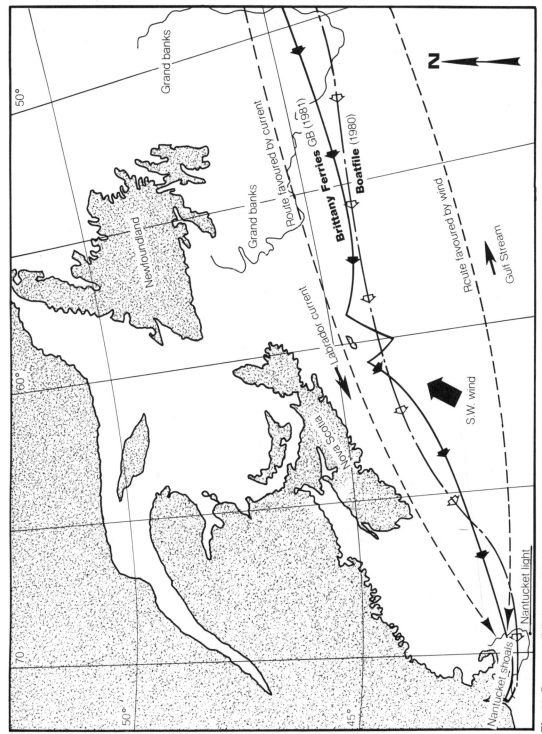

**Fig 11** *Route possibilities over last 1000 miles*

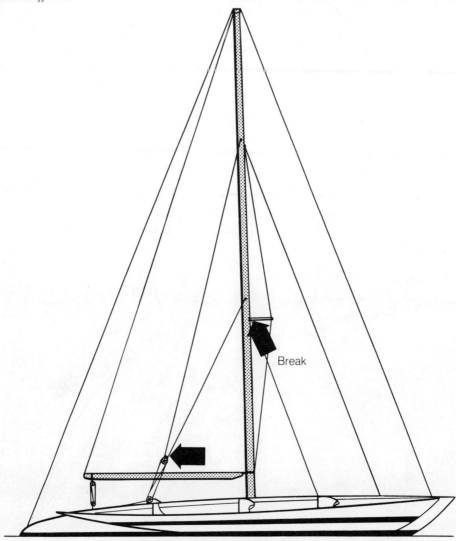

Break

**Fig 12** *Runner and jumper breakages on* Brittany Ferries GB

Our navigation at this stage was becoming a bit of a headache. For the first part of the voyage we had switched on the satellite navigator every morning to get a fix. This was easier and less time consuming than using a sextant – important when one is continually tired, and after sailing, cooking, maintenance and sleep were next on the agenda. However, halfway across, the satellite navigator packed in and we had to take a few sights. Our position was then confirmed, unnecessarily I hasten to add, during our daily talks with England when Naomi would read us the positions of all the leading boats. But at this stage we were suffering from bad horizons or no sun. We really needed perfect sights to cross the Nantucket Shoals accurately and approach the finish. Our only resource was RDF and we were delighted to pick up Sable Island that morning.

On the domestic scene our water and food was holding out as planned, though we'd finally run out of sugar.

*Day 13* 19 June
Noon 41° 30' N 65° 00' W   Run 190 miles

Once again we were able to lay the course in a light north-easterly which gave us the opportunity to work south. We were sailing with the light spinnaker and making a series of 'tacks' downwind. By gybing through 60 degrees we could bring the apparent wind from 10 degrees aft of one beam to 10 degrees aft of the other. In such light conditions it definitely paid to tack downwind.

Our lead had remained at 190 miles and *Elf Aquitaine* and *Gauloise IV* were reported as equal second. Mike Birch and Walter Green on *Tele-7-Jours* had dropped to tenth place having totally stopped or even sailed slightly in a south-easterly – backwards – direction. Of course, we had no idea why but assumed damage.

*Day 14* 20 June
Noon 41° 05' N 68° 45' W   Run 175 miles

Needless to say, a very exciting day. The new wind came up from the south, not south-west, so we were able to close reach. By noon we had only 135 miles to go with a

*Four miles to the TwoSTAR finish.* Brittany Ferries GB *with her full rig.*

lead of 180 miles. We still worried: about damage, hitting a fishing boat and lots of other minor things that would not enter one's head if it were a close race to the finish.

We averaged 11 knots for the last 135 miles so we approached the shoals very fast. I picked up the DF station on Nantucket Island and we steered to pass 20 miles south of it. As we were without a very accurate fix and the visibility was very poor we dared not go near the shallows. Despite steering to clear the land the DF bearing stayed constant for several hours, making me believe the DF was faulty. We altered course to clear by a greater margin and slowly at first, then rapidly, the bearing opened. Right on the shallows the fog cleared and the buoy we were aiming for appeared dead ahead. The Lokata DF had indeed been accurate and the discrepancy between our dead reckoning and DF positions was explained as we got closer to the buoy and saw the vicious tidal set across our course. Much relieved, we set course directly for the finish 60 miles distant.

The race was now against daylight as we hoped to finish before dark. From 40 miles away we made VHF contact and gave an ETA for two and a half hours' time. Our first view of the finish was at sunset when Brenton Reef tower started to flash. With about four miles to go the first spectator boat found us. It was rapidly getting dark and the wind was heading which created a problem. By this time we were close-hauled, surrounded by spectator craft and totally blinded by photographers' flood-lights and could barely lay the nearest end of the finishing line. There was a lot of yelling and shouting and a few inebriated drivers directly under our bows – 'get closer for a better picture'. We identified Naomi, Chay's wife Maureen and his daughter Samantha shouting congratulations. We still didn't look very happy; unable to see the finishing buoy and with no idea how close it was I rushed forward and lowered the staysail in case we had to put in a crash tack – although how we might have managed that successfully with so many boats hemming us in is anybody's guess. Finally we spotted the buoy and in the ever-dying wind we squeezed across the line.

Our time for the voyage was 14 days and 14 hours (350 hours). We'd sailed 3214 miles through the water to make good 2983 miles at average speeds of 9.2 and 8.5 knots.

The next to finish was Mark Pajot's *Elf Aquitaine* just ahead of *Gauloise IV*. *Elf* was 16 hours behind us representing a speed difference of five per cent. Eric Loiseau's performance on *Gauloise* was staggering. His trimaran at only 44ft had lost out considerably during the gales earlier on (lying fourteenth after seven days) but had gained later in the lighter airs by taking a more southerly route. A week before the finish she was 180 miles behind us and held the same distance till the end. Robin Knox-Johnston finished in fourth place – giving the cats second and fourth placings – an interesting come back. The first monohull followed in fifth place.

And of the other favourites, there were 23 multihulls over 40ft LOA at the start of the race; there were 5 monohulls of 65ft LOA or more which could have been in the first few places but none got closer than fifth. Of the 23 potential front runners of trimarans, catamarans and proas, 11 retired, eight were beaten by one or more monohulls and four made the top places. The details are given in Table 3 (page 90).

*Delighted to have won.*

**TABLE 3**

*TWOSTAR ANALYSES*

| Class | Mono | | Tri | | Cat | | Proa | Total multis | | Total all | |
|---|---|---|---|---|---|---|---|---|---|---|---|
| | Start (retired) | | | | | | | | | | |
| Class 1 (61'–85') | 5 | (1) | 2 | (1) | 2 | (0) | | 4 | (1) | 9 | (3) |
| Class 2 (46'–60') | 10 | (2) | 7 | (4) | 1 | (1) | 2 (2) | 10 | (7) | 20 | (8) |
| Class 3 (41'–45') | 11 | (2) | 8 | (3) | 1 | (1) | | 9 | (3) | 20 | (5) |
| Class 4 (36'–40') | 23 | (4) | 6 | (3) | | | | 6 | (3) | 29 | (7) |
| Class 5 (31'–35') | 15 | (4) | 1 | (0) | | | | 1 | (0) | 16 | (4) |
| Class 6 (25'–30') | 6 | (0) | 3 | (0) | | | | 3 | (0) | 9 | (0) |
| Totals | 70 (13) | | 27 (11) | | 4 (1) | | 2 (2) | 33 (14) | | 103 (27) | |

From a statistical point of view the samples are fairly small yet it is worthwhile pointing out some of the facts that emerge.

1. Ocean-racing catamarans can now be built strong and fast enough to compete well for speed and reliability against their three-hulled counterparts.

2. Proas are still pretty dodgy bets (100 per cent failure rate).

3. 18 per cent of the monohulls retired and 42 per cent of the multihulls retired. These figures are, regrettably, to be expected. On the other hand if more than half the racing cats and tris entered in a race reach the finishing line at least one of these survivors will beat the monohulls of a similar size – to windward as well.

4. While 16 per cent of the English entries retired, no fewer than 33 per cent of the other European entries did not finish the course.

So much for statistics. Let us now look at the performance of our list of favourites at the start of this chapter.

*Jacques Ribourel*, 80ft trimaran (ketch).
She appeared fast in the early stages but seemed either unable or unwilling to sail close to the wind. Her northerly route put her in the wake of *Sea Falcon* until losing her mainmast on the sixth day at sea. Had she continued to race without damage I doubt that she would have made the first three places. Her light-airs speed (on paper) looked unlikely to match that of the leaders.

*Sea Falcon*, 70ft catamaran (sloop).
Sailing very fast in the early stages and close to the lead for the first week. However, her major gain was in sailing down the Great Circle route which allowed her to sail freer in the predominant southerly winds of the first few days. It turned out to be a false investment as she was forced to work close-hauled south, dropping to eleventh place, then later recovering to fourth.

*Elf Aquitaine*, 63ft catamaran (sloop – fractional rig).
Finished second. Different and better than *Sea Falcon* in respect of her rig – hence faster in light airs and closer winded. In heavy airs off the wind she was also very fast (as she was

90

*Joined by our families after an absence of only 14 days – an east-west sailing record. On Chay's left are his wife Maureen and daughter Samantha. Naomi is on my left.*

later to prove). I think *Brittany Ferries GB* had a very slight speed advantage in all conditions, but mainly in heavy airs to windward. During the first week we gained on her at a rate of 15 miles a day and in the lighter weather ten miles a day.

*Royale*, 60ft trimaran (sloop – fractional rig).
A similar boat to *Brittany Ferries GB* but with a more 'state-of-the-art' rig and foil stabilization. There is no doubt that sailing to windward just after the start in force 6 she was both faster and closer winded than us. Alas her 'state-of-the-art' rig fell down after a few miles. The interesting and unanswered questions are:

1. If her rig had been similar to ours – i.e. slower but reliable – would she have been faster than us with her foil stabilization?
2. If so, would we have made up the ground in light airs when her foils (though retractable) would not have helped her?
I believe she may have won the race.

*Sudinox*, 55ft proa.
Collided at the start with *D'Aucy* and holed the main hull. Repairs were made and she set out again a day late only to retire for good that same day with 'sail problems'.

*Eterna Royale Quartz*, 55ft proa.
I saw her after the start sailing at the same speed to windward as *Brittany Ferries*. She was dismasted on day 5 (and then sank) while lying over 300 miles behind the leaders – not very impressive.

*Tele-7-Jours*, 53ft trimaran (sloop).
She was going well and would probably have finished second but, 600 miles from Newport, the bow of her port float broke off at the join of the leading edge of the crossbeam. Mike Birch was fortunate in having as crew the designer and builder of his boat, Walter Green, which must have been handy for discussing warranty claims! But first they had to get to shore and much credit is due to them for superb seamanship in this respect. They partly filled the starboard (good) float with water, using a bucket and funnel, in order to prevent a capsize over the port float, and then, tacking on to port to put the good hull firmly to leeward, they made a good landfall in Nova Scotia, where the boat was repaired and strengthened.

*Starpoint*, 53ft trimaran.
A sister ship to *Tele-7-Jours*. Perhaps not sailed so hard, she finished seventh.

*Paul Ricard*, 52ft trimaran.
As noted she retired with a damaged main hull. Nothing conclusive was proved about her design. It is probably out of date by now (although only three years old).

*Lesieur Tournesol*, 52ft trimaran.
She finished eighth which was near the limit of her potential.

*Gautier II*, 45ft trimaran.
When she lost her rudder she was lying fourth, way ahead of any other vessel her size which tends to prove that her foils were working well. How she would have behaved in light airs was never discovered.

*Bonifacio*, 45ft trimaran.
She capsized while still sailing to windward in conditions her crew did not consider extreme. Her skipper, Phil Steggall, was below at the time and did not think the waves were of a dangerous size. There is an element of chance in racing any multihull; there will always be the odd wave peak capable of causing disaster. The skipper who runs off before meeting any of those waves will live to fight another day – but he won't win the race.

*Gauloise IV*, 44ft trimaran.
Despite having disregarded this entry as being too small to worry us, Eric Loiseau gave us quite a fright. He proved his boat to be as fast as any other competitor in light airs. A great performance that brought him to within 50 minutes of second place.

*Brittany Ferries FR*, 44ft trimaran.
Sailed well to tenth place but 24 hours behind *Gauloise*.

*Mark One Tool Hire*, 30ft trimaran.
In easily winning Class IV she proved again that a small trimaran can race to windward in gale conditions. Her time of 22 days 8 hours compares with my time of 22 days 22 hours on the 31ft *Boatfile* in the 1980 OSTAR.

On the monohull scene I should mention that the wide ocean-racing yachts did as well if not better than the ultra thin, deep-keel yachts designed solely for speed. Especially disappointing was *Kriter VIII*, described as being 'as far as monohull can go'. As a 'monomaran' this 79 footer suffered badly from pitching and finished eleventh, almost two days behind the winner. The results of the race can be found in Table 4.

As an interesting epilogue to the story of the TwoSTAR one should look briefly at the race from New York back to England and France. This event was conceived as a return race to get the yachts back to Europe and, more interestingly, to follow that route considered to be the Atlantic record, Sandy Hook to the Lizard, a distance of nearly 3000 miles. *Brittany Ferries* was not entered and it was left to *Elf Aquitaine* and *Sea Falcon* to lead the ten entries racing to beat the record of ten days ten hours set by Eric Tabarly on *Paul Ricard* in 1980.

As a race it was a non-event but as a record attempt it was very dramatic. *Elf* proved to be the fastest in the fleet and set up a very fast pace in conditions perfect for breakneck speeds. At times she averaged 17 knots for several hours. She passed the Lizard in nine days ten hours, and broke the record rather conclusively. Her average speed was over 13 knots. It was a pity none of the fast trimarans – particularly *Brittany Ferries GB* – were in the race. We shall have to wait till next year to see if the tris can equal the speed of the cats in a similar event.

**TABLE 4**

## 1981 OBSERVER/EUROPE 1 TRANSATLANTIC RACE

| Position | No | Yacht | Skipper/Crew/Country | Type | Class | Class pos. | Elapsed D | H | M |
|---|---|---|---|---|---|---|---|---|---|
| 1 | 345 | Brittany Ferries GB | Chay Blyth/Rob James (GB) | 65' T | I | 1 | 14 | 13 | 54 |
| 2 | 117 | Elf Aquitaine | Marc Pajot/Paul Ayasse (Fr) | 63' C | I | 2 | 15 | 06 | 03 |
| 3 | F115 | Gauloises IV | Eric Loiseau/Halvard Mabire (Fr) | 44' T | III | 1 | 15 | 06 | 52 |
| 4 | 350 | Sea Falcon | Robin Knox-Johnston/Billy King-Harman (GB) | 70' C | I | 3 | 15 | 21 | 38 |
| 5 | 22 | Faramserenissima | Bruno Bacilieri/Marc Vallin (Italy) | 66' M | I | 4 | 16 | 01 | 25 |
| 6 | 128 | Monsieur Meuble | Florence Arthaud/Francois Boucher (Fr) | 69' M | I | 5 | 16 | 03 | 57 |
| 7 | 21 | Starpoint | Paolo Martinoni/Enrico Sala (Italy) | 53' T | II | 1 | 16 | 04 | 58 |
| 8 | 32 | Lesieur Tournesol | Eugene Riguidel/Jean-Francois Coste (Fr) | 52' T | II | 2 | 16 | 05 | 22 |
| 9 | F15 | Charles Heidsieck III | Alain Gabbay/Andre Beranger (Fr) | 65' M | I | 6 | 16 | 05 | 59 |
| 10 | 5 | Brittany Ferries FR | Daniel Gilard/Lionel Pean (Fr) | 45' T | III | 2 | 16 | 07 | 21 |
| 11 | 28 | Kriter VIII | Michael Malinovsky/Joel Charpentier (Fr) | 75' M | I | 7 | 16 | 08 | 48 |
| 12 | 67 | Gepe Papiers Peints | Gerard Pesty/Jean Pierre Griziaux (Fr) | 43' T | III | 3 | 16 | 23 | 54 |
| 13 | 25 | Chaussettes Kindy | Philippe Poupon/Charles Capelle (Fr) | 38' T | IV | 1 | 17 | 21 | 30 |
| 14 | 64 | Tuesday's Child | Warren Luhrs/Jim Stanek (USA) | 54' M | II | 3 | 18 | 07 | 24 |
| 15 | 130 | Skyjack | Philip Walwyn/Frances Walwyn (St Kitts) | 45' C | III | 4 | 18 | 23 | 35 |
| 16 | 84 | Inkel Hi Fi | Fred Dovaston/Jeff Taylor (GB) | 38' M | IV | 3 | 19 | 14 | 54 |
| 17 | 100 | Voortrekker | Bertie Reed/John Martin (S. Africa) | 49' M | II | 4 | 19 | 20 | 49 |
| 18 | 51 | S Marine | Oliver Moussy/Louise Chabaz (Fr) | 44' M | III | 5 | 20 | 00 | 28 |
| 19 | 35 | Technica | Philippe Fournier/Yann Nedellec (Sw) | 36' T | IV | 4 | 20 | 06 | 40 |
| | | | (Time penalty: 36 hours for crew change according to Rules 6.3/8) | | | | | | |
| 20 | 24 | Super Marches Bravo | Annick Martin/Annie Cordelle (Fr) | 45' M | III | 6 | 21 | 04 | 28 |
| 21 | 60 | BMW Marine | Patrice Charpentier/Jean-Michel Charpentier (Fr) | 38' M | IV | 4 | 21 | 05 | 28 |
| 22 | 30 | Fleury Michon | Jean-Pierre Derunes/Andre Wilmet (Fr) | 44' T | III | 7 | 21 | 10 | 42 |
| 23 | 38 | Philips Radio Ocean | Patrick Elies/Dominique Hardy (Fr) | 34' M | V | 1 | 21 | 14 | 51 |
| 24 | 20 | Mark One Tool Hire | Mark Gatehouse/Michael Holmes (GB) | 30' T | VI | 1 | 22 | 08 | 26 |
| 25 | 91M | Tri-Dextrostrix | Simon Frost/Eugene Wade-Brown (GB) | 40' T | III | 8 | 22 | 12 | 58 |
| 26 | 12 | Launet Entreprise | Alain Petit-Etienne/Michel Liot (Fr) | 56' M | II | 5 | 22 | 18 | 00 |
| 27 | 66 | Transports Jet | Patrick Morvan/Jean-Pierre Vambacas (Fr) | 39' M | IV | 5 | 22 | 18 | 35 |
| 28 | K988 | Blackjack | Rodney Barton/Mike Pocock (GB) | 38' M | IV | 6 | 23 | 05 | 38 |
| 29 | K3999 | Poppy II | Jean Dean/Richard Reddyhoff (GB) | 35' M | V | 2 | 23 | 05 | 46 |
| 30 | F57 | First | Yvan Griboval/Francois Carpente (Fr) | 35' M | V | 3 | 23 | 10 | 22 |
| 31 | F42 | Dictionnaire Robert | Michel Horeau/Olivier Despaigne (Fr) | 56' T | II | 6 | 23 | 10 | 52 |
| 32 | 50 | F Magazine | Claire Marty/Catherine Hermann (Fr) | 37' M | IV | 7 | 23 | 15 | 31 |
| 33 | 102 | Festival de Lorient | Marie Noelle Dedienne/Isabelle Bernadin (Fr) | 41' M | III | 9 | 23 | 15 | 33 |
| 34 | N117 | Nor-Am Friendship | Gustav Brun Lie/Thorlief Thorleifson (Nor) | 37' M | IV | 8 | 23 | 19 | 00 |
| 35 | 71 | Lady of Sailomat | Joe Seaton/Sylvain Vergnot (Fr) | 40' M | IV | 9 | 23 | 20 | 47 |
| 36 | 22287 | Misanthrope | John Sweeney/David White (USA) | 43' M | III | 10 | 23 | 21 | 14 |
| 37 | 142 | Gipsy Moth V | Giles Chichester/Brian Gladstone (GB) | 57' M | II | 7 | 24 | 03 | 09 |

| | | | | | | | | | |
|---|---|---|---|---|---|---|---|---|---|
| 38 | D166 | *Ville de St Nazaire* | Dominique Montesinos/Malou Montesinos (Fr) | 39' M | IV | 10 | 24 | 04 | 51 |
| 39 | E1840 | *Picanel* | Enrique Curt/Bernard Oliva (Spain) | 38' M | IV | 11 | 24 | 09 | 12 |
| 40 | B644 | *Patrick III* | Paul Vinck/Gerrit D'Haeseleer (Belgium) | 46' M | II | 8 | 24 | 09 | 53 |
| 41 | 29 | *Heart* | Tom Perkins/Phyllis Aschenbrennen (USA) | 29' T | VI | 2 | 24 | 17 | 23 |
| 42 | 19024 | *Bella Blu* | Valerio Monaco/Giorgio Masala (Italy) | 39' M | IV | 12 | 24 | 17 | 45 |
| 43 | 68 | *Namar V* | Edoardo Guzzetti/Sergio Rigo (Italy) | 41' M | III | 11 | 25 | 07 | 21 |
| 44 | F7555 | *Coathalem* | Marc Guillemot/Bertrand de Broc (Fr) | 30' M | VI | 3 | 25 | 08 | 19 |
| 45 | K3694 | *Sherpa Bill* | Alan Perkes/Tim Rees (GB) | 36' M | IV | 13 | 25 | 08 | 24 |
| 46 | K64 | *Assassin* | Brian Wells/Barry Sanders (GB) | 39' M | IV | 14 | 25 | 08 | 27 |
| 47 | 36 | *Olympus Camera* | Kai Granholm/Klaus Koskimies (Finland) | 35' M | V | 4 | 25 | 09 | 40 |
| 48 | 1 | *Port du Crouesty* | Didier Greggory/Alain Caudrelier-Benac (Fr) | 35' M | V | 5 | 25 | 09 | 57 |
| 49 | 262M | *Livery Dole II* | Peter Phillips/Keith Brimacombe (GB) | 35' T | V | 6 | 25 | 10 | 25 |
| 50 | PZ900 | *Kapitan II* | Jan Pinkiewicz/Wojciech Krupski (Poland) | 43' M | III | 12 | 25 | 13 | 12 |
| 51 | 5661 | *Airstrip* | Gerard Hannaford/Michael Stockwood (GB) | 29' M | VI | 4 | 25 | 13 | 48 |
| 52 | 5649 | *Thunderer RAOC* | John Ross/Carl Hoe (GB) | 32' M | V | 7 | 25 | 14 | 44 |
| 53 | 17 | *Alcatel* | Olivier Dardel/Emmanuel Callico (Fr) | 38' M | IV | 15 | 25 | 15 | 22 |
| 54 | 847 | *Hello World* | Eve Bonham/Diana Thomas-Ellam (GB) | 35' M | V | 8 | 25 | 18 | 21 |
| 55 | 79 | *Ratso II* | Guy Bernadin/Andrew Herbert (Fr) | 38' M | IV | 16 | 25 | 18 | 34 |

(Time penalty: 36 hours for crew change according to Rules 6.3/8)

| | | | | | | | | | |
|---|---|---|---|---|---|---|---|---|---|
| 56 | 43 | *Moody Blue* | Jacques Jean/Benoit Jean (Fr) | 49' M | II | 9 | 26 | 02 | 45 |
| 57 | K879 | *Carte Blanche* | Jeremy Tetley/John McCormick (GB) | 36' M | IV | 17 | 26 | 04 | 53 |
| 58 | 3958 | *Adfins Rival* | Graham Adams/Stewart Murdoch (GB) | 38' M | IV | 18 | 26 | 07 | 24 |
| 59 | 53 | *Betelgeuze* | S. C. J. Van Hagen/Rob Jaspers (Holland) | 42' M | III | 13 | 26 | 08 | 28 |
| 60 | 34 | *Wild Rival* | Kitty Hampton/Rachael Hayward (GB) | 34' M | V | 9 | 26 | 17 | 15 |
| 61 | 555 | *Carmen* | Jerzy Colojew/Jacek Borkowsky (Poland) | 30' M | VI | 5 | 27 | 05 | 21 |

(Time penalty: 3 hours 26 minutes for late arrival according to Rule 6.11)

| | | | | | | | | | |
|---|---|---|---|---|---|---|---|---|---|
| 62 | PZ648 | *Retman III* | Wojciech Jeziorski/Anna B. Jeziorski (Poland) | 53' T | II | 10 | 27 | 09 | 49 |

(Time penalty: 9 hours 26 minutes for late arrival according to Rule 6.11)

| | | | | | | | | | |
|---|---|---|---|---|---|---|---|---|---|
| 63 | 1952 | *Puerto Principe* | Jose Luis Ferrer/Xavier Kirchner (Spain) | 40' T | IV | 19 | 27 | 10 | 27 |
| 64 | K3477 | *Phantom* | Cyril Simpson/Fred A. Brown (GB) | 36' M | IV | 20 | 27 | 12 | 57 |
| 65 | 120 | *Exchange Travel* | Martin Minter-Kemp/Michael Wingate-Grey (GB) | 38' M | IV | 21 | 27 | 17 | 32 |
| 66 | 63 | *Thistledowne* | William McClure/Bud McClure (USA) | 28' M | VI | 6 | 27 | 22 | 20 |
| 67 | 8 | *Bollemaat IV* | Kees Roemers/Nancy Roemers (Holland) | 44' M | III | 14 | 28 | 05 | 02 |
| 68 | 4 | *Dancing Dolphin* | Bob Menzies/Christine Brouet (GB) | 37' M | IV | 22 | 28 | 10 | 54 |
| 69 | 48 | *Therm-A-Stor Mermaid* | Julian Benson/Nick Robinson (GB) | 32' M | V | 11 | 29 | 12 | 17 |
| 70 | 233 | *Melmore* | Frank Esson/Martin Walker (GB) | 46' M | II | 11 | 30 | 07 | 52 |
| 71 | 92 | *Telstar* | Slade Penoyre/Tony Blofeld (GB) | 26' T | VI | 7 | 31 | 01 | 24 |
| 72 | 226 | *Bourlingeur III* | Luc LaFortune/Pierre Turenne (Canada) | 27' M | VI | 8 | 32 | 00 | 49 |
| 73 | 27 | *Fiskars-Finnsailer* | Lennart Koskinen/Gustaf Flegge (Finland) | 34' M | V | 12 | 32 | 07 | 02 |
| 74 | 107 | *Miss Alfred Marks* | Anne Hammick (GB)/Elizabeth Hammick | 33' M | V | 13 | 32 | 22 | 23 |
| 75 | 11 | *Wild Thyme of Durham* | Joseph Kayll/David Kayll (GB) | 42' M | III | 15 | 33 | 18 | 04 |
| 76 | 0 | *Yang* | Jean Lacombe/Toni Austin (USA) | 25' M | VI | 9 | 41 | 16 | 12 |

# 5

## Colt Cars GB

I stayed in Newport for two weeks after our arrival on *Brittany Ferries GB*. My association with the Shuttleworth trimaran ended as soon as John Oakeley and Laurel Holland finished the race in the Freedom 70, *Kriter Lady II*. While Chay prepared *Brittany Ferries* for a fast West to East return journey, Naomi and I turned our attention to preparing the Freedom for the same voyage. The Atlantic crossing was to be crew training for the Whitbread Round the World Race, due to start in two months' time.

Before leaving Newport I went for a last sail on *Brittany Ferries*. It was a 'jolly' with several guests, including designer Dick Newick. The day was perfect for showing off the tri and we achieved some impressive speeds. Newick was heard to remark that the vessel was more powerful and faster than any of his designs to date – very pleasing praise for John Shuttleworth, her designer.

Our trip back to England in the Freedom 70 took only 13 and a half days (very fast for a monohull) and ironically we nearly beat Chay who set sail on the same day. Approaching England we heard via VHF link calls that Fairways Marine, the owners of the Freedom, had gone bankrupt. I decided to put into Dartmouth to find out our legal position. Sure enough the morning papers enclosed a small paragraph relating the demise of Fairways Marine; it also mentioned that their only asset was in mid-Atlantic and wouldn't Rob James get a rude surprise when he returned.

Within hours our arrival in the UK was discovered and the first writ was nailed to the mast. All we could do was return the yacht to its owners and try to salvage something from the wreck. It soon appeared the best – indeed the only – way to save our entry in the Whitbread was to find a company interested in buying the yacht from the appointed receivers and to enter her under a new sponsored name. While exploring this possibility we renewed contact with Michael Orr, the chairman and managing director of the Colt Car Company. We had known him for several years and had in fact broadly discussed the possibility of sailing under the Colt banner at a dinner a few months earlier. After several hastily organized meetings Colt decided to buy the Freedom and I recommended the maximum price to which they should go. To our surprise this offer was turned down by the receiver and that was the end of our round the world race entry.

My crew joined Chay on *United Friendly* and Naomi and I went back to Colt Cars to

*I sail the* Freedom 70 *back to disappointment in England – her owners bankrupt and the yacht to be sold.*

discuss possible alternatives. Within a few days a perfect proposition presented itself: we were to buy or build a trimaran for the 1982 Round Britain and Ireland Race and the Route du Rhum in the same year. Various avenues were explored and Michael Orr finally decided to build a 60ft trimaran (the maximum size for OSTAR '84). After considerable thought and discussion with designers I decided to co-design the new boat with Ron Holland. The design situation itself was interesting: Shuttleworth had shown himself to be the most up to date trimaran designer with *Brittany Ferries,* and yet that would be the boat I would have to beat in the Round Britain Race. At the same time, I had a few ideas of my own, and our neighbour in Cork, Ron, was keen to turn his undoubted skills in monohull design to something new.

So, Ron and I sat down to produce the drawings of a racing multihull. The chapter on multihull design (Chapter 6) goes into some detail on our design concept. Briefly, the aim was to produce a high power-to-weight ratio without becoming too radical. The main area for improvement over *Brittany Ferries* would be in the rig. A tall fractional spar by Stearn was specified and a deck layout to allow close sheeting angles for windward work. In fact the deck – cockpit, sheet tracks, chain plates etc – was one of the first things we considered. We decided on two crossbeams, with the mast on the forward one, which were to be narrow top to bottom (low windage, good water clearance) and yet very stiff; even at a weight and cost penalty. The hulls would be fairly conventional but finer forward with more rocker than the norm to improve speed in light airs. The ghosting performance of the boat would also be aided by a masthead spinnaker and genoa.

Looking back, it's fair to say that we chose a trimaran rather than a catamaran because I had more knowledge of the former; we chose a composite construction for the same reason.

As time was short – six months to the May '82 qualifying deadline – we rushed out enough drawings to be able to approach potential builders. Altogether, I had detailed conferences with ten boatyards and they each put in quotations for the yacht. We were after a price for the three hulls and two crossbeams assembled using a glass/Kevlar/carbon lay-up over a foam or balsa core. Some yards suggested variations to the lay-up and it was made clear that any changes to the nature of the composite would allow appropriate adjustments to the price.

The result was an education: the cheapest price was less than 50 per cent of the highest. The most interesting was put forward by SP Composites of Cowes. As an alternative to the other standard quotes, they suggested using Nomex core, instead of foam or balsa, and recommended using 50 per cent carbon and 50 per cent Kevlar in a hybrid cloth instead of glass fibre with some carbon and Kevlar fibre. Michael Orr was impressed with the proposal and having met Paul Rudling and Tim Gurr, who would respectively organize and build the vessel, he gave the go-ahead. Contracts were drawn up, SP organized premises and the final design work was done. Tony Marchant Associates, a firm of composite consulting engineers, were employed to do all the stress calculations and to specify the detailed laminates and joints. With four months to the deadline building started.

During this period it was my job to organize and buy all the deck gear, rig and sails and have them available when they were required by the builders. By the end of March the hulls and crossbeams were complete and ready for assembly. A lot of hours had been put

*An unlikely looking bunch of builders! They worked nearly 100 hour weeks to make the deadline.*

in in a relatively short time to achieve the high quality Tim Gurr demanded. It was not unusual for the builders to work from 6 a.m. to 8 p.m. seven days a week.

In order to bond the pieces together successfully it was necessary to work indoors. There are few sheds available with 41ft-wide doors so it was decided to build an air building over the 'bits' after moving them to a site near the water. The building – polythene sheets, rope, a ground seal and a fan – was put up in a day, and it blew down that night. The problem turned out to be a combination of lack of pressure due to a poor ground seal, a temporary door allowing a rip to start and high winds. The flogging polythene was threatening to knock the main hull off its cradle so we reluctantly had to cut it away. Within two days a new sheet had been made, with a better door and seal and we ended up with a perfect 70ft-diameter bubble which stayed intact for the time we needed it. Inside this hothouse, the boat was completed.

There were the usual last minute hitches, which were mainly overcome by endless telephoning, trips to London, visits to a local fabricating shop and more telephoning. With the qualifying deadline approaching (we had to sail 200 miles by 9 a.m. on 10 May) the pace hotted up. We were unable to fit the electrics, paint the interior or finish the paint work outside in the time available so these jobs were left till later. On the evening of 6 May we lifted the trimaran up to fit the expensive German rudder into the rudder bearings (from the same manufacturer) which had already been fitted. It didn't fit. With three and a half days to go before the qualifying deadline we had no rig, no deck gear in place and a rudder that wouldn't fit.

*The bubble air building is deflated over the completed yacht.*

We finally launched at 9 a.m. on 7 May having adjusted the rudder bearings. That day we fitted all the deck gear, the centreboard and one bunk, while Spencers rigged the mast which had arrived from the USA a few days previously.

There were several things wrong with the mast that obviously had to be rectified before it could be rigged. One of the diamond jumper struts had to be rewelded; the mast step, fixed to the mast, had to be cut off as we had already bonded a mast step to the trimaran, as

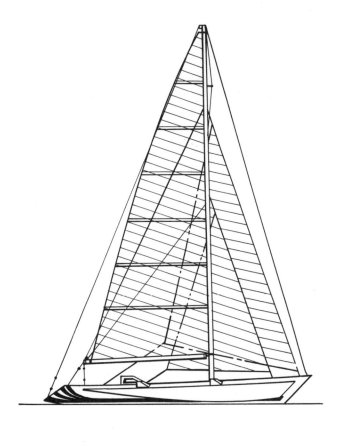

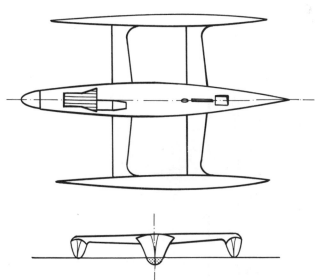

**Fig 13** Colt Cars GB

per specification, with the result that the mast ended up 3ins shorter than designed; finally we had to remove the spinnaker halyard non-chafe crane (as ordered) as it was quite impractical and would not allow a sail to be hoisted (see fig. 14).

When at last the boat was craned into the water we found her to be bow down on the designed waterline. To help rectify this we set up the mast with a certain amount of rake. Therefore, when the rig was lifted on to the step on deck we had to mark it, lift it off and cut the base at the correct angle. Finally, though, the mast and boom were there and the

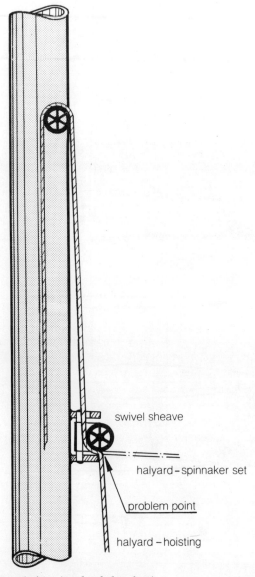

swivel sheave

halyard–spinnaker set

problem point

halyard – hoisting

**Fig 14** Colt Cars GB—*'Non chafe' spinnaker halyard exit*

hydraulic vang – an addition to the design to double up with the vang track – was carefully put in its correct place.

Peter Bateman arrived from Hood Sailmakers with our mainsail, genoas and staysail. The mainsail came with six full-length battens to support a certain amount of roach and also to improve sail shape, especially in light airs. The battens themselves (the longest 26ft, the shortest 6ft) were a composite construction using carbon fibre either side of a honeycomb core. It was made clear to me that the battens would need looking after although I must confess I was not at all sure about gybing a 1200 sq ft mainsail on a fractional – and hence with running backstays – rigged boat. Anyway, we shoe-horned the battens into their pockets and carried the sail aboard. The foot was loose with the clew attaching to a strong slider on top of the outboard end of the boom; this slider was hydraulically controlled to tension the foot. The luff was a tape system, i.e. no slides but a continuous bolt rope that slid up a groove in the mast. Six strong plastic cups were fitted just behind the bolt rope to take the forward compression from the battens on to the mast. Once set the sail was beautiful, but hoisting, lowering or controlling it while lowered, was very difficult.

The staysail was conventional and intended to double as our storm jib. The three genoas included a heavy no.1, a light no.1 and a Solent jib (no.2). The light no.1 was a loose-luffed mylar sail set from the masthead and intended for up to 5 knots of apparent wind. On inspection it felt far too heavy for the proposed job. The heavy no.1 was a conventional fractional jib with low foot and overlap. This we would use as a furler jib when unable to change down to the Solent jib – which was full hoist, no overlap and low-footed, ideal for winds from 20 to 35 knots apparent.

Our two spinnakers had arrived earlier from Miller and Whitworth. The all-round sail was a conventional 1½oz triradial to be set from the fractional halyard, and the light runner was a ¾oz radial head of massive proportions, to be set from the masthead. Both sails used a spi-squeezer system – see Chapter 12 (fig. 15 shows the complete sail plan and fig. 16 the mainsail details).

On 8 May we went out on to a flat Solent for our first sail. It was somewhat of an anticlimax as there was absolutely no wind. We set full main and heavy no.1 genoa and drifted with the tide till we were eventually towed back to Cowes again.

The next day we were out at the crack of dawn in order to give ourselves enough time to complete the 200 miles in the 27 hours left. It was still calm as Naomi, Tim, two more builders and I tried to get away from Cowes. A very light breeze soon came up from the west and we hoisted our all-round spinnaker for the run east. After a series of reaches and gybes we found manoeuvring easier with only two, or at most three, people in the cockpit rather than the full crew. Providing we kept out of each other's way the sail-handling systems worked well – indeed in flat water and only 5 knots of wind they should do!

Once clear of the Solent we came on the wind and tried the light no.1. Hoisted loose-luffed to the masthead in 8 knots apparent, not only did the luff fall off, precluding beating, but the top of the spar was bending alarmingly. Obviously, we could only use the sail in very light airs and for that requirement the cloth weight (over 4oz) was far too heavy. We put the sail back in its bag and unfurled the heavy no.1 again.

For the rest of the voyage the wind stayed in the west and blew no more than 12 knots. This allowed us to reach back and forth across the Channel clocking up the miles,

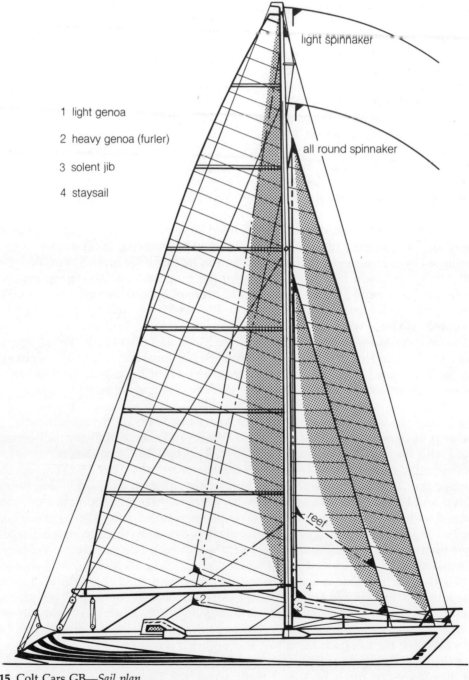

light spinnaker

1 light genoa

2 heavy genoa (furler)

3 solent jib

4 staysail

all round spinnaker

reef

1

2

4

3

**Fig 15** Colt Cars GB—*Sail plan*

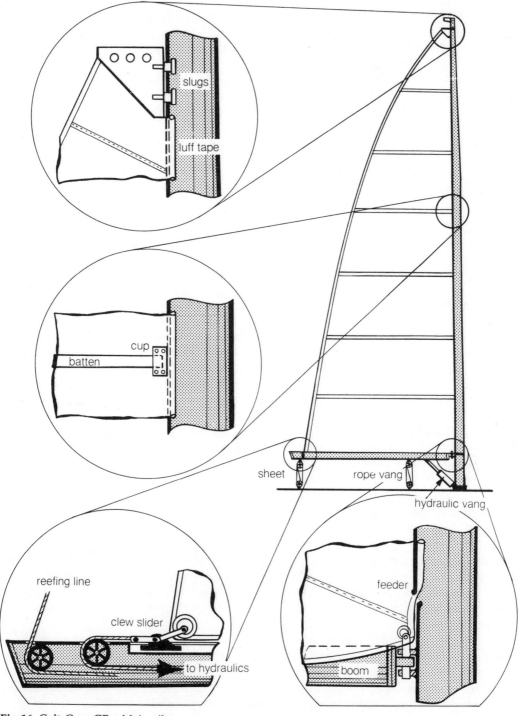

slugs

luff tape

cup

batten

sheet

rope vang

hydraulic vang

feeder

reefing line

clew slider

to hydraulics

boom

**Fig 16** Colt Cars GB—*Mainsail*

including, at one point, sailing into Cherbourg harbour and out again. I had been very keen to see how our bow down trim would effect performance. It certainly felt right in light airs and as we started to heel on to the float in the puffs the bow came up exactly as it had been designed to do.

My early reactions to the boat were several and mixed. I felt that we were incredibly close-winded when beating – better than any previous multihull I'd sailed; I felt our light airs speed was better than *Brittany Ferries*'s had been before she re-rigged but not as magic as I'd dreamed it might be; our medium airs speed appeared to me to be slower than that of *Brittany Ferries*. These were only feelings as we had no instruments on *Colt Cars* at the time and anyway, it is virtually impossible to decide whether you're fast or slow until you have competition. Chay Blyth has a saying 'all boats are fast on their own', and I have to agree with him.

We were back in Cowes by 3 a.m. on 10 May – six hours inside the limit. We were woken a few hours later by Ron Holland rowing anxiously round and round his latest creation. We all retired to the yacht club for breakfast to discuss what needed to be done to the boat. Immediately after breakfast we took the mast out and hoisted *Colt Cars* back on to her building pad. The mast was undoubtedly stiff and strong enough but there were various things wrong. To begin with it was necessary to go up the mast with a hammer to encourage the headboard slugs to move up or down past the mast-join at mid point, where the tracks did not quite line up. Also, the spreader angle was wrong, the lower tang angle was incorrect and the second diamond strut had come unwelded.

While these problems were being attended to the builders finished the boat. With the help of a colleague, Jeff Houlgrave, Naomi and I fitted the electric lighting, solar panels, instruments, satellite navigator, autopilot and radio direction finder. Within a week we were re-rigged and ready to go training.

We sailed daily from Cowes and slowly came to grips with the boat. Our instruments indicated a good performance. In flat water we could tack through a little under 80 degrees and still make 10 knots to windward in a true breeze of only 8 or 9 knots. We found it paid to reef rather than change jib – as our main was so large and powerful. Off the wind we could reach 20 knots in a true wind of much less. The spinnaker system, with the squeezer, worked very well and Naomi and I found we could tack and gybe quite satisfactorily with just the two of us pulling the strings while I steered with the tiller between my knees.

On 27 May we took *Colt Cars* to Lymington for the official naming ceremony. I had been nervous of manoeuvring our 60ft by 41ft square around the confines of Lymington river but by that time we had perfected the manoeuvring techniques. With the dinghy and its 25hp outboard strapped alongside the main hull near the stern we found that not only could we motor at 8 knots but we could also go astern and steer using the main helm plus engine angle.

The ceremony was performed by Michael Orr's wife Pat, the bottle smashed at first go and the contents of many more were consumed by the end of a successful launching.

Twenty-four hours later Naomi, Tim, Jeff and I set sail for Cork in Ireland. The purpose of the trip was training (nothing to do with the desire to moor the new boat up outside our front door) and to give Ron and his design team the opportunity to sail her. The trip over was quite slow due to very light head winds, followed by light winds dead astern. (With

*Naomi and I look apprehensive as we go for our first sail on* Colt Cars GB.

*The first sail. Note the lack of name (left off in the rush to meet the qualifying date), the modern fractional rig, fully battened main, and her bow down trim.*

*After completing* Colt Cars *we trained every day. Here we close reach at speed.*

the light, following wind it seemed best, and VMG instruments confirmed it, to reach downwind keeping the apparent wind angle between 100 degrees and 120 degrees off the bow and gybing through about 60 degrees). At Land's End a breeze came up from the beam and we shot off. We were doing 20 knots with full jib and one reef in 25 knots apparent when a wave hit the fairing of the port aft beam with a terrific whack and it exploded into pieces. A batten broke in sympathy so we slowed down to 12 knots for the rest of the night and arrived in Cork early in the morning.

The fairings were light-weight structures designed to convert the square crossbeams into aerodynamic shapes. The fairing shape itself was good, but we had tried to get away with a very light structure. I had felt uneasy about them when they were made and had requested more strength but the builders had thought it worth a try keeping it as light as possible so we had made a deal that they would keep the mould and make stronger ones if necessary – it was. Tim flew back to England and returned six days later with two new fairings strapped to the roof of his car! Meanwhile, we mended the batten and sailed every day with designers and sail makers. Two sails were recut – the leech of the heavy no.1 hollowed to clear the top spreader and the fractional spinnaker lengthened three feet to allow for the revised halyard exit. Those few days were most useful and a lot of good ideas came my way from the experts.

To fit the new fairings we beached *Colt Cars GB* at Johnny Minchin's boathouse where Naomi and I had refitted *Boatfile* two years earlier. Johnny, a friend in Currabinny, had very kindly offered the use of his fore-shore and boathouse.

Not surprisingly, with a vessel worth nearly 20 times as much as the Val we were very careful indeed. We dropped the rudder out while still on the mooring – a relatively easy manoeuvre as the rudder and its stock actually float – and brought it ashore. The ground was measured and cleared of stones. Anchors were laid out in the river and lines tied to strong points on the shore and to the near-by slipways to act as springs. Johnny rounded up 15 tyres and these we lashed in a 30ft line with ropes out each side ready to tie to the main hull. Finally we motored in at high tide with an outboard dinghy on each float to provide power and steering. Without mishap (albeit with a certain amount of shouting) we got her tied into position. She settled gently on the tyres while we lashed props to each beam end to hold her upright.

For two hours at high water she floated, and took the ground perfectly by herself between times, remaining seven or eight hours high and dry each tide, which afforded Tim ample time to complete the work.

While ashore one morning, a garden mysteriously appeared down the side of the saloon! Naomi and Rob Jacobs from the design office had conspired together and Rob had painted a superb mural on the side of the boat – flowers, bumble-bee and leprechaun. It certainly relieved a somewhat plain interior.

The work, which had to be completed in a week, was hampered by the occasional rain shower and by continual Minchin hospitality. There was no time to change the fairing attachment system so we glued the new fairings on to the old points, using a 2in overlap between fairing and beam, top and bottom, along the length from float to hull.

After some deliberation Ron and I decided not to alter the trim of the trimaran. To do so would have been time-consuming and difficult as it would have involved adding more buoyancy forward. Not only that, we felt the boat was better as it was. We eventually solved the problem by repainting her in Colt colours (four black stripes) aligned with the new water-line.

Once the fairing work was complete we refloated and refitted the rudder. To achieve this last manoeuvre we made a cradle of sail ties round the rudder and suspended a weight underneath it. With a further line on the weight it could be lowered until the buoyant rudder was forced in sink to the vertical position. With a swimmer in the water the stock was then positioned under the tube and the rudder floated up into its bearings as weight was taken on the line. The head of the stock came up above the cockpit floor so it was an easy matter to replace the retaining nut and tiller head.

On 14 June we set sail for Cowes again. The wind was strong, and this combined with a steep sea made Naomi badly seasick; she only recovered when we rounded Land's End 12 hours later. As she was trying a new type of seasickness remedy, one that is absorbed by the skin behind the ear, she was very put out by its singular lack of success. The trip was otherwise uneventful and the boat behaved well in the rough seas; we were not pushed for time just then so speed was no consideration. We got back to Cowes and prepared for our first race – the 60 mile Round the Island classic.

At Cowes we saw for the first time our three major competitors in the Round Britain. Standing in the Island Sailing Club, staring intently through their powerful binoculars, I watched *Brittany Ferries* mooring up offshore. Of course I knew the trimaran well but I was interested to see how her new rig looked. Chay, in an attempt to keep ahead of newer designs, had increased *Brittany Ferries*'s mast by seven feet, thereby increasing her sail area from 2100 sq ft. to 2500 sq ft. The proportion of the new rig to the hull did look pretty impressive. Comparing *Brittany Ferries* with *Colt Cars* the figures were:

|  | *Colt Cars* | *Brittany Ferries* |
|---|---|---|
| LOA | 60ft | 65ft |
| LWL | 48ft 9 ins | 55ft |
| Beam | 40ft 6ins | 40ft |
| Displacement | 12,000lbs | 15,000lbs |
| Mast height | 80ft | 80ft |
| Rig | Fractional | Masthead |
| Sail area | 2,000 sq ft | 2,500 sq ft |

On paper this would indicate two yachts of similar performance.

*Livery Dole*, Peter Phillips's new Shuttleworth trimaran was also moored nearby. She looked very similar to *Brittany Ferries* but with only two crossbeams, and a smaller rig. At 60ft LOA, a published weight the same as *Colt Cars GB*, but with a slightly smaller sail area, she would certainly be good competition.

The third trimaran to arrive was *Exmouth Challenge*. This Phil Morrison design was considerably different from the other three favourites. Like *Colt Cars* she was drawn by an unknown multihull designer. But in this case, her architect was a champion dinghy sailor and designer. Morrison had been limited in size to 54ft but had overcome this by drawing a trimaran with longer than usual floats and a 40ft beam. This gave her skipper, Mark Gatehouse, a boat potentially as fast as her larger adversaries in a breeze. Her relatively small rig would also help her out in heavy conditions but in medium airs she would be underpowered. My first impression, to be honest, was that she didn't have the power-to-weight ratio to do that well – a rash analysis.

The night before the Round the Island race I made another rash judgment – I accepted a bet from Chay that the loser buy dinner for the winner (between our two boats) and his crew.

I was hoping for light to medium airs for the race. The last thing I wanted was a lot of wind for our first showing in competition and with three people on board who'd not sailed the boat yet. On Saturday morning it was blowing about force 6. We manoeuvred out of the river into Cowes Roads and picked up a spare buoy in order to get the mainsail up tidily and to prepare the Solent jib. Once most of the monohulls had started we let go the buoy, hoisted the jib and started to reach back and forth at crazy speeds.

With just a few minutes to our gun we tacked at the outer end of the line, and as we started to sheet in there was a loud crack and the windward runner collapsed around our ears. The mast must have been bending alarmingly until we eased the jib sheet and got the sail down – all of which time the only thing holding the mast back was the leech of the mainsail. Having seen the cause of the failure, a sheered swivel on the runner block, it was obvious the race was over for us. It was a shock to see the others shooting over the line as the gun went and we couldn't help momentarily feeling that we'd suffered a great setback. There was nothing for it but to moor up again and be thankful it hadn't happened at the start of the Round Britain.

Investigation subsequently showed that the runner block was rated at 11 tons with a swivel of twice that strength. The manufacturers were sufficiently upset to replace the four swivel blocks in the running backstay system with four fixed head types. As there was no alignment problem I should have specified fixed head blocks at the outset.

The race was won easily by *Exmouth Challenge* in a record time of four hours and 30 minutes. She was more than half an hour ahead of the second boat, *Brittany Ferries*, who suffered spreader damage. *Livery Dole* came fourth with sail damage. The result didn't show anything conclusive about relative performances except that *Exmouth Challenge* was a force to be reckoned with in strong winds. A few weeks earlier she had been dismasted, and she'd also needed strengthening in the deck between the beams to reduce twisting; consequently, the opinion prevailed prior to the Round the Island was that she would not stand being pushed too hard. Yet, she was the only front-runner not to sustain damage.

The following week the Royal London Yacht Club held a multihull series. Alas, as they insisted on using IYRU racing rules most of the fast multihulls were excluded (because of commercial names) but we went out every day anyway to spar with *Livery Dole*. Despite having a commercial name she had been allowed to enter officially but, finding that there was no one to race against, she elected to drop out and match race against us. We joined in the first race on the first reach about a quarter of a mile behind *Livery Dole*. We slowly closed the gap and by the time we got to the leeward mark we were right on her stern. The moment of truth came as we sheeted in for the beat; to my immense relief we found ourselves sailing higher, out of her dirty wind dead astern, and passing her to windward. We beat her in that race, and the others, by an average of three minutes in every hour.

The most exciting race included a very fast reach from mid Solent off Southampton Water to a mark 12 miles to the east, off Seaview. The apparent wind was 25 to 30 knots and we carried the Solent jib and one reef. *Livery Dole* was pushing very hard behind us so

Exmouth Challenge *the 54ft Morrison design, sailed by Mark Gatehouse, that won the heavy weather round the Isle of Wight race in 1982 beating out of the Solent.*

we held on and tore down the reach with the lee float nearly completely submerged and the main hull beginning to lift – great sheets of spray everywhere. We touched 26 knots, averaged 20 for the stretch, and overtook two commercial ships on the way. The water was flat so there was no wave effect to contend with; it was exhilarating but also nerve-wracking. I remarked to Naomi that we couldn't afford to push the boat like that in the Round Britain as it would be too risky. Little did I know then.

After the series we replaced the two forward beam fairings, manufactured a new set of battens and overhauled the mainsail. The battens were a cause for great concern: they were breaking either when we hoisted the sail or when gybing. A particular point of destruction was at the running backstays; if the battens hit the runners they would fold up around them, inevitably breaking two or three. Another problem area was the luff of the mainsail which was being chewed up in its groove on the mast where the forward end of each of the six battens pushed on to it. These problems were destined to stay with us for a long time.

Finally prepared, we sailed down to Plymouth at the end of June and entered Milbay dock for the pre-race week of scrutiny and social functions. It was a good week for us as *Colt Cars* was ready to race and we could relax as much as possible and take a look around at the rest of the competition. The complete entry list is shown in Table 5.

## TABLE 5
# *THE BINATONE ROUND BRITAIN AND IRELAND RACE 1982*
### List of entries by sail number

| Sail No | Skipper | Crew | Boat | LOA | Type | Nation | Class |
|---------|---------|------|------|-----|------|--------|-------|
| 00 | Bertrand Harin | Herve Harin | *Arraok* | 36 | T | Fr | IV |
| 001 | G. Tatton-Brown | John Everton | *Whisperer* | 30 | M | Br | VI |
| 1 | Robert James | Naomi James | *Colt Cars GB* | 60 | T | Br | II |
| 2 | Fred Dovaston | John Weatherup | *Kurrewa* | 34¾ | M | Br | V |
| 3 | Stephanie Merry | Kate Clegg | *Christian Saul II* | 34 | T | Br | IV |
| 4 | Bob Menzies | Henry Pottle | *Dancing Dolphin* | 37 | M | Br | IV |
| KAT4 | Ian Johnston | Cathy Hawkins | *Twiggy* | 31 | T | Aus | V |
| 5 | Cees Visser | Chris Court | *Triple Trappel* | 31½ | T | NL | V |
| 6 | Robert Denney | Tony Smith | *Jan II* | 35 | C | NZ | V |
| 7 | Mark Gatehouse | Peter Rowsell | *Exmouth Challenge* | 53 | T | Br | II |
| SA8 | Bertie Reed | John Martin | *Voortrekker II* | 60 | M | SA | II |
| 9 | Guy Howard Williams | Edward Mackeson | *Foxtrot Kilo* | 44 | M | Br | III |
| 10 D2 | Bent Lyman | Ulla-Britt Lyngkjaer | *Ghoster* | 57 | M | Den | II |
| 11 | Luke Fitzherbert | Jeremy Fordham | *Falmouth Bay II* | 29 | M | Br | VI |
| 12 | Bernard Letellier | J.-P. Strowski de Linka | *Heliode* | 42 | T | Fr | III |
| 13 | Simon Beeson | John Gill-Murray | *Passing Wind* | 40 | C | Br | IV |
| 14 | Patrick Tiercelin | Francois Tiercelin | *Trimama* | 40 | T | Fr | IV |
| 15 | Andrew Bray | Hugh Cartwright | *Footloose* | 28½ | M | Br | VI |
| 17 | Marc Pajot | Patrick Toyon | *Elf Aquitaine* | 59 | C | Fr | II |
| 18 | Jeffrey Houlgrave | Nicholas Mott | *United Friendly II* | 44 | M | Br | III |
| 20 | Nicholas Grey | Julian Mustoe | *Applejack* | 30 | T | Br | VI |
| H23 | John Simonis | Alexander Simonis | *Boomerang* | 44½ | C | NL | III |
| 29 | Martin Sadler | Peter Foot | *Sadler Two-Niner* | 28½ | M | Br | VI |
| 30 | Andre Wilmet | Lauren Becquevort | | 45 | T | Bel | III |
| 33 | John Oakeley | Robert Oakeley | *Freedom Flight* | 33 | M | Br | V |
| 34 | Mary Falk | Fiona Wylie | *Wild Rival* | 34 | M | Br | V |
| 35 | Walter Greene | Joan Greene | *A Cappella* | 35 | T | USA | V |
| 38 | Stewart Hatcher | Sarah Methew | *RTZ Computer Systems* | 37½ | M | Br | IV |
| 40 | Andre de Jong | Dick van Geldere | *La Peligrosa* | 31 | M | NL | V |
| 41 | Martin Walker | Frank Esson | *Moody Eagle* | 41 | M | Br | III |
| 42 | Donald Clark | Nick Starkey | *Abacus* | 41½ | M | Br | III |
| 45 | Chay Blyth | Peter Bateman | *Brittany Ferries GB* | 65 | T | Br | I |
| 47 | Roger Burt | Christopher Hughes | *Grey Wanderer* | 29½ | M | Br | VI |
| 48 | Max Ekholm | Johan von Willebrand | *Gefion* | 30 | M | Fin | VI |
| 48M | David Bains | Humphrey Tresswell | *Aqua Blue* | 40 | T | Br | IV |
| 55 | Bob Brooks | Bob Harris | *'apenny Dip* | 45 | M | USA | III |
| 56 | Christopher Shaw | C Cannon Brookes | *Micro Metalsmiths* | 56 | M | Br | II |
| M59 | Paul Jeffes | B. Collins | *S L Simpson-Lawrence* | 33½ | T | Br | V |
| 64 | Warren Luhrs | John Luhrs | *Tuesday's Child* | 54 | M | USA | II |
| 69 | Herman Struijk | Dick Struijk | *Sagitta* | 33½ | M | NL | V |
| 77M | Kitty Hampton | Geoff Hales | *Quest* | 54 | T | Br | II |
| 78 | George Jepps | Denis Marcharris | *Seamiste of Rhu* | 25¼ | M | Br | VI |
| 81 | Adrian Thompson | Max Noble | *Alice's Mirror* | 30 | M | Br | VI |
| 82 | Tony Bullimore | Nigel Irens | *IT '82* | 40 | T | BR | IV |
| 84 | Robert Nickerson | Jeffrey Taylor | *RJN Marine* | 39 | M | Br | IV |
| 87 | John Chaundy | Christian Delaisse | *Roo* | 32 | M | Br | V |
| 101 | Brian Law | Dick Gomes | *Downtown Flyer* | 38 | T | Br | IV |

| | | | | | | | |
|---|---|---|---|---|---|---|---|
| M111 | John Perry | Charles Prendergast | *Crusader Sea Wolf* | 50 | C | Br | II |
| 130 | Philip Walwyn | Francis Walwyn | *Skyjack* | 45 | C | St Kitts | III |
| 200 | Nigel Wollen | Mick Bettesworth | *Wish Hound* | 33 | M | Br | V |
| 138 | M. J. Whipp | P. T. Whipp | *Gordano Goose* | 40 | T | Br | IV |
| 310M | John Ward | Peter Coombes | *Cheers Dears* | 38 | T | Br | IV |
| 330M | Frank Wood | Michael Hampson | *Triple Jack* | 45 | T | Br | III |
| 350M | Robin Knox-Johnston | Billy King-Harman | *Sea Falcon* | 70 | C | Br | I |
| 371M | Terry Cooke | Andrew Hall | *Triple Fantasy* | 34 | T | Br | V |
| 372M | Mike Ellison | David Ellison | *Sabu* | 26½ | T | Br | VI |
| K495 | Rob Adamson | Sam Oliver | *Tigris* | 52 | M | Br | II |
| 679 | Walter Ehn | Kurt Meierhofer | *Scheat* | 31 | M | Swi | V |
| C0718 | Nigel Southward | R. H. Devitt | *Skat* | 32 | M | Br | V |
| 808 | Michael Cozens | George Whisstock | *Gemervescence* | 39½ | M | Br | IV |
| K808 | Leslie Williams | Bob Fisher | *Challenger* | 80½ | M | Br | I |
| 810 | Richard Moncad | David Craddock | *Mr Speedy* | 25½ | M | Br | VI |
| 888 | Donald Young | Shirley Weese | *Humdinger* | 35 | T | Br | V |
| 988 | Rodney Barton | Peter Johnson | *Blackjack* | 38 | M | Br | IV |
| 999 | Peter Phillips | Andrew Herbert | *Livery Dole III* | 60 | T | Br | II |
| 1143 | L. M. K. Ward | R. Wood | *Tradewind of Lyner* | 32 | M | Br | V |
| 1224Y | Mike Butterfield | Bill Howells | *Advocat* | 35 | C | Br | V |
| 1300 | John Oswald | Richard Oswald | *Pepsi* | 39½ | M | Br | IV |
| 1542 | S. Whiting | R. Davies | *Gibbs II* | 27¾ | M | Br | VI |
| G1554 | Wolfgang Quix | Lothar Kohler | *Jeantex II* | 54 | M | W Ger | II |
| 1966 | Bobby Lawes | John Reid | *Camelot of Wessex* | 36 | M | Br | IV |
| 2202 | Michael Hall | Michael Moulin | *P & O Cruising West* | 35¼ | M | Br | IV |
| K2300 | E. Southby-Tailyour | Roger Dillon | *Caressa* | 36½ | M | Br | IV |
| 2615Y | Jocelyn Waller | Brian Hall | *Plunder* | 31½ | M | Br | V |
| 3219 | Eve Bonham | Diana Thomas-Ellam | *Blue Nun* | 32 | M | Br | V |
| K3340 | Richard Linnell | Russell Calderwood | *Quelle Surprise* | 26 | M | Br | VI |
| 3447Y | Derick Nesbit | John Beharrel | *Clairella* | 31 | M | Br | V |
| K3747 | Geoffrey Cook | Peter Porter | *Anouki* | 35 | M | Br | V |
| 3885 | Eric Jaques | Nigel Williams | *Wilybird* | 36 | M | Br | IV |
| 3999 | John Dean | Richard Reddyhoff | *Poppy II* | 35 | M | Br | V |
| K4230 | Robin Sargent | Terence Jenkins | *Sea Nymph of Southwick* | 34 | M | Br | V |
| 4294 | Mark Heseltine | Mick Underdown | *Proven Sharpe II* | 33 | M | Br | V |
| K5000 | Edward Bourne | Richard Clifford | *Elia Rose* | 38 | M | Br | IV |
| 5038 | Robin Tatam | Ian Atkins | *Ancasta Marine* | 30 | M | Br | VI |
| K5232 | Ann Fraser | Jan Robson | *Gollywobbler* | 32 | M | Br | V |
| K5235 | John Dungey | John Mullins | *Ocean Beetle* | 28 | M | Br | VI |
| K5672 | David Searle | Roger Downham | *Ruined Bruin II* | 30 | M | Br | VI |
| 5691Y | Hardy Classen | John Clark | *Laurel* | 29¾ | M | Br | VI |
| 5856Y | Jane Ashe | David Ashe | *Stormy Rival* | 34 | M | Br | V |
| 5958Y | John Boyd | Geoffrey Dean | *Foreign Exchange* | 34 | M | Br | V |
| K6459 | Barry Sullivan | David James | *Maritime England '82* | 27 | M | Br | VI |
| 6994 | Hywel Price | Keith Fennell | *Taal* | 35 | M | Br | V |
| 6726Y | Mike Cox | John McKillop | *Delta Shrike* | 34½ | M | Br | V |
| 7076 | June Clarke | Vicki de Trafford | *Moondog* | 30 | M | Br | VI |
| K7266 | Alexander Allan | Katie Clemson (Allan) | *Uncle John's Band* | 25½ | M | Br | VI |
| 9100 | Niall Morrow | Roy Barber | *Morrow Yacht Charter* | 34 | M | Br | V |
| K9107 | Richard Tolkien | David Tolkien | *Douchka* | 34 | M | Br | V |
| K9115 | Greg Bertram | John Bruwer | *Quinta* | 34 | M | SA | V |
| K9539 | Jerry Freeman | Roger Utting | *Tortoise* | 28 | M | Br | VI |

CLASS I = Over 60ft (18.29m) to 85ft (25.91m)  CLASS IV = Over 35ft (10.67m) to 40ft (12.19m)
CLASS II = Over 45ft (13.72m) to 60ft (18.29m)  CLASS V = Over 30ft (9.14m) to 35ft (10.67m)
CLASS III = Over 40ft (12.19m) to 45ft (13.72m)  CLASS VI = Over 25ft (7.62m) to 30ft (9.14m)

The following are the most interesting entries in their classes:

## Class 1

*Brittany Ferries GB.* Chay's 65ft trimaran with a larger rig. At this stage no one knew if she would be faster in light airs or possibly slower in a breeze. She certainly looked powerful. Peter Bateman, the managing director of Hood Sails and ex dinghy world champion, was crewing for Chay. I was disturbed, not only by his obvious skill, but also by the fact that they would lack nothing in the sail department both in terms of quality, quantity and ultimately, the setting thereof. Most people rated her the favourite.

*Sea Falcon.* The same 70ft cat sailed by Robin Knox-Johnston and Billy King-Harman in the TwoSTAR. *Sea Falcon* had just competed in the La Rochelle to New Orleans race and, in order to get back in time for the Round Britain, Robin had stayed only 24 hours in the USA before setting out on the 5000 mile return journey. He arrived only 24 hours before the start (thereby incurring a severe time penalty) and he was subsequently ill-prepared for another marathon event. Given the instance of considerable periods of light airs, an expected feature of the race, she was not considered a great threat. Light airs were her weakest point.

*Stevens and Liffield Challenger.* When Les Williams and his crew Bob Fisher announced their intention to sail the 80ft maxi in the race, everyone thought they were crazy. No changes were made to the monohull to facilitate short-handed sailing so Les and Bob were short of 14 crew. To get around the course would be considered an achievement, to be the first monohull most unlikely, and to win – impossible!

## Class II

*Livery Dole.* We now felt we had her fairly well sized up after the Solent racing. The only unknown was whether she would out-perform us in a blow. Shuttleworth designs are good in a gale – the unknown was really our own potential in those conditions.

*Exmouth Challenge.* The previous few weeks, especially her fine performance in the Round the Isle of Wight race, had changed my view of Mark Gatehouse's entry. Her secret in a breeze was her broad beam, long floats and small rig. The rig did not need to be reefed till much later than ours and her pitching, with less mast aloft, was quite a lot less pronounced. Still, in medium to light airs she had to rely on a masthead genoa to her normally fractional rig. This genoa, loose-luffed, was sure to suffer from a sagging luff and hence lose efficiency. Nevertheless, she looked dangerous.

*Voortrekkar II.* A 60ft monohull sailed by Bertie Reed from South Africa. She had already managed second place in the South Atlantic race and was the favourite for the monohull honours. There was little to no chance of her beating the bigger multihulls.

## Class III

*Heliode.* A Newick Creative 42ft design, sailed by Bernard Letellier from France. On paper she looked the fastest in the class.

*Skyjack.* Philip and Francis Walwyn, who live in St Kitts, West Indies, had entered their Spronk-designed 45ft fast cruising catamaran. They had done the race before in a different boat and had competed in the 1981 TwoSTAR in *Skyjack*, so they knew what they were up to.

## Class IV

This class for 34ft to 40ft yachts looked to be the most competitive of the fleet.

*Gordano Goose.* Nigel Irens designed and sailed her in the 1981 TwoSTAR. A damaged rudder forced him to retire. The small 40 footer was now chartered to Michael Whipp (the same chap who would have bought my Val 31 trimaran but never took delivery – see Chapter 15).

*It '82.* This was Nigel's development of *Gordano Goose*. Like its predecessor she was built by her designer. The major difference between the two boats was in the apparent sizes; the new boat was a large 40 footer. She looked impressive and was rumoured to be as fast as the bigger multihulls. In my view, she was too small to win overall, but one had to watch her.

*Downtown Flyer.* A 40ft Newick design very well built by her crew, Brian Law and Dick Gomes. They won their class in the multihull regatta in La Trinité (apparently *It '82* had been measured by the French as being a fraction of a millimetre too big for the class). Both crew were experienced ocean racers.

## Class V

*Humdinger.* Designed and built by Walter Green, this 35ft trimaran had a good pedigree, being similar to the third- and fourth-placed boats in the 1980 OSTAR. It would be interesting to see if Donald Young could keep her ahead of his designer and builder.

*A Cappella.* Walter Green back again with his wife sailing the same trimaran which had done so well in the same race four years before. She later won the Route du Rhum sailed by Mike Birch. With their vast experience of the boat and race they had to be favourites for the class.

*Triple Fantasy.* An interesting 35ft Derek Kelsall design sailed by two unknowns to multihulls, Terry Cook and Andrew Hall. She was a small-hulled, home-built vessel with a generous rig.

*Twiggy.* A remarkable entry. We heard that Ian Johnston and Kathy Hawkins had sailed their 31ft Lock Crowther design from Australia to England to take part in the race. If ever there was a safe, ocean-going multihull with an experienced crew, this was it.

## Class VI

The only multihull of note in the smallest class was *Applejack*. This small trimaran was the old *Mark One Tool Hire* which Mark Gatehouse had sailed so brilliantly in the 1981 TwoSTAR. This time she was entered by Nicholas Grey.

The saddest omission from the fleet was Mark Pajot's catamaran *Elf Aquitaine*. This cat, which had been second to us in the TwoSTAR, had been re-rigged and lengthened for the recent La Rochelle to New Orleans race. *Elf* was originally launched with a masthead rig, changed to fractional and longer bows for '81, changed to masthead again and longer sterns for '82, and still found time to experiment with a wing mast! After the New Orleans race Mark decided to ship his boat back to be sure to arrive in time for the Round Britain. Pajot himself made the deadline but his trimaran didn't. It had been arranged for the cargo ship to call in at Brixham to drop the yacht over the side. This she was prepared to do but owing to a slip up in communications there was no one there to receive the boat so she left again and sailed on to Hamburg taking *Elf* with her. There was apparently nothing to be done to divert the ship so Pajot had to withdraw from the race.

The pity was that we wouldn't know how fast the improved *Elf* was. She had been placed second in the New Orleans race to another catamaran, *Charante Maritime*, which had been sailed on the more successful southerly route. On the other hand, his absence reduced the serious competition by one.

During the final week of preparation there was an enormous amount of pre-race psyching out. The press made a big thing about the rivalry between Blyth and James and we certainly didn't disappoint them in our pre-race interviews. A usual question was 'Who do you think will come second?', or 'Who is your major competitor?'. Not wishing to name the other Chay and I would usually reply, *'Exmouth Challenge'*. Mark himself stayed well away from this aspect of the event which he described as 'rather ridiculous'. However, having, in our case, a sponsor to provide with publicity, it was essential to go along with it. Towards that end I agreed to take a small 16mm film camera for the BBC and promised to take lots of film during the race.

On the Friday morning the Colt Car Company held a champagne breakfast for the press and some of the competitors. It was a most enjoyable do and with reluctance we left to attend the crew-briefing at 11 a.m. The briefing covered details of the start and course which were all admirably covered in the sailing instructions anyway. The course was the same as the race four years earlier. That is:

Leg 1. Plymouth to Crosshaven, Cork, leaving Eddystone and Scilly Islands to starboard. 230 miles.

Leg 2. Crosshaven to Castlebay, Barra, Outer Hebrides, leaving Ireland to starboard. 460 miles.

Leg 3. Castlebay to Lerwick, Shetlands, leaving St Kilda and Muckle Flugga to starboard. 420 miles.

Leg 4. Lerwick to Lowestoft. 470 miles.

Leg 5. Lowestoft to Plymouth. 305 miles.

In each port each yacht stops for exactly 48 hours before restarting.

The most important aspect of the briefing was the metereological report. The forecast was for a south-westerly, going north-westerly force 4 to 5. This would mean a dead beat for the whole leg to Crosshaven. Probably because of memories of the Fastnet storm there was some hedging in the long range forecasting, *maybe* force 8 later, *maybe* even later. . . . It wasn't going to take us long to get to Crosshaven so we ignored what was coming later and concentrated on the unwelcome idea of an uncomfortable beat.

Saturday 10 July. 7 a.m. Outside our hotel window a complete calm in Plymouth Sound beckoned us. Just the job, I thought, to make it easy to get the main hoisted and *Colt Cars* under way. Down at Milbay it was already busy as we all had to be out of the dock gates by 08.30. The entire James family came on board at the last minute for a quick look before we left the quay. Out in the Sound there was still no wind so we used our dinghy, with the help of Tim and Jeff, to continue out towards the breakwater while we wrestled with the main. The start was not till 11 a.m. so there was plenty of time to kill. A light breeze came up from the south-east so we dropped Tim and Jeff off and proceeded slowly out through the eastern entrance under main alone. We made for the line to get a transit off the shore

*The apprehensive crew prior to the start of the 1982 Binatone Round Britain and Ireland Race on* Colt Cars.

Colt Cars GB *leaving Millbank Dock.*

and a feeling for the sailing time from the breakwater. We were both nervous, drinking cups of tea and watching competitors reaching up and down around us. A weather forecast heard later on VHF giving gale force 9 in Fastnet did not exactly make us feel better! Half an hour before the start the wind was up to 15 knots and I was sure it would rise further so I put in the first reef – the first mistake of the race. The starting line was between two vessels anchored in Plymouth Bay, and was divided by a large orange mark. Multihulls had to start to port of the mark. This suited me very well as the south-easterly wind favoured our end, and as it was not possible to clear the line on a starboard tack, it would be the perfect place for a port tack start.

With five minutes to the gun we sailed back from the line on a starboard tack. The other large multis were all approaching us on port, heading for the line. Beating the gun in this case would be disastrous as the penalty was $\frac{1}{2}$ hour for every second over, so the main thing was to keep ahead of everyone else, but behind the line. I tacked in front of *Brittany Ferries* with the others still behind her and with 30 seconds to go shouted to Naomi to take the helm while I wound madly on the genoa sheet. There were two small trimarans just ahead of us sitting practically on the line but we accelerated underneath them as the gun went. A glance back at the others and we saw we were clear in the lead. The course was a close fetch to the Eddystone so we concentrated on steering and trimming sails till I felt we were moving well. Another cautious look astern to see *Exmouth Challenge,* to my relief, dropping back. *Livery Dole* was behind *Brittany Ferries* and Chay didn't appear to be gaining on us. Michael Orr was buzzing overhead in his helicopter giving us the thumbs

*The start of the Binatone, Round Britain Race.* Brittany Ferries *(behind our jib),* Livery Dole *(directly astern) and* Exmouth Challenge *(the float to the left of the picture) all well covered by* Colt Cars.

up and we waved to the TV crews and photographers.

After about 20 minutes we were a quarter of a mile ahead of *Brittany Ferries* but the wind I had expected to rise was, in fact, falling. Everyone else who'd had a reef in had shaken it out so we hurriedly followed suit while our lead diminished. We soon picked up again with full sail and finally I was happy that we had the speed edge in these light conditions. Obviously 2000 miles was a long way to go but I still felt intense relief that there would be some conditions in which we were fastest – in short, we definitely had a chance of winning.

We had a two-minute lead as we shaved the rocks at the Eddystone and bore away towards Land's End. The wind went slowly round to the south so no spinnakers were needed. We continued to sail nearly close-hauled at 12 to 16 knots with *Brittany Ferries* and *Livery Dole* in sight, dead on our stern, but slowly falling back. The visibility was fairly

*A worried look astern just after the 1982 Round Britain start – are we pulling ahead?*

poor, but navigation was made relatively easy by the fact that I'd decided to stay directly ahead of the competition astern. Only when we lost sight of the two in the squall cloud did I nip below to do a quick check on the RDF and set a course to clear the Lizard.

Fortunately the water was flat despite a moderate breeze so there was no spray on deck, no sail changing to do, just continual trimming and steering. All this made lift fairly easy but even so I couldn't bring myself to stay below for more than a few minutes before gazing astern again. Are we pulling ahead? Are they gaining? we repeatedly asked ourselves.

By the Lizard, 70 miles from the start, we were, by my estimation, ten minutes in the lead. We could see both *Brittany Ferries* and *Livery Dole* close together but their hulls were indistinct and we couldn't tell which was which. Naomi and I were steering one hour on, one hour off, and, as is the way when there are competitors in sight, never relaxing during the off-watch hour.

Towards evening we sighted the Scillies to starboard just off our lee bow. As the apparent wind direction was 60 degrees off the port bow and the strength down to 10 to 12 knots I thought about trying a spinnaker. We prepared the smaller of the two, connected

*Despite a reef we gained an early lead.*

the guys, sheets and halyard and hoisted it to leeward of the genoa. Naomi lifted the squeezer bell and tube to the top of the sail while I juggled the guy and sheet while the autopilot steered. Once the spinnaker was set, we then quickly furled the jib and settled down to trim for a very close reach. Throughout the operation (which is described in detail in Chapter 12) it had been necessary to make only small adjustments on the hand control of the autopilot to keep the boat under perfect control. As usual, as soon as one of us was free from sail handling, we took over the steering again and limited the autopilot's use to when we were both occupied or too tired to steer a good course.

Despite being able to bear away slightly and still clear the rocks off the Scillies the apparent wind was light, between 57 and 65 degrees. To keep the spinnaker set careful trimming was required so Naomi stood on the windward forward crossbeam calling the curl of the luff while I steered. We kept this up for over an hour by which time we were 200 yards to windward of Bishop Rock. At that moment the spinnaker decided to collapse. I was determined to hold on to it as we'd need it as soon as we bore away around the rocks. I immediately ran off directly towards the shore for a few seconds till the sail set and then rapidly rounded up again. We were now 100 yards from jagged grey fingers pointing out of the sea but we slid by and a few minutes later were past the lighthouse and on the new course for Ireland. It was the first of several corners we shaved uncomfortably close in order to make the shortest distance round the course.

Hoisting the spinnaker when we did definitely seemed to have paid off; by Bishop Rock we were probably 20 minutes or more ahead of the next trimaran which we could see reaching with a genoa. The wind was still south-easterly, giving a dead run of 120 miles to Cork. As the wind was forecasted to go north-easterly force 5 (the northerly force 9 once forecast was now forgotten), we should obviously have favoured the starboard gybe. However, as the sails behind us appeared to be staying on port gybe, heading 30 degrees to the west of dead downwind, we did the same. Within an hour it was dark and as soon as we lost sight of the others – and they of us – we did a safe gybe through 60 degrees to follow our planned route. They, we heard later, gybed at precisely the same time.

The wind continued fairly light, 6 to 7 knots apparent, and we averaged 10 to 11 knots for a number of hours. As there was little to do but steer, whoever was off-watch tried to sleep. Several times during the night I attempted to pick up the RDF beacons at Kinsale and Ballycotton but the signals were too weak for accuracy. The race ruled out satellite navigation and Decca, so RDF was very important.

As predicted the wind slowly backed so that by daylight we had the apparent wind on our starboard beam. After what seemed like hours of peering through the murky visibility

*Our main competitors in the Round Britain Race.* **Brittany Ferries GB** (*Blyth and Batemen*). *A 65ft Shuttleworth design, rerigged with more sail but still old fashioned cutter rig.*

Exmouth Challenge (*Gatehouse and Rowsell*).

searching for the Kinsale gas rigs we sighted one right ahead about two miles away. I had hoped to be well to windward of the field but this hope had been based on optimism, not navigation. We were 28 miles from Cork harbour with the wind rising and heading us rapidly. We unfurled the genoa, doused the spinnaker and headed up slightly to compensate for any compass error or leeway. The last thing I wanted was to end up to leeward of the entrance and have to beat up to it.

Our speed was pretty good but we were being slowed by a steep sea building up. As we hit one wave, there was a loud snap and the shackle at the clew of the mainsail parted. Fortunately the wind was just over 20 knots so we put in a reef and left it at that. Ninety minutes after passing the gas field we sighted land ahead. It was extremely difficult to identify – despite the fact that we had lived in Cork on and off for three years – and as we were exactly between the two RDF beacons they couldn't tell us if we were to right or left of the harbour entrance. Naomi argued that as she didn't recognize the lump ahead it couldn't be on the west side which she knew well, but I still kept up on course to be quite sure of staying upwind. By the time I was quite sure in my mind where we were I had to bear away 40 degrees towards the harbour mouth five miles away. Our speed shot up and

Livery Dole III *(Phillips and Herbert). A 60ft development of* Brittany Ferries GB.

we were doing 18 to 20 knots for the last 20 minutes but if we'd headed off sooner we could have gained considerably more – so much for local knowledge.

As we approached Roaches Point lighthouse, one end of the finishing line, I could see a sail ahead. I was sure it was another multihull and became convinced it was either Chay or Peter Phillips. Naomi chastised me for being stupid. She was equally convinced it was a tiny monohull creeping along the coast – and she was right. Even so, we were both afraid of seeing another multihull moored up somewhere past the finish.

We crossed the line at 09.04, having completed the leg in 22 hours and four minutes, an average speed of over 10 knots. A dinghy in the vicinity sailed up and offered to organize a tow in while we began the arduous task of lowering the mainsail – and made a dreadful hash of it. Half of it was pulled out of Naomi's hands by the strong wind and streamed out by the lee float and the other half remained obstinately up the mast. While we drifted, Naomi hauled me up to the second spreaders from where I could reach the head of the mainsail. I could only persuade it to move by means of violent hammering which didn't do the headboard much good. By this time we had nearly drifted on the rocks so we unfurled some jib and sailed on up the river. Soon we spotted a motor boat coming out to meet us with friends on board from Currabinny, our village across the water, and Jeff who'd flown over the night before. As soon as they were within range we could see by

*IT'82 (Irens and Bullimore). Small at 40 feet, but this Irens' design could be fast.*

their large grins and single fingers raised in salute that we were first in. We picked up a neighbour's mooring just off the Currabinny pier and rushed to get tidied up and ashore. As we stepped onto the pier we saw *Brittany Ferries* coming in the entrance accompanied by a rain squall which put paid to our plans of leisurely mowing the lawn as Chay and Peter went past, thus giving the impression we'd been there for hours. We were, in fact, 48 minutes ahead (some journalist reported it as 'only 48 minutes ahead' but I thought it was a reasonable lead in 22 hours sailing, almost 5 per cent speed difference); as we had been doing 15 or so knots at the finish, that 48 minutes was represented by 12 miles – good enough for us.

We were, though, realistic enough to realize that the leg had been an easy one, and ideal conditions for us. Although our supporters were euphoric about our success so far I felt it necessary to say that I thought the lead would change several times during the next four legs; we could not hope to stay ahead all the way, but we had to count on doing well in the last stages if the weather was unkind to us in between.

The stop-over in Crosshaven was a very pleasant one for us as we could stay at our house and still keep *Colt Cars GB* in view on her mooring and watch the rest of the fleet rapidly fill up the estuary. One morning's work on the boat was enough to get her back into shape for the next leg. We replaced the mainsail clew shackle with a larger one which involved drilling and filing out the hole in the clew slider on the boom. We temporarily solved the track line-up problem on the mast (which prevented the headboard sliding past) by filing down the slides. For the rest of the time in port we relaxed, enjoyed the hospitality of our neighbours and friends, and the great atmosphere of the Royal Cork Yacht Club.

The order and times of arrival of all the yachts in Crosshaven are shown in Table 6. From this table several interesting points became apparent. First, it appeared that *Livery Dole* was not as fast and/or well sailed as the older Shuttleworth design, *Brittany Ferries*, but also B.F.'s increased rig had not made her quite as fast as Chay had hoped in light winds. Second, *Exmouth Challenge*, despite her unbeatable performance in the Round the Island race in a breeze, was not fast in light and medium conditions. (Later on in the race we would come to regret sincerely that assessment). Third, as expected, Robin Knox-Johnston's *Sea Falcon* was no threat, except perhaps in a gale. And last, again as expected, no monohulls looked likely to contest the lead.

We were up at the crack of dawn on the morning of the 13th to get ourselves organized for the 9 a.m. start. Several friends helped us out and assisted with the mainsail so we were ready much sooner than expected. To our consternation there was almost no wind which would effectively reduce our theoretical 12-mile lead to almost nothing.

This was the sort of race where the leader wishes for calm finishes and windy starts and those behind hope for the opposite. It took ages to do the last quarter of a mile to the line. There was no need to control our approach, we just arrived and went over a good few minutes late. On the line we hoisted the light spinnaker and with that the wind dropped to zero. Chay was just coming around the headland and his joy at seeing us becalmed could only have been matched in intensity by our own frustration. For 30 minutes we struggled to get the spinnaker to set, before giving up. At last a light breeze came up from the south-east and we were able to move slowly away from the harbour entrance. Forty-five minutes after our start we were only three miles from the line – a real dent in our lead.

The visibility was less than a mile so we could see nothing astern. The wind was now a light easterly so we set the all-round spinnaker and reached downwind, gybing regularly to stay on the best course towards the south-west corner of Ireland. The visibility was so bad that once we gybed less than half a mile from the rocky shore and even then could only just see it.

During the afternoon the wind died away to almost nothing so we decided to try the light spinnaker. The change went very smoothly. To minimize time without a sail we hoisted the new spinnaker in its squeezer while still flying the old one. Then I squeezed down the old, swapped sheets and unsqueezed the new. By evening the wind was non-existent and we drifted to within a few miles of the Fastnet Rock. We couldn't see it but could hear its fog signal which then mysteriously stopped. I called on VHF to find out why and Mizzen Head coastguard answered to confirm that the signal was 'stood-down', but gave no explanation. We reported who we were and assumed they would pass the message on.

Five hours later we were still drifting near the Rock, which was now sounding again, and we could clearly see its light flashing. We had experienced only one puff of wind in

**TABLE 6**
## *FLEET ORDER AT CROSSHAVEN*

| Yacht | Type | Class | | | Yacht | | Class | | |
|---|---|---|---|---|---|---|---|---|---|
| Colt Cars GB | T | 2 | 0904 | 11th | Pepsi | M | 4 | 2158 | |
| Brittany Ferries GB | T | 1 | 0952 | | Kurrewa | M | 5 | 2210 | |
| Livery Dole III | T | 2 | 1048 | | Gemervescence | M | 4 | 2218 | |
| Sea Falcon | C | 1 | 1050 | | Ghoster | M | 2 | 2236 | |
| Exmouth Challenge | T | 2 | 1138 | | Aqua Blue | T | 4 | 2247 | |
| IT'82 | T | 4 | 1236 | | Poppy II | M | 5 | 2249 | |
| Gordano Goose | T | 4 | 1256 | | Taal | M | 5 | 2313 | |
| Downtown Flyer | T | 4 | 1314 | | Moody Eagle | M | 3 | 0001 | 12th |
| Skyjack | C | 3 | 1318 | | Proven Shape II | M | 5 | 0025 | 12th |
| Triple Fantasy | T | 5 | 1318 | | Freedom Flight | M | 5 | 0041 | |
| Jan II | C | 5 | 1335 | | Blackjack | M | 4 | 0042 | |
| A Cappella | T | 5 | 1338 | | Kreepy Krauly | M | 5 | 0140 | |
| Arraok | T | 4 | 1401 | | Eila Rose | M | 4 | 0141 | |
| Triple Jack | T | 3 | 1410 | | Abacus | M | 3 | 0159 | |
| Twiggy | T | 5 | 1412 | | Alice's Mirror | M | 6 | 0203 | |
| Humdinger | T | 5 | 1424 | | Camelot of Wessex | M | 4 | 0235 | |
| Voortrekker II | M | 2 | 1626 | | Whisperer | M | 6 | 0326 | |
| Quest | T | 2 | 1631 | | Sea Nymph of Southwick | M | 5 | 0339 | |
| Crusader Sea Wolf | C | 2 | 1638 | | RTZ Computer Systems | M | 4 | 0453 | 12th |
| Trimama | T | 4 | 1648 | | Roo | M | 5 | 0456 | |
| Tuesday's Child | M | 2 | 1651 | | Sadler Two-Niner | M | 6 | 0459 | |
| Heliode | T | 3 | 1722 | | Tortoise | M | 6 | 0539 | |
| RJN Marine | M | 4 | 1821 | | Ruined Bruin II | M | 6 | 0543 | |
| Challenger | M | 1 | 1828 | | Ancasta Marine | M | 6 | 0605 | |
| S-L Simpson Lawrence | T | 5 | 1854 | | Blue Nun | M | 5 | 0621 | |
| Jeantex II | M | 2 | 1926 | | Footloose | M | 6 | 0625 | |
| Triple Trappel | T | 5 | 2000 | | Mr Speedy | M | 6 | 0638 | |
| Boomerang | C | 3 | 2010 | | Skat | M | 5 | 0702 | |
| Applejack | T | 6 | 2037 | | Maritime England | M | 6 | 0813 | |
| Micro Metalsmiths | M | 2 | 2143 | | Uncle John's Band | M | 6 | 0819 | |
| Ocean Beetle | M | 6 | 0925 | | Wild Rival | M | 5 | 1647 | |
| P & O Cruising West | M | 4 | 0928 | | Gollywobbler | M | 5 | 1918 | |
| Gefion | M | 6 | 0929 | | Delta Shrike | M | 5 | 1928 | |
| Falmouth Bay II | M | 6 | 1046 | | Foreign Exchange | M | 5 | 1930 | |
| Anouki | M | 5 | 1053 | | Gibbs II | M | 6 | 2039 | |
| Stormy Rival | M | 5 | 1109 | | La Peligrosa | M | 5 | 2121 | |
| Plunder | M | 5 | 1216 | | Grey Wanderer | M | 6 | 2245 | |
| Dancing Dolphin | M | 4 | 1310 | | Advocat | C | 5 | 1016 | 13th |
| Quelle Surprise | M | 6 | 1330 | | Seamist of Rhu | M | 6 | 2259 | |
| Moondog | M | 6 | 1410 | | Sabu | T | 6 | retired | |
| Scheat | M | 5 | 1449 | | Passing Wind | C | 4 | retired | |
| Wish Hound | M | 5 | 1500 | | Douchka | M | 5 | retired | |
| Laurel | M | 6 | 1610 | | | | | | |

that time accompanying a rain squall. We had just got the spinnaker up in time to catch the last of the puff and to get both it and ourselves soaking wet.

Eventually wind appeared from the north and strengthened very quickly to force 5. We reefed the main once, then again, and finally had to attend to the headsail. The choice was to stop and change to the Solent jib or just roll in a few feet of genoa. It was pitch dark and Naomi was already feeling the dreaded effects of seasickness so I chose the easier, but less efficient, option. By morning we had a force 6 on the nose and a very uncomfortable sea. We were heading south-west on an offshore tack at dawn and we could see a yacht on our port beam out to sea. Although we couldn't identify it, it was clearly sailing faster, if a little freer. We lost sight of it in a rain squall.

We steered an hour on and an hour off into a sea that made us pitch badly and slow down with every violent motion. *Colt Cars GB* lacked power in the partly furled jib and with Naomi obviously feeling terrible, her crew lacked the will power to do anything about it.

About mid-morning another trimaran, or the same one, approached us on a port tack and passed about a mile under our stern. It was *Brittany Ferries*. We tacked on to her weather beam in order to take the same route as Chay back inshore. The course was a dead beat with no tack favoured. Chay and Peter were sailing away from us but falling off to leeward. They were still in sight on our starboard bow when another sail crossed about four miles to windward of us. It was hard to identify but with straight leech mainsail and low genoa it had to be either *Exmouth Challenge*, or *Sea Falcon* with only a staysail forward of the mast. Most likely the former, I thought. Either way, she was obviously going very fast. We were most depressed. I kept as much genoa set as I could but I didn't feel we were 'in the groove' at all.

During the afternoon *Brittany Ferries* crossed very close ahead of us as she headed again out to sea. She had gained about a mile in four hours – not too disastrous. I elected to continue on inshore towards the Aran Islands, looking for flatter water. Although we didn't know it then, this move helped us along a lot. Just before dark we tacked under the lee of a headland and made a two-hour starboard hitch in order to clear the north-west corner of Ireland. Before the light failed we saw a trimaran about two miles ahead of us. Not believing that we could have caught *Exmouth Challenge* (which was in fact the case) I assumed it was *Sea Falcon*. At worst we realized we could have dropped to fifth place.

At dawn on the third day we'd cleared the corner and eased sheets slightly for the 180-mile reach to Barra. It was immediately apparent on bearing away, that we were in for some hair-raising sailing. *Colt Cars* charged at and through the waves at a ferocious pace, sending great sheets of water into the air when the waves hit the beams.

Naomi was feeling a lot more cheerful when she woke me at 8 a.m. Our speed was excellent – around 18 to 20 knots – and there was a sail in sight about two miles ahead which she was holding. The waves hitting the forward beam fairings were slowing us down a bit (see fig. 17a) but the only alternative was to reduce sail, thereby reducing heeling and giving more beam clearance. However, we found that full power, despite the slamming, gave us a better speed. Of course the strain on the beam fairings was great but I was not unduly worried about them as they were new, and strong fairings. Consequently I was surprised and dismayed to detect a break in the join between the beam and the fairing, which rapidly came unstuck altogether along its lower edge (see fig. 17b). Very soon, with the continual pounding, the fairing had bent to the shape shown in fig. 17c. The result was a severe jerk every time a wave came into contact with the deep, vertical face which now presented itself. The effect was alarming: our speed would go up to 18 knots between each wave but then there'd be a smash as the crossbeam took a wave full on and our speed would drop instantly to 12 knots. Standing below by the chart table unable to anticipate the impending jerk, I would be thrown violently against the bulkhead each time. I was most concerned about the rig. It didn't seem to be moving very much but how much more of that punishment could it take before it kept going at full speed and left the trimaran behind? There was only one sensible course of action and that was to reduce sail. Reluctantly I furled in a bit more jib. The yacht ahead of us started to pull away. The situation, with over 120 miles to Barra and with such bad progress already (so we

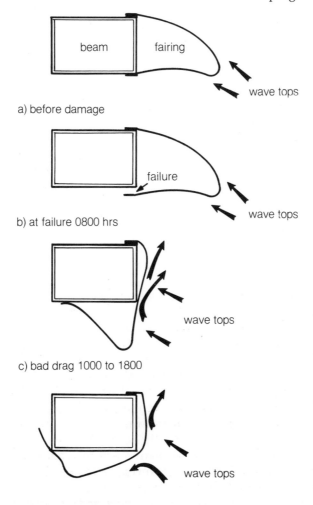

**Fig 17** *Beam. Fairing damage*

thought), was desperate. Thirty minutes later I decided to stop and attempt to cut the fairings away altogether. It would mean exposing the square beam but it could not be as bad as the fairings hanging down to within inches of the water.

Leaving the jib sheeted to starboard I downed the helm and put *Colt Cars* about. Hove-to on a port tack we were making 5 knots back towards Crosshaven while I attacked the fairings. My efforts were fruitless. The bottom flange had come unglued but the top one was still as solid as ever and refused to be pried loose. After 15 frustrating minutes I gave up and we got the boat back on course. Wild with anger Naomi suggested we cram on sail, ignore the jerking, and either dismast or, if we were lucky, lose only a few more hours and still be in the race. She was right, of course. So we hammered on.

The whole day was a most anxious one. Knowing that we were losing ground and risking the whole race was disheartening and discouraging. Naomi sat for long spells at the helm seemingly not caring about our wild motion while I brooded by the chart table waiting for the inevitable to happen. By the time we sighted Barra at 18.00 the fairing had started to crack up and fold round the beam. This was a help as it reduced somewhat the area of the 'brake'. The wind held all the way to Barra Head and there in the lee of the island, and in flat water, we heaved sighs of relief and shook out the last reef for the final ten miles to Castlebay.

We crossed the line at 21.00 exactly two and a half days since leaving Crosshaven. A launch was quickly out to meet us and very obligingly held us head to wind while I lowered the mainsail. Again I started to go aloft to encourage the mainsail headboard down but I'd scarcely left the deck when the main fell down with a rush. Delight turned to dismay when I saw that all three headboards slugs were in pieces and the luff tape had ripped off the sail for two feet down the luff. My annoyance was tinged with relief, though, when I realized that the luff, in the absence of headboard slugs, had been supporting all the leech tension, which it was obviously unable to do, and had only just started to go. It could easily have ripped all 78ft of luff tape off. It was repairable, although I only had one spare slug instead of the three required.

Once safely under tow we dared to ask what our position was. *Exmouth Challenge* had won, 30 minutes ahead of Chay and Chay was only 90 minutes ahead of us! We couldn't believe it. We had seen both *Exmouth Challenge* and *Brittany Ferries* twice; we had gained on them by going well inshore and they'd pulled ahead again after that. At the time we'd stopped to try and remove the fairing, *Brittany Ferries* was the sail we saw ahead, and Chay could see *Exmouth Challenge* ahead of him. The heavy beat had cost us the lead but we'd not lost as much time as I'd feared because of it. The finishing order of the leaders is shown in Table 7.

Once anchored in the bay we went ashore and had a drink with Chay, Peter, Mark Gatehouse and his crew Spud Rowsell before a late dinner. It was wonderful to relax totally and discuss the various aspects of the leg and the problems we'd all had. Mark had had to go over the side with a knife in his teeth to cut away a fishing net they'd become entangled with. Chay had blown out a spinnaker, but otherwise it had been a excellent leg for them. I began to wonder what we could do about the mainsail situation. The fairings, I thought, we could just cut off and leave on the beach; but the headboard was a different matter as it had to be rebuilt properly or it wouldn't stand the strains imposed on it. Regretting I had not fitted a headboard car did not help. We desperately needed more

**TABLE 7**
## EARLY ARRIVALS AT BARRA (CASTLEBAY)

| | | | |
|---|---|---|---|
| 1 | *Exmouth Challenge* | Gatehouse/Rowsell | 1906 15th |
| 2 | *Brittany Ferries GB* | Blyth/Bateman | 1930 15th |
| 3 | *Colt Cars GB* | James/James | 2100 15th |
| 4 | *Livery Dole III* | Phillips/Herbert | 0043 16th |
| 5 | *IT '82* | Irens/Bullimore | 0151 16th |
| 6 | *Sea Falcon* | Knox-Johnston/King-Harman | 0910 16th |
| 7 | *Downtown Flyer* | Law/Gomes | 0921 16th |
| 8 | *Gordano Goose* | Whipp/Whipp | 1114 16th |
| 9 | *Skyjack* | Walwyn/Walwyn | 1242 16th |
| 10 | *Voortrekker II* (monohull) | Reed/Martin | 1250 16th |
| 11 | *A Cappella* | Green/Green | 1340 16th |
| 12 | *Tripple Jack* | Wood/Hampson | 1415 16th |
| 13 | *Twiggy* | Johnston/Hawkins | 1541 16th |
| 14 | *Tripple Fantasy* | Cooke/Hall | 1614 16th |
| 15 | *Humdinger* | Young/Weese | 1617 16th |
| 16 | *Tuesday's Child* (monohull) | Luhrs/Luhrs | 1832 16th |
| 17 | *Quest* | Hampton/Hales | 1926 16th |

slugs to replace the broken ones, there was no other way. I phoned Michael Orr with the bad news and he suggested we get some sleep and call again at 8 in the morning if I needed his help. We then crashed out and a few minutes later, so it seemed, the alarm woke us again. Explaining our problem to Michael was easy: we needed at least ten new slugs, in case the same thing happened again; I knew Hood Sailmakers had them in stock; they had to be in Barra within 36 hours. Michael's reaction was forthright and immediate. 'Leave it to me. You'll have them.'

There was only one flight a day to the Island and the timetable depended on the tides as the plane had to land on the beach. The arrangement did not fill me with confidence, especially as my experience with 'jet cargo' and 'express mail' had been less than successful in the past. There was nothing more I could do but wait.

After breakfast Naomi and I went out to the boat to begin the work. Getting rid of the fairings turned out to be simpler than I'd thought, now that I had time to think about it calmly and a still platform to work on. Our cut-out kit consisted of a drill, a half-inch bit and a tungsten-tipped saw. The theory was that in the event of a capsize one member of the crew leaps below for safety and then cuts a hole in the bilge, now the roof, as an escape hatch. Using this saw it didn't take too long to slice through both forward fairings, whereupon a friendly local towed them ashore and left them on the beach – like a couple of stranded whales.

The next job was to repair one batten and replace another two with spares. We had four spares with us, all of assorted sizes, but it was necessary to repair any breaks in batten nos. 5 and 6 (the two longest at 20ft and 26ft respectively).

By mid-afternoon we had only the headboard and the luff-tape rip to work on. I was in the process of wondering how I could best botch the job if our spares didn't arrive when Naomi pointed to a helicopter approaching from the east. It came in low over the bay and we could clearly see several arms waving down to us. Hardly believing it we got a lift ashore and walked a few hundred yards to a school playing field where the chopper had landed. Sure enough it was Michael, accompanied by two friends, Paul Rudling from SP Composites, and our spares. Michael handed over the spares, laughed hugely at our amazement and said he couldn't imagine a better excuse to get out of the office for a few hours and take his friends for a jolly to the Hebrides.

As we wandered back to the boat Michael related the events since 8 that morning. He had taken a helicopter from his home in Devon to his office in Cirencester as usual; a second helicopter was despatched to Lymington to pick up the slugs from Hood's; the same helicopter went on to Cowes to pick up Paul (Michael thought he might have some intelligent comments on the fairings), and then went on to Cirencester. By this time Michael had done his day's work, rounded up a neighbour a· J a colleague to come along for the ride and the whole team set off by helicopter to Staverto· .. They there transferred to a fixed wing and flew to Inverness, and on to Barra by yet another helicopter. The whole operation had taken only eight hours to organize and execute.

Back on board, Paul (who knew something about sail repairs) gave us some good ideas on how to go about the luff repair and inspected the two aft fairings for signs of damage. We decided to leave well alone. Michael cleaned up the forward beams where I'd left a fairly jagged edge and one of his colleagues went ashore for a pot of paint and some beers. After a very enjoyable afternoon they climbed back into the chopper and headed home, leaving us open mouthed in the school yard. I was very grateful for Michael's extraordinary enthusiasm.

That evening we joined the others for dinner at the Isle of Barra Hotel and as usual chewed over performances in the race. Chay thought we were trying to sail too close to the wind in heavy airs and I had to concede that he may have been right. He had freed off slightly and Mark Gatehouse even more. Perhaps we (Naomi and I) were reacting too strongly against the old maxim that multihulls will only go really fast if you sail them free; it is imperative to sail as close as a monohull in light to medium winds and flattish seas, but perhaps we should relent a little in the heavy stuff . . . I wondered. We had been sailing at 9 to 10 knots and tacking through 85 degrees. Chay reckoned he was sailing at 11 to 12 knots and tacking through 100 degrees – an actual improvement in VMG to windward of nearly half a knot. Whether we could have matched his speed by sailing freer I couldn't say. At any rate, after this discussion I put on my thinking cap and decided to move the sails not in use back into the main accommodation. This should help to reduce our pitching moment, even though it made the saloon floor 18ins higher.

The next morning we devoted solely to sewing up the mainsail luff – a tedious job – and fixing the slugs to the headboard. It was impossible to push a needle through the mainsail head due to the dozens of layers of reinforcing cloth, therefore each hole had to be punched with a spike and hammer, which made for a long-winded and boring process.

Later in the afternoon we dozed in our bunks on board before starting preparations for the evening departure. The previous night it had blown very hard from the north-west – the last thing we wanted – and even in the afternoon it was still blowing hard enough for several yachts to drag their anchors. But by 19.00 there was an improvement in the weather and the wind dropped to a force 3 westerly.

We arranged our tow out good and early so that we could watch *Exmouth Challenge* and *Brittany Ferries* start. The wind direction meant there was a half-mile run from the line before clearing the island at the entrance of the bay and coming on to a close reach south, down to Barra Head. Neither of the two leaders set a spinnaker for the first half mile and each was encouraged, as a result, to reach close into the lee of the little island before clearing their course down to Barra Head. I decided to set a kite, go wide of the lee, and hopefully gain some ground.

After hoisting full mainsail we dropped the tow and for the next hour reached back and forth across the narrow bay entrance. Naomi made supper and we ate well before starting. At last the time came and although we were a little late for the line because of a lull, the spinnaker was drawing well and we slid past the island. All too soon it had come down and we hardened up on course. Because the squeezer – in its tube – was blowing aft to leeward of the jib, it was reluctant to come down. I pulled the tube forward round the headstay, and back to the base of the mast to windward of the genoa, but still it wouldn't budge.

'Knock on the autopilot and come up here', I shouted to Naomi. Within seconds she was up forward and after putting our combined weight on the halyard it reluctantly came down. It looked like a future source of trouble although I couldn't see anything wrong.

As we approached Barra Head we could see both the leading boats out to the west. They had rounded the Head and were visible through the gap between the islands. Not too far away, I thought. Coming out of the lee of Barra produced no more wind (it remained at 15 knots apparent) but a rather large, steep sea. I was keen to tack from our south-westerly course as soon as possible to get on to the favoured tack for St Kilda. It was getting dark when we tacked but I could clearly see that we would pass about half a mile to windward of the headland and be on our way. That was the theory anyway. By some cruel twist of fate no sooner were we directly to windward of the cliffs than the wind just died to nearly zero. The 12ft waves were still there plus their backwash off the rocks so we were being rocked about relentlessly. We could just about build up to 4 knots when the wind would be knocked out of the sails and *Colt Cars* would stop dead. The best I could do was to make a course parallel to the shore, only just managing steerage way. We tried tacking and simply stopped. With the seas and no wind it took at least 20 minutes to get under way again, and that was 2 knots back the way we had just come. The situation was desperate. We could not work away from the cliffs no matter how hard we tried. The tide was beginning to run east towards the islands which brought us closer and closer to the rocks. I was beside myself in fury and frustration and have never tried so desperately to make way in *any* direction, just to get away from the cliffs which were getting dangerously close.

It took two hours before the sound of the waves breaking against the rocks grew less loud and we finally escaped from that black hole. A good breeze sprang up from west-south-west which set us going in the right direction again, but we regretted bitterly the two hours we'd lost. After analysis, it was easy to see why we'd got into such trouble; the wind, blowing towards the cliff, had had to rise over it. We were so close to windward of the cliff when the general lull came (as Chay and Mark afterwards confirmed) that we completely missed what little breeze there was as it went over our mast top. A fine example of the effects of a wind shadow and why one should give headlands a wide berth.

We pressed on for the rest of the night, close reaching at about 16 knots under full sail. Sometimes we had to ease the mainsheet as the anemometer registered over 25 knots in the puffs. St Kilda appeared dead ahead shortly after daylight and we had to harden up to clear it. I was determined not to pass too close to windward of it. The wind was increasing quite rapidly so it was a relief to bear away around the most desolate-looking heap of rocks you could ever imagine. By 07.00 we were clear and on a very broad reach north.

After a hasty breakfast Naomi encouraged me, despite a large following sea and rising wind, to get the spinnaker up. Shamed into action I went forward somewhat cautiously. We were already surfing on nearly every wave so working on the narrow foredeck was not that easy. With the spinnaker in its squeezer tube, though, it was at least easy to control while the guys, sheets and halyard were organized. I hoisted it behind the genoa in the normal way. Naomi furled the jib and took some weight on the windward guy while the autopilot steered. As I pulled up the squeezer, Naomi sheeted in and the sail set with a bang; I tore back aft to grab the tiller. We were going great guns.

Our course lay dead downwind which in normal circumstances would have meant a series of reaches; but in this case we had power to spare. We surfed on every wave anyway so sailing 20 degrees off downwind appeared to be the safest course. That was as near dead downwind as we dared to go without risking broaching to leeward and yet it was sufficiently far off a reach for the trimaran not to be overpowered. Our speed varied between 12 knots and occasionally over 20 on the surfs; the apparent wind varied between 12 knots down to virtually nothing as we out-surfed it. It was tricky steering to keep the spinnaker set. The true wind was at least force 6 but when everything was steady there was no problem. As we surfed, though, one of two things happened: either *Colt Cars* came up slightly on course, in which case the increase in boat speed drew the apparent wind ahead and the spinnaker flogged, or she would go down on course putting the wind dead astern, in which case the apparent wind would drop to zero, we would overtake the spinnaker and the main would try to back (we had it prevented so it couldn't go far). The secret was to try and keep on the knife edge between the two.

The BBC had given me a severe telling off in Crosshaven for not having taken enough film, so, reminding Naomi how pleased everyone would be with some nice heavy weather shots, I persuaded her to dig it out of its hole and do some filming. In the ever-increasing wind *Colt Cars* was hurtling along with spray flying in all directions. A great sight, Naomi assured me as she perched on the stern and filmed over my shoulder. Suddenly we picked up a bigger wave than usual and all thought of filming, along with the camera, was dropped. The wave had caught me steering up slightly on course. The surf started and to my annoyance I couldn't get the yacht to bear away. Naomi leapt into the cockpit and leant her weight on the tiller but it was too late. We had shot down the wave and as the apparent wind drew to the beam the lee float started to dig in. This would normally trip the boat back to leeward (see Chapter 6) but this time there were two other factors involved. The wave crest was throwing the stern around and our degree of heel had put the rig so far to leeward that its drive was outside the lee float and contributing to the broach. Within a few seconds we were beam on, stopped, with the spinnaker and full main driving the lee float completely under. Keeping the helm hard over with a foot I released the spinnaker sheet and shouted to Naomi to try and get the spinnaker down. She ran forward but with the sail flogging as it was (the sheet had not released completely so it wouldn't collapse entirely), she couldn't get the squeezer down.

'It's no good, we've got to bear away again', she yelled above the terrific noise of flogging sail.

I held the tiller up and the next wave knocked us off wind; we picked up speed and the spinnaker filled with a noise like a rifle shot as we bore away back on course. We were back under control. After a few minutes breather Naomi urged me to get rid of the spinnaker while we were all still in one piece. I gave her the helm and lowered the undamaged sail without any trouble.

With the full furler jib pulled out there was no appreciable difference in our speed. I went below to check the charts, estimate our position and decide what to do next. We had run north for three hours and it looked as though, if we gybed, we could lay a course to Muckle Flugga, 300 miles away. Having decided this we looked at each other and wondered how we were going to tackle the problem of gybing a fully battened main on a fractional rig, short-handed in near gale conditions. The biggest problem is that the mainsail has to be right in to the centre-line before the lee backstays can be wound up and the others let off, otherwise there's simply nothing holding the mast up. It is impossible to get the lee stays on sooner because the battens will all break if the stays are winched into them and, anyway, the boom is in the way.

While I steered and looked after the backstays, Naomi winched in the main. It took her about 20 minutes and we had barely reached the critical point with the lee stays still just slack and the sail threatening to gybe, when we lost control. Sailing dead down wind with no spinnaker to pull us along the mainsail took over. The effect was rather like a weathercock; we simply spun through 180 degrees and ended up amid flayling sheets and running rigging – facing upwind! It was at this point that we realized the incredible effect a fast multihull has on the apparent wind; with everything under control and the boat speed anything from 15 to 25 knots the apparent wind is a manageable 10 to 15 knots. Turn round though and you find yourself in 35 knots of wind, and with full sail!

We ignored the battens and got the backstay up tight – the other one was still tight. I had no idea which way the boat would go. *Colt Cars* was stationary directly head to wind with the sails and rig shaking violently.

'Back the jib to starboard – standby to let off the port runner!' I shouted as we started to move backwards. Before I had a chance to reverse the helm it was wrenched out of my grip as we surfed stern first down a wave. The tiller hit the stop with a tremendous crack but the effect was perfect; as we dropped back the bows swung off to port – we had tacked instead of gybed.

'Runner off – *Main out!*' I yelled at Naomi, and added: 'Get some jib in!' *Colt Cars* started to move forward on a starboard tack with main and jib sheets free. I was hesitant about bearing away with the wind steadily increasing as we picked up speed.

'Here goes – either she will or she won't – hold on!' Quite what I thought she might do if she didn't bear away (luff up again or turn over?) I left Naomi to worry about.

With all my weight on the tiller she ground around on one float, accelerating like a turbo-charged car with the other float whistling through the air. I'm sure the main hull came clear of the water at the worst angle of heel before we lurched back upright in the relative calm of dead downwind.

The next priority was to get a strong preventer on the boom to supplement the normal preventer which probably wouldn't take the strain of an accidental gybe. Having done that I took the windward boom preventer, clipped a snatch block on to its end and put the block around the windward genoa sheet, using it as a barberhauler to goose wing the genoa. Set up like that we could steer anything, from dead downwind to 30 degrees off, in comparative safety. There were still over 250 miles to go to our turning point north of the Shetlands so we had to settle down as best we could to a nerve-wracking stretch of sailing.

We could each steer for only about half an hour at a time. Although the trimaran steered well it sometimes needed all our weight on the tiller to prevent a gybe. We normally sat down to steer but the strain on our arms made it necessary to alter position. Naomi sometimes steered standing up with the tiller between her knees, gripping the front of it with both hands and sometimes going through contortions to stay on course. She was not enjoying the ride at all at that stage, but her blood was up and she maintained a pitch of fierce concentration for the whole 24-hour run.

At least once every 15 minutes a rogue wave would lift some part of the vessel and try to screw us off course and it was impossible not to waver slightly. Either the jib or, more worrying, the main would back but the preventers held and we managed to straighten up each time without mishap. I told Naomi the routine should the preventer break – it had nothing to do with sailing or rig security either – it was just duck!

The mainsail was looking sorry for itself with broken battens starting to come through the sail like bones of a broken limb. There was nothing we could do about it though.

I estimated that we were averaging 15 knots (it turned out to be just under 14) although it felt like a lot more with the surfing. The waves we liked were those we picked up at the bottom of their faces; we could ride them comfortably for long periods. The frightening ones where those that almost got past before *Colt Cars* would decide at the last second to go for it; we would start to career down the face of the wave in an alarming bow down attitude. It felt as though we must drive under and pitch-pole but somehow, although we occasionally lost the floats and once or twice the whole bow, she always kept going forward. On these wild surfs the crossbeams would sometimes catch a subsidiary wave top, slice it clean off and send it in a sheet of solid water into the cockpit. It was a wet ride.

Whoever wasn't steering tended, initially, to stay in the cockpit ready to help with the tiller when required. Much later, though, we would go below and lie fully dressed on the floor just inside the hatch, ready for instant action. I slept a bit – Naomi not at all. I also managed to cook a meal which we both ate, Naomi having got over her seasickness by this time.

Later that day we were beginning to have more control problems. The mainsail tended to turn the yacht upwind causing the genoa to back. While this was quite safe (the backed genoa would blow the bows off down wind again) it was annoying and not very good for the rig, especially as it was too easy to over compensate and then we would swing to leeward, which sometimes called for both of us pushing on the tiller to prevent a gybe. I decided it might help to put in a reef, something I imagined would be pretty difficult. In fact, getting the main down was much easier than I'd thought; with the halyard slack I waited for a good surf and yanked down some main as the apparent wind decreased. Of course the leech then goes slack, which allows the battens to bend around the lee rigging, but winching in on the leech line at the same time prevented that. With a reef in we were a lot better balanced and steering was somewhat easier.

I was able to get reasonable DF bearings as we careered northwards. There was a good beacon on Muckle Flugga which was just as well because the visibility was less than a mile and giving a wide berth to the corner would waste miles. By the time it got dark I had estimated we would reach the corner by 05.00 and, also, that we could afford to alter course 10 degrees towards the land. The advantage in this was that we could take the jib across to leeward and broad reach instead of run. This would make steering in the dark safer as it would remove the danger of a broach to leeward.

We reached for an hour like this. Naomi was steering and I was dozing on the cabin floor when I was abruptly woken by a horrified shout from on deck.

'Rob! The float's gone! Shall I luff up or bear away?'

Before she'd even finished speaking we had borne away and the danger had passed. Apparently a steep wave on the quarter had tried to twist the boat up and as Naomi fought the tiller over, we heeled on the face of the wave and the lee float dug in. Immediately the boat began to slow and pivot around the float and before Naomi could really make up her mind what to do the tiller was amidships and we'd run off to a dead run. The front of the float appeared again and Naomi pushed the tiller hard the other way to avoid gybing.

'So, what's the problem?' I asked. Naomi grimaced and sent me below again to finish my snooze.

Instead, I decided to check our position and found we were about 30 miles from the corner but our course really needed to be more downwind than our reach. Reluctantly we winched the genoa back over to windward and resumed dead running. There was just enough light to see the waves so steering wasn't too bad.

At daybreak – fortunately there were only a couple of hours of real darkness at 60 degrees north in summer – we found the visibility to be worse than ever. We were running slightly by the lee now in order to make the course. I was determined not to gybe, reach out and gybe back, unless absolutely necessary. The wind strength was still force 7, the waves very big but we had become somewhat inured to the conditions by then. Naomi particularly, I think, had lost much of her apprehension that we might pitch-pole or capsize; we'd got into difficulties and out of them again and it was now just a case of hammering on till we got away round the corner and into milder conditions.

Eventually we saw land to starboard about a mile away. It soon became recognizable as North Neaps Head. Squeezing the course round slightly more to port and by now sailing definitely by the lee we closed on Muckle Flugga which appeared ahead. We sailed within yards of the headland and offlying rocks before rounding up to a beam reach in the lee of the cliffs. The lee meant flat water but the wind was as strong as ever. The cliffs looked amazing in the hazy morning light with not another living soul around but for thousands of wheeling seabirds. We shot along at over 20 knots to the next headland, four miles away, where our course became due south for the 60 miles down the east coast of the Shetlands to the finish.

We came hard on the wind then, just laying the southerly course. We put in a second reef and rolled up some jib to cope with the nasty squalls coming off the land. Our speed was now not very good, mainly because of the mainsail which looked a very sorry sight – more like corrugated iron than an aerofoil shape.

Halfway down the coast the course turned west of south round the Outer Skerries Rocks so for this last part we had to beat into a desperately frustrating sea. With no power left in the mainsail it was necessary to keep up full jib and luff in the worst puffs. The waves were viciously steep and close together, and we hobby-horsed and pitched till I thought I'd go crazy.

We had no idea how the opposition were faring, of course, but we felt that our two hours lost at Barra Head added to what we were already behind, presented a gloomy enough picture. We were relieved, therefore, to hear Chay on the VHF giving the Lerwick coastguard his ETA at 08.30. I reckoned our ETA at 11.00 which would mean we lost only an hour on the leg, not two. There was no word from *Exmouth Challenge*.

As we sailed on, Naomi monitored Chay's conversations with the coastguard. He was asking if anyone knew where we were so we sent him a message saying, 'Well done. We are down but we're not out yet'. We could hear Chay laughing as it was relayed. *Brittany Ferries* was obviously experiencing slower conditions than they had expected, as their ETA slowly went back, till they eventually finished at 09.35. By then we had 15 miles of dead beating plus the short reach to the line. Progress was slow so I gave my ETA as 11.30.

The visibility was now excellent so we could see the point we had to round, off to starboard, as we battled on on a starboard tack, only making about 8–9 knots. Naomi finally persuaded me to tack but it was clear we were not going to make the headland; still we headed inshore and as the water grew flatter our speed improved and it even looked at one point as if we might be lifted round the point. Half a mile from it we were headed and had to put in a hitch. It was one of the worst tacks we ever did – in irons, unable to go one way or the other for a few minutes – we really seemed to be making a hash of things. After a few minutes we tacked back and were headed once more. Determined to make it though, we managed to squeeze up in the heavy squalls now reaching 35 to 40 knots, feathering like mad to avoid being overpowered. Finally the shore curved away north and we could ease away slightly and then come on to a broad reach for the last two miles.

We were three minutes away from our ETA at that point and I was about to ask Naomi to change it when the water started to churn as a vicious squall headed our way. There was no time to reduce sail  Naomi sat by both sheets while I tried to edge further and further off the wind.

'Ease the main!' The squall hit us and we accelerated like a rocket.

'Ease the jib!' I yelled, as the water level came up to the top of the float.

'*Ease the main!* Look at that water!' It was rushing past at an incredible speed; the boat felt as though she'd left the water except for little quivers and jumps as small waves collided with the beams. I glanced at the speedo, it was hard against the 30 knot stop. We crossed the line.

Immediately I bore right away into the lee of the town and we got the jib furled away. We were both somewhat shaken by the experience. Under main only we reached up to the dock entrance, whereupon a tug came out and took our bow line. He held us head to wind while we lowered the mainsail and then towed us alongside.

Our time for the leg had been fast, including a spell of 330 miles in 24 hours. Chay and Peter were one hour 55 minutes ahead. *Exmouth Challenge* came in over an hour behind us. At least we were back in second place. Table 8 shows the order of the early arrivals in Lerwick.

The hospitality in Lerwick was tremendous. We were taken away to eat at one house, our laundry was taken care of, bedding went somewhere else to be aired and we went to yet another house to sleep. Which we did – for a long time.

The first job to be attended to was the battens. All the old broken bits which had got lodged in the pockets had to be laboriously worked out by shuffling and tugging. Two

**TABLE 8**
*EARLY ARRIVALS AT LERWICK*

| | | | |
|---|---|---|---|
| 1 | *Brittany Ferries GB* | Blyth/Bateman | 0936 19th |
| 2 | *Colt Cars GB* | James/James | 1131 19th |
| 3 | *Exmouth Challenge* | Gatehouse/Rowsell | 1247 19th |
| 4 | *Livery Dole III* | Phillips/Herbert | 2056 19th |
| 5 | *IT '82* | Irens/Bullimore | 2257 19th |
| 6 | *Sea Falcon* | Knox-Johnston/King-Harman | 0227 20th |
| 7 | *Downtown Flyer* | Law/Gomes | 0414 20th |
| 8 | *Gordano Goose* | Whipp/Whipp | 0835 20th |
| 9 | *Skyjack* | Walwyn/Walwyn | 1135 20th |
| 10 | *A Cappella* | Green/Green | 1202 20th |
| 11 | *Tripple Fantasy* | Cooke/Hall | 1300 20th |
| 12 | *Voortrekker II* (monohull) | Reed/Martin | 1453 20th |
| 13 | *Humdinger* | Young/Weese | 1713 20th |
| 14 | *Tripple Jack* | Wood/Hampson | 1831 20th |
| 15 | *Quest* | Hampton/Hales | 0330 21st |
| 16 | *Tuesday's Child* (monohull) | Lurhs/Luhrs | 0334 21st |

people on the quay offered help and within seconds they were struggling with us – they turned out to be our hosts. The mainsail itself wasn't so difficult to mend using sticky cloth over the rips in the pockets and hand sewing on the pocket seams. The battens presented a greater problem. By utilizing our last spares and, whenever possible, moving part of a broken large batten into a smaller pocket, we made a complete set except for the two longest. These I finally manufactured in our host's workshop by splicing and gluing lots of short bits together. They looked a bit lumpy and not exactly straight but we were back in action.

The 48-hour stop-overs in this race do give competitors the chance to effect repairs, but this, in my view, makes the race harder, not easier. First, one pushes the boat much harder and take more risks with equipment, knowing it can be repaired in the next port and second, the difficulties involved in getting a large multihull in and out of harbour without an engine, short-handed, make for nerve-wracking experiences. What the ports boiled down to was some long hours of much needed sleep, a little too much socializing when the frantic repairs were finished and some harrowing hours short tacking or gybing in confined waters wishing to goodness you were 100 miles out in the ocean. These were my feelings but perhaps many of the other competitors preferred the interest of the ports to a simple ocean race.

The forecast at 06.30 on the morning of our departure gave a northerly 4–5, good conditions for us, but by the time we got down to the dock at 09.00 it was blowing 5–6 from the west, which must have pleased Chay a lot. I went out in a dinghy to watch *Brittany Ferries* start and they shot off to the south depressingly quickly.

Eventually we were towed out and held to windward while we had our usual battle with the main. We hadn't even got it completely up before I noticed two more broken battens. I was disgusted because they were two new short ones, made at a later date and supposedly better; they obviously couldn't even take the strain of the mainsail flapping as it was hoisted. I managed to get a message across to a launch to ask our builders for replacements, to be sent out to Lowestoft by the time we got there. We then did our best to ignore the hard chines in the mainsail.

We'd made a mistake going out too early and now had an hour to kill. The wind was blowing 25 knots true so we put in a reef and reached out over the line into the harbour and back about five times to while away the time. We had only the main up and several times found ourselves in irons, making it necessary to ease out some jib, back it, to blow the bows off and then get going again having refurled the jib in order to keep the speed down. At last we went for the line, let out full genoa and blasted away in the wake of Chay, who, we estimated, was now about 25 miles ahead.

As we sheeted in we picked up a good speed but as soon as we got away from Lerwick the wind fell away to under 20 knots. Thankfully I shook out the reef and settled down to a fast reach. By now I felt that we had the fastest boat in the fleet provided we could carry full sail – as soon as we had to reduce sail I wasn't so sure. Two hours later we sailed into a fog bank and the wind dropped to 5 knots. Having reached up a bit to clear the fog the wind surprised us by going dead astern and piping up to force 4 again. Up with the spinnaker and on with the long run south.

This leg turned out to be the most enjoyable. The sailing was perfect; we executed a series of long reaches at an average of 12 or 13 knots, with not a single worrying moment or problem. We had regular meals, a lot more sleep than before and were able to find time to film and do general maintenance.

The conditions remained the same that night and throughout the following day. The clouds broke occasionally and I took a few sun sights to check our position. I was keen to get plenty of accurate fixes as the approach to the Norfolk coast and the run down to Lowestoft were riddled with sandbanks. The safety aspect didn't concern me as much as a possible loss of time and distance if we had to make large course alterations to avoid unexpected banks.

During the second night we approached land, our navigation helped along by the dozens of brightly lit oil rigs dotted along the way. We gybed several times with the spinnaker up (the wind was well below the force 6 impossibility bracket) to keep on the best course through the rigs and sandbanks. I decided to approach the finishing line at the offshore end – a buoy just outside the sandbanks – rather than sailing down the inshore, deep-water channel to the inner end close to Lowestoft harbour entrance. It would create a problem after finishing as we would be the wrong side of the bank and faced with a five-mile beat to the nearest deep water crossing but it meant we could reach in fast to the line from our position to the north-north-east. The unacceptable alternative was to lower the spinnaker, close reach up until we were inside the sandbank and then dead run down the shore for a few miles. The speed difference between running and reaching in those lightish conditions could have made a not inconsiderable difference of ten minutes or possibly more.

At 20 miles from the line we turned on the VHF and overhead Chay calling the coastguard with his position. They were about six miles ahead of us. We listened with amusement to their conversation. The coastguard was trying to persuade Chay to take the safer inshore channel to the finish (he later tried to convince us as well). Chay was fishing around nervously for news of us. As they'd had spinnaker problems they fully expected to have been overtaken. We let them stew a bit longer and then came on the air with our position. Chay's voice was a great mixture of relief and disbelief when he realized we weren't ahead.

They crossed the line at 04.30, just before daylight. At that point we had picked up a squall – in answer to my desperate entreaties to the wind to be fair – and were reaching along at 15 knots. A very strong adverse tide was just starting to run and if the wind dropped we'd lose miles on him. We were also having great difficulty identifying the flashing red buoy at the end of the line. The buoy marked the limit of navigable water so it was pretty important to keep close to, otherwise we'd go aground. The shore lights, plus the approaching dawn made it very difficult to find but Naomi finally shouted that she'd spotted it. It looked in the right place so I headed for it. Concentrating on keeping the spinnaker set on a beam reach was taking up most of my attention but I suddenly noticed with a shock that the water around us was very brown – we were on the bank. I quickly bore away and at the same moment Naomi saw another red flashing buoy half a mile away on our port bow. I ran off towards it, sweating at the thought of going aground at 15 knots.

We finished at 04.49, 19 minutes behind Chay, thanks to that last lucky burst of speed. Crossing the line though, was not the end of our problems. We had very little room to get the sails down. The squall had stayed and the true wind was 20 knots, making quite a choppy sea with the wind against a fast tide. First I squeezed down the spinnaker; then leaving it hoisted we had to gybe the main quickly and point our bows away from the bank. Over the VHF we were told that a boat would come out and tow us through a channel over the bank to avoid having to go around. With relief we tackled the mainsail – with the usual dire results. This time it came halfway down and a puff caught the bow and put us beam on which pressed the top half of the sail tight against the rigging. Meanwhile the rest of it disappeared over the lee float with Naomi spread-eagled in in the centre of it trying to stop the middle part ballooning up. Cursing and vowing I would never have another luff grove system or full battens in a mainsail I helped Naomi out and bit by bit we got the luff back under control. Naomi sat on it while I stuffed the spinnaker down its hole, which reduced the windage forward, and finally managed to haul the mainsail the rest of the way down. By the time we'd got lashings around it we were exhausted. The tow was standing by so we passed a line, hoisted the centreboard as far up as it would go, and made our way into the harbour.

Naomi immediately crashed out for a couple of hours but I felt more like a shower and a cup of tea, both of which the yacht club provided even at that hour of the morning. At 8 a.m. I began the usual 'phone calls to Michael Orr, home, batten makers, etc.

For the rest of the day we took it easy. Michael and several others from Colt came down to organize a promotional function, with the boat as star guest, for the following day and that evening Michael hosted a dinner for us and the crews who had come in by then – actually there was only Mark and Spud from *Exmouth Challenge* (they'd come in four hours behind us and were well out of it by now, so we thought). Chay and Peter had another engagement but as all Mark's family were down we had quite a party. It was an occasion that typified the feelings between the crews. There was tremendous, even cut-throat, rivalry, and yet great friendship fostered by the fact that we were all up against the same problems.

Next morning, Saturday the 24th, we enlisted the help of Paul Yeadon, who'd done a lot of work and sailing on the trimaran already, to fix reinforcing patches on the luff of the main, badly chaffed. In the meantime, Rob Lipsett arrived from SP Composites with the new battens we'd hurriedly ordered. My brother and his wife and three daughters came to help with odd jobs on the boat so we were all happily kept busy on board, with a short break for the Colt promotion at lunch-time. After an early dinner friends and relatives departed and we climbed into our bunks with the alarm set for 3 a.m.

As soon as the alarm rang I leapt on deck to view the weather – flat calm! The tide would be against us for hours so it looked as though we had a problem, so did Chay, of course. The only person who could afford to laugh about it was Mark Gatehouse, who soon had ample reason for delight. We hoisted the mainsail alongside the quay in absolutely breathless air and got our tow out only 20 minutes before our start, by which time Chay should have been away. He'd dropped the tow at five minutes before his start and was drifting rapidly down past the harbour entrance. I asked our tow to hold us on a transit somewhere near the line and at five minutes to our off we dropped anchor. *Brittany Ferries* had also anchored but not till she'd drifted 200 yards downtide. We had regained the lead!

But any jubilance we felt was soon squashed by the growing certainty that the wind wasn't going to come up till the tide turned. The time passed. Every now and then I would imagine a puff and I would heave up on the anchor. Naomi, her eyes glued to a transit on shore, would tell me after a few minutes to drop it again. After four hours we'd just about made the line, having pulled up and dropped the anchor five times; but at last a tiny breeze set in from the east. We pulled up the anchor for the last time and crept up the shore. By the time *Exmouth Challenge* started we were two miles ahead of her with Chay a quarter of a mile behind us. The race had started all over again.

I always expected the last leg to be the most tricky and most telling, and I was proved right. Mentally and physically it was the hardest part of the race, not because of bad weather, but simply because of the flukey conditions and the close proximity of the other two front-runners. As far as we were concerned the race was between the three of us. The fleet had become very spread out (the finishing order of the first 8 boats into Lowestoft is shown in Table 9 – only eight had arrived by the time we left) and the closest boat to *Exmouth Challenge* was *It '82*, many hours back.

As we slowly reached down across the Thames Estuary, Chay stayed further to leeward close inshore. Mark was heading further out to sea and was definitely gaining on us; so we decided to stay out as well, assuming there must be more wind out there. *Exmouth Challenge* picked up on a puff and came right up behind us till the puff died out and she

## TABLE 9
### *LOWESTOFT ARRIVALS BEFORE OUR DEPARTURE*

| | | | |
|---|---|---|---|
| 1 | *Brittany Ferries GB* | Blyth/Bateman | 0433 23rd |
| 2 | *Colt Cars* | James/James | 0452 23rd |
| 3 | *Exmouth Challenge* | Gatehouse/Rowsell | 0901 23rd |
| 4 | *Livery Dole III* | Phillips/Herbert | 2341 23rd |
| 5 | *IT '82* | Irens/Bullimore | 0029 24th |
| 6 | *Sea Falcon* | Knox-Johnston/King-Harman | 0251 24th |
| 7 | *Downtown Flyer* | Law/Gomes | 0804 24th |
| 8 | *Gordano Goose* | Whipp/Whipp | 1013 24th |
| 9 | *A Cappella* | Green/Green | 0029 25th |

slowed down again. *Brittany Ferries*, meanwhile, disappeared in the haze; when we last glimpsed her she was just aft of our beam, moving well and apparently in more wind. We later discovered that Chay had found a steady breeze inshore and had reached away from us under spinnaker. Pretty soon we had our large spinnaker up but were having great difficulty keeping it set in almost zero air. Whenever we picked up a little puff we would pull out on *Exmouth Challenge* but, when there was no wind at all, she seemed to move better. This was most annoying as we had far more sail area than her and should have been better off. Our problem, we had to conclude, was the light spinnaker; it was just too big and too full. It wouldn't lift in the calm patches. A smaller, flatter spinnaker would have hung in a better shape when there was virtually no wind, ready to catch the slightest zepher; ours caught nothing but a load of abuse from me. Occasionally we came within shouting distance of *Exmouth Challenge* but such was our concentration that no one said very much. We could not shake her off.

All day and all that night we crept on. Outside the Goodwin Sands and into the Dover Straits we fought the variable wind every inch of the way. Off Dover we were beating and still *Exmouth Challenge*'s lights were within yards of us.

Suddenly a squall came off the shore, nearly 20 knots, and at last we blasted away. It stayed with us, and from Dungeness onwards we made a steady 16 knots. We lost *Exmouth Challenge* against a maze of shore lights and by daylight there was no sign of any other sails. We hoped we'd got the breeze before Mark and hence stolen a few miles on him. We had no idea where Chay could be. As the wind rose we were forced to put in a reef but we held full jib and pressed on. There was a lot of spray coming off the square face of the forward beam (we really missed the fairing in these conditions) but at least we felt we were driving as hard as possible.

Soon we had passed the Royal Sovereign and before long the Isle of Wight hove into view. We were looking ahead and behind us constantly for another sail but not, oddly enough, to windward. So it was well after daylight before we suddenly saw, with something of a shock, a yacht exactly north of us on our windward beam, about four miles away. For an hour we tried to identify her in the poor light – *Brittany Ferries* or *Exmouth Challenge*? Eventually, through the binoculars, I decided she had three beams and was therefore Chay. He seemed to have only a staysail, no jib and one reef in. The wind was becoming very puffy – one minute 26–28 knots then down to 20 so that we were alternatively under-canvased and over-pressed. But I started to feel that the wind might actually be dropping so we smartly got the reef out. In his upwind position Chay seemed to be getting the better of the puffs and was, if anything, drawing ahead. Soon after we'd got near enough to see each other clearly he'd rolled out his jib and soon he also took out the reef. We were both powering along between 15 and 20 knots but I felt there was no sense in staying where we were. Although it meant losing ground we had to get close enough to him to experience exactly the same wind pattern. We hardened up and I set the mainsail with more twist to reduce the power somewhat. The lee float was well pressed down at times but the effect of the main twisting off seemed good and our speed was excellent. I think I had always been setting the main with too little twist, being used to masthead rig. With a fractional rig the main needs more twist to allow for the varying angle of the apparent wind. The lower part of the sail is in effect headed by the jib whereas the upper part is not.

145

Suddenly we were 'in the groove' and really going. By the time we were in line with *Brittany Ferries*'s stern we were a mile behind. But now, each time a puff came through, I was able to work out to windward and gain some ground. Within an hour we were abeam of them and edging past. As we drew level the wind died. Peter and Chay prepared to change to their large Mylar genoa and I decided we'd go for a spinnaker. I quickly got it hoisted and pulled on the bell line – nothing. It was jammed. This was the first time it had failed us and it chose this particular time. *Brittany Ferries* was less than 100 yards to leeward and with a staysail only forward of the mast as they struggled to get the new headsail up. Still the squeezer jammed and I was forced to lower it – at least our jib was still set. At that moment, the wind, by now only 6 knots, swung from the beam to 40 degrees on the starboard bow: What luck! I stuffed the spinnaker down the hatch and sheeted in. Chay had his new sail setting by now but by the time we were on the proper course we were 50 yards right in front of him. We watched anxiously, afraid that their big genoa would give them the power to pull ahead but very slowly, we increased the lead. Although we were only at Anvil Point, over 100 miles to the finish, I was determined to cover his every move.

Initially, we could lay the course making 7 or 8 knots almost close-hauled. Carefully trimming the sails we pulled away to a quarter of a mile lead. I had to get a few minutes sleep so I left Naomi to it with the instructions to 'do whatever he did'. Within half an hour the wind had headed to a dead beat. The true wind was about 5 knots and we were sailing close-hauled in 9 or 10 knots apparent. Naomi went to pull on the control line to lower the

*The winning crew – tired but happy.*

centreboard to its fullest extent and ended up on her back in the cockpit; the downhaul line had broken at the end fitting – the one seven feet down in the centreboard box. This was a problem. The board immediately floated up and no amount of jumping on it could overcome its buoyancy. With the full board we knew we could pull away from *Brittany Ferries* – without it. . . . It was a case of wedging it down as far as we could force it, by luffing hard and standing on it. The result was a board 2ft short of maximum.

Despite the light westerly the forecast was for northerlies. I intended to cover Chay tack for tack to the finish but so as not to be caught out if the wind did go northerly, we tried to stay directly ahead of him on the inshore (north-westerly) tack and on his windward beam on the offshore tack. I hoped this way to stop him passing us by better tactics. In fact, even with our centreboard arrangement we were pointing slightly higher and sailing a fraction faster. Shortly after Portland Bill our lead was up to about three miles. Chay took a long tack inshore, we covered, he tacked out again and we covered, but this time he appeared to be gaining on us and climbing up on our stern. Slowly he came up and despite our pointing ability we were having trouble matching him. I had almost decided they must have managed some magic sail trim or found themselves miraculously 'in the groove' when I asked Naomi to check the centreboard. It was up. It had obviously popped up on the previous tack and for the last two hours we'd sailed with only half of it down. Quickly we pushed it down and put in a ten-minute port hitch to get back on *Brittany Ferries*'s weather, but our lead had dropped to three quarters of a mile.

Conditions remained the same and by late afternoon we were tacking in towards Start Point. During the day I'd made several calls to let everyone know where we were, where Chay was, and, hopefully, to find out where *Exmouth Challenge* was. No one had heard from her. Naomi called Michael Orr just before dark to revise our ETA to 2 a.m. Michael's wife Pat reported that he was already out looking for us and simultaneously we heard a helicopter approaching, then another, and another. Michael had mobilized all three Colt Aviation helicopters, one of which contained a BBC film crew hanging out of the windows, to find us before dark. They kept well out of Chay's and our way, we were glad to see. It was a great welcome.

Tactically, the race was approaching a critical stage. Still beating in the light variable wind, it was essential to stay on the same tack as *Brittany Ferries* to avoid the possibility of her picking up a different wind pattern. I also knew that Chay would not put his navigation lights on after dark so we would have to guess at their position. In fact, Chay played into our hands at this stage by making a long port tack into Start Bay out of the tide. So as soon as it was dark there was only one tack to be on – starboard back out to Start Point. As soon as we lost sight of them completely we tacked, so did Chay (they could still see us against the Western sky yet had no alternative but to tack).

The wind started to lift soon after we tacked and to our relief, increased. Soon we were reaching up past Start Point and as the wind seemed quite strong enough we went very close to it, our sails brilliantly lit up every few seconds by the flash of the light. From there we reached all the way past Bolt Head at 17 knots and by the time we hardened up for the last 12 miles the wind had freed further. We both experienced panic as pinpoint red and green nav lights appeared behind us and rapidly drew near, but it was a motor boat, we realized, as a powerful spot light lit us up like a Christmas tree. Whoever it was identified us and shouted across,

'Where's Chay?'

'No idea', we replied.

As we neared Plymouth breakwater the wind dropped. Small nav lights appeared from everywhere, making us very twitchy but one by one they turned into motor boats. It was a very dark night, made even darker whenever someone turned on a brilliant spot light, which blinded us momentarily and made navigation all the more difficult. The wind headed as we neared the western entrance to the Sound and it was obvious we were going to have to put in a few tacks. Naomi took the helm and the runners while I saw to the jib sheets. Fortunately we didn't miss a tack and slowly we edged our way past the harbour entrance and tried to identify the buoys. More flood light blinded us as the TV crews moved in. 'Well done', someone shouted.

The wind proceeded to die and we slowed to a crawl. 'Do you think we should ask them if we're first?' Naomi whispered. 'They might be congratulating us for coming second.' It was true, no one had said anything yet.

We were moving very slowly indeed.

'Don't bloody stop now', came Michael Orr's voice out of the darkness.

Concentrating hard to keep ghosting towards the line we heard the magic question. 'Where are Chay and Mark?' We looked back into the darkness. 'Probably just back there', Naomi ventured.

'When did you realize you were going to win?'

'Not until we pass that buoy ahead', I replied.

'Can we turn on the lights again?'

'Go for your life', I said, suddenly prepared to believe we had actually done it. 'We've won', said Naomi. 'How absolutely extraordinary'.

Seconds later we drifted sideways over the line, the gun went and pandemonium broke out all around.

Coming ashore at 02.30 in the morning to be met by an overjoyed owner, family and friends put the seal on a great event. Immediately the questions started.

'Would you have won in stronger winds?'

'Maybe, maybe not. But we did break the overall record for the race so it couldn't have been that light, could it?'

'Did you enjoy it, Naomi?'

'No. It was too hard, both physically and mentally. The way you have to drive these boats now is beyond my strength and skills. I'm going to retire now – while I'm ahead'.

'How did you manage, with a wife as crew?'

'Very well. Between us, we were short on physical strength but Naomi is a very good helm and very determined. I agree with her though. It's tough. She should give it up now if she wants to'.

'What's next?'

'A holiday – and a book to finish. Then the Route du Rhum single-handed race'.

'What do you think of your boat now?'

'Great. And we've nowhere near reached her full potential. For instance, we did the whole race with a heavy genoa, furling in heavy airs and using it in the lightest stuff as well. We never got round to changing to the heavy or light genoas – and we still won'.

Chay and Peter finished nearly an hour later. It would have been only 20 minutes but for the frustrating calms inside the breakwater. Only an hour after that, Mark and Spud brought in *Exmouth Challenge*. Nearly a whole day went by before the next boat finished.

Chay was asked, 'Was there any way you could have beaten Rob?'

'Yes', he replied with a wry grin. 'Hit him over the head with a mallet!'

The full results are shown in Table 10. Fig. 18 illustrates the route of the whole race and fig. 19 shows the key points of the last leg.

**TABLE 10**
### BINATONE ROUND BRITAIN RACE 1982
### FINAL RESULTS

| Item | Yacht | Plymouth H. M. Day | Class M multihull |
|---|---|---|---|
| 1 | Colt Cars GB | 02 03 27th July | 2M |
| 2 | Brittany Ferries GB | 02 46 27 | 1M |
| 3 | Exmouth Challenge | 03 42 27 | 2M |
| 4 | Livery Dole III | 22 15 27 | 2M |
| 5 | IT '82 | 01 26 28 | 1M |
| 6 | Downtown Flyer | 02 17 28 | 4M |
| 7 | Gordano Goose | 02 43 28 | 4M |
| 8 | A Cappella | 09 15 28 | 5M |
| 9 | Triple Fantasy | 18 21 28 | 5M |
| 10 | Skyjack | 18 27 28 | 3M |
| 11 | Sea Falcon | 20 08 28 | 1M |
| 12 | Voortrekker II | 03 10 29 | 2 |
| 13 | Humdinger | 08 37 29 | 5M |
| 14 | Triple Jack | 09 40 29 | 3M |
| 15 | Arroak | 13 40 30 | 4M |
| 16 | Crusader Sea Wolf | 14 01 30 | 2M |
| 17 | Tuesday's Child | 14 03 30 | 2 |
| 18 | RJN Marine | 14 13 30 | 4 |
| 19 | Quest | 14 23 30 | 2M |
| 20 | Challenger | 15 57 30 | 1 |
| 21 | Boomerang | 16 23 30 | 3M |
| 22 | Triple Trappel | 17 31 30 | 5M |
| 23 | S-L Simpson Lawrence | 19 54 30 | 5M |
| 24 | Jeantex II | 20 20 30 | 2 |
| 25 | Pepsi | 20 22 30 | 4 |
| 26 | Kurrewa | 04 00 31 | 5 |
| 27 | Micro Metalsmiths | 04 53 31 | 2 |
| 28 | Poppy II | 21 51 31 | 5 |
| 29 | Gemervescence | 15 20 1st Aug | 1 |
| 30 | Ghoster | 22 06 1 | 2 |
| 31 | Freedom Flight | 22 10 1 | 5 |
| 32 | Moody Eagle | 03 21 2 | 3 |
| 33 | Kreepy Krauly | 04 38 2 | 5 |
| 34 | Blackjack | 06 22 2 | 4 |
| 35 | Applejack | 12 24 2 | 6M |
| 36 | Alice's Mirror | 12 42 2 | 6 |
| 37 | Proven Shape II | 00 46 3 | 5 |
| 38 | Whisperer | 03 13 3 | 6 |

| Item | Yacht | Plymouth H. M. Day | Class M multihull |
|---|---|---|---|
| 39 | Ancasta Marine | 06 37 3 | 6 |
| 40 | Camelot of Wessex | 08 37 3 | 4 |
| 41 | Sadler Two-Niner | 09 51 3 | 6 |
| 42 | Eila Rose | 09 54 3 | 4 |
| 43 | Abacus | 11 09 3 | 3 |
| 44 | Taal | 15 11 3 | 5 |
| 45 | Sea Nymph of Southwick | 15 36 3 | 5 |
| 46 | Roo | 01 56 4 | 5 |
| 47 | Blue Nun | 05 07 4 | 5 |
| 48 | Scheat | 10 11 4 | 5 |
| 49 | Ruined Bruin 2 | 10 26 4 | 6 |
| 50 | Tortoise | 11 35 4 | 6 |
| 51 | Uncle John's Band | 12 06 4 | 6 |
| 52 | Footloose | 13 32 4 | 6 |
| 53 | Mr Speedy | 22 15 4 | 6 |
| 54 | Gefion | 23 24 4 | 6 |
| 55 | Skat | 00 14 5 | 5 |
| 56 | Quelle Surprise | 01 14 5 | 6 |
| 57 | Falmouth Bay II | 02 04 5 | 6 |
| 58 | RTZ Computer Systems | 03 14 5 | 4 |
| 59 | Stormy Rival | 03 25 5 | 5 |
| 60 | P & 0 Cruising West | 18 00 5 | 4 |
| 61 | Wish Hound | 01 15 6 | 5 |
| 62 | Wild Rival | 05 27 6 | 5 |
| 63 | Moondog | 16 34 6 | 6 |
| 64 | Plunder | 04 15 7 | 5 |
| 65 | Foreign Exchange | 18 51 7 | 5 |
| 66 | Dancing Dolphin | 16 47 8 | 4 |
| 67 | La Peligrosa | 00 27 9 | 5 |
| 68 | Gibbs 2 | 06 17 9 | 6 |
| 69 | Gollywobbler | 13 25 10 | 5 |

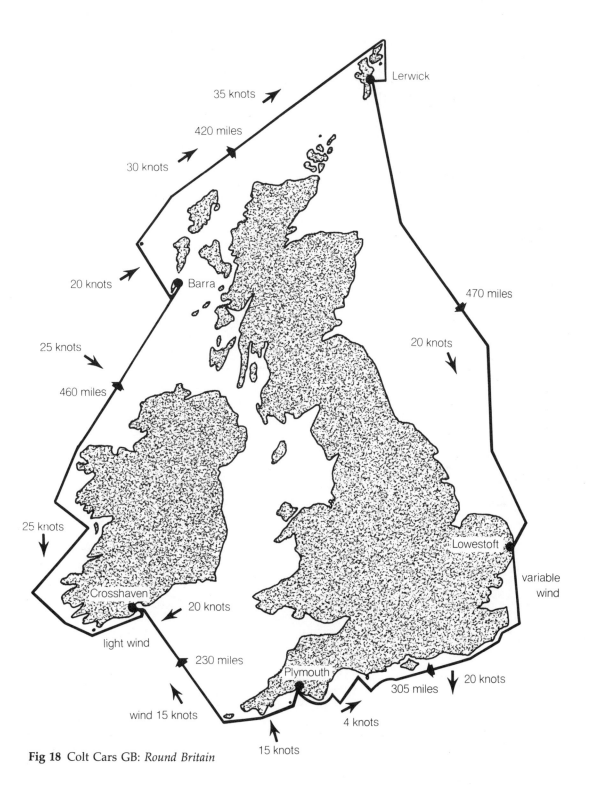

**Fig 18** Colt Cars GB: *Round Britain*

*151*

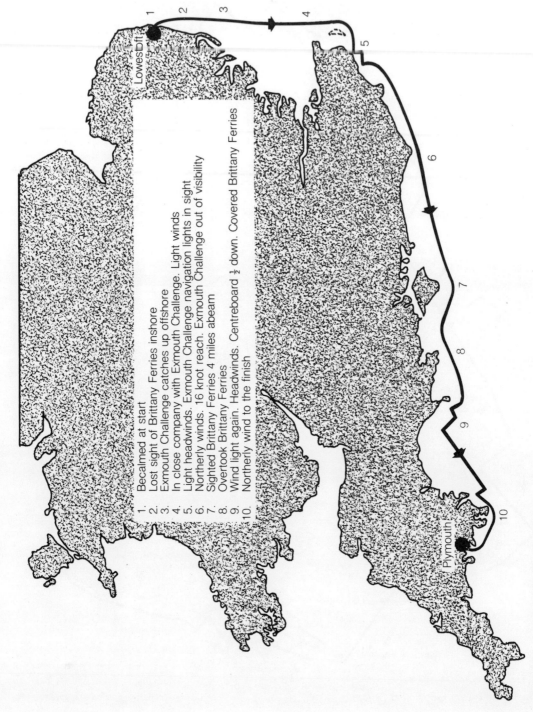

Lowestoft

Plymouth

1. Becalmed at start
2. Lost sight of Brittany Ferries inshore
3. Exmouth Challenge catches up offshore
4. In close company with Exmouth Challenge. Light winds
5. Light headwinds. Exmouth Challenge navigation lights in sight
6. Northerly winds. 16 knot reach. Exmouth Challenge out of visibility
7. Sighted Brittany Ferries 4 miles abeam
8. Overtook Brittany Ferries
9. Wind light again. Headwinds. Centreboard ½ down. Covered Brittany Ferries
10. Northerly wind to the finish

**Fig 19** *Last leg 1982 Round Britain*

# PART II

# 6

# *Trimaran Design*

In the early days of trimaran development there was an air of mystery surrounding the design and sailing of these strange vessels. This was because the first multihull sailors were experimenters and pioneers rather than yachtsmen; the yachtsmen tended to steer clear of the 'ugly and unseaman-like' craft then being built. The change in attitude came about largely as a result of the advent of prestigious, long-distance open races. Multihulls and multihull sailors began to develop from the 'fast reaching everywhere brigade' into a more all-round performance mode. By the beginning of the 1980s it had become apparent that all future mixed races would most probably be won by multihulls, provided that enough entered; even with a 50 per cent retirement rate there would still be the other 50 per cent to get through and at least one of those would beat the monohulls. Why is this so?

Although the answer to this question is the same for all multihulls I will concentrate on trimarans in this chapter and then make comparisons with cats and proas in the following two chapters.

## Speed

Racing trimarans are faster than racing monohulls of the same size for two reasons: they have a greater power-to-weight ratio and less wave-making resistance. To appreciate this it helps to compare the way in which trimarans and monohulls achieve sufficient stability to stand up to the driving force of their sails.

As a monohull heels under pressure from the wind a righting moment is produced between the centre of buoyancy acting upwards, the centre of gravity acting downwards and the lever arm between these two forces (see fig. 20). This moment can be increased for a given angle of heel in two ways. Adding weight to the keel has the effect of increasing the magnitude of the two forces (gravity *and* buoyancy) and, by lowering the centre of gravity, lengthening the lever arm. Alternatively, increasing the beam of the yacht will also lengthen the lever arm, as the centre of buoyancy will necessarily move further from the centre-line as the boat heels. Therefore, to achieve sufficient stability a monohull has either a heavy keel, a broad beam, or, most likely, a combination of the two. The heavy keel obviously reduces the power-to-hull-weight ratio of the yacht. This heavy weight

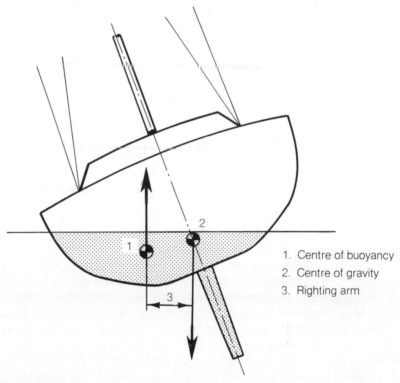

1. Centre of buoyancy
2. Centre of gravity
3. Righting arm

**Fig 20** *A monohull heels*

would not be too disastrous – effecting only acceleration not top speed – were it not for the obvious fact of the hull having to displace more in order to support the weight of the keel, which in turn means more wetted surface area and, even more damaging to speed, further hull width.

As the speed of the boat increases, so does the wave-making resistance of its wide hull, to the point where the displacement craft reaches a speed in knots equal to 1.4 (2.5) times the square root of its water-line length in feet (metres), and can accelerate no more. For instance, a 40ft vessel with a water-line of 32ft cannot sail faster than 8 knots. The wave-making resistance at this point is approaching infinity and no amount of extra power will overcome it. The only way for a broad-beamed boat to break the speed barrier is to lift clear of the water and plane like a dinghy or speedboat. Unfortunately, the yacht is held in the water by its keel weight and remains, with the exception of the smaller performance yachts, a displacement craft. With wave assistance a monohull may achieve considerably higher speeds by surfing but for a few seconds only.

A trimaran's stability is created in the same way, i.e. a righting moment between buoyancy and gravity, but the geometry is quite different. As the multihull heels increasingly more of the displacement is supported by the lee float and less by the main hull. In the situation shown in fig. 21 the float is providing half the buoyancy, thus the centre of buoyancy of the whole vessel has moved rapidly to leeward of the position

*A trimaran, a speed boat (hidden) and a displacement craft all travelling at 14 knots. Note the differences in wave making.*

shown. If the boat continued to be pressed over, a situation would be reached in which all the buoyancy was being provided by the lee float, as the main hull lifted clear of the water (see fig. 22). Because of the length of the beams connecting the hulls, this righting arm is automatically very long and hence there is not the need for a lot of heavy weight like a keel, to increase the moment. The individual hulls can be narrow as the shift of the centre of buoyancy comes from the beam of the whole vessel, not that of individual hulls, and there is no keel weight to carry. In turn, the narrow hulls (provided that their water-line beam is less than 10 per cent of their water-line length) are not subject to a speed limitation from wave making resistance.

The stability of a multihull can be increased by extra weight or extra overall beam. The way to gain potential speed, therefore, is to design a yacht as wide and as light as sufficient strength will allow, with a maximum of sail area. Fine, in theory, but a perilous route to follow as stability will become dangerously low if the sail area is too great for the

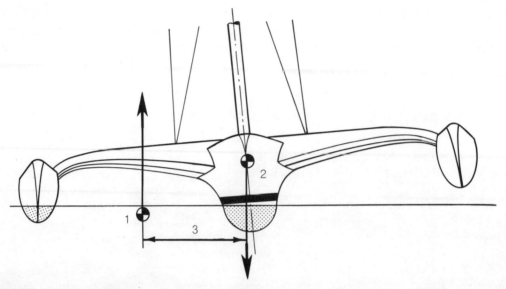

**Fig 21** *A trimaran heels*

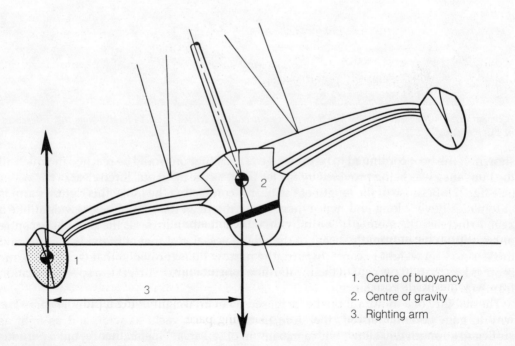

1. Centre of buoyancy
2. Centre of gravity
3. Righting arm

**Fig 22** *The main hull lifts*

size and weight of the yacht. The ultimate, yet reasonably safe, limit is reached by building with only just enough weight to get the required strength, having enough beam to provide stability (but not too much as otherwise the engineering of the crossbeams will add too much weight) and adding a manageable sail area – i.e. one equivalent to the area on a similar sized monohull.

## Length, beam, weight and sail area

*Length.* The potential top speed of a monohull, as has just been discussed, is dependent on its water-line length. To increase top speed from 8 knots to 16 knots, say, it would be necessary to increase the water-line from 32ft to a staggering 130ft. But with a trimaran there is no theoretical limit. So, why not design a small, and therefore cheap, multihull? Is there any advantage in size? The answer to the last question is, yes. In general, larger trimarans beat smaller ones in long, ocean races but not necessarily when racing inshore. The reason for this is the greater ability of the longer, larger multihull to power through waves which would slow down its smaller counterparts. This applies to waves of 1ft (35cm) which would affect a 30ft (9m) trimaran but not a 60ft (18m) one, up to waves of 30ft and above which would completely stop the smaller vessel. When a race is predominantly downwind the effect is not so marked; witness Mike Birch's victory in the 1978 Route du Rhum in the smallest (and best-sailed) trimaran in the fleet.

However, length does pay in multihulls, though not as markedly as in monohulls, with the gain probably tapering off around the 70–80ft (23m) mark as construction, not to mention handling, problems assert themselves.

*Beam* and *Weight.* It has been shown that stability depends on overall beam and total weight. By increasing the beam the weight may be reduced for a given stability. Conversely, if the weight is unchanged an increase in the beam will give greater stability, thus allowing more sail to be carried. Theoretically, for a given length the more the beam and sail area the greater the potential speed. The trend of the modern design is in that direction but there are, of course, practical problems. The greatest of these is the necessity of making the crossbeams strong enough: if they are too long the weight required in the engineering structure may counteract any increase in sail carrying ability. The problems of mooring and handling the craft also dictate practical limitations to overall beam. (For more on crossbeams see the appropriate section later within this chapter.)

Assuming, then, a given minimum stability for safety and sail carrying purposes, weight in a trimaran will serve no useful function at all. Obviously there is no point in making the vessel so light that it capsizes with full sail in 20 knots of breeze; also, there is no point in making it so light that it lacks sufficient strength to stand up to a gale on the nose. Within the limits dictated by common sense a designer should attempt, therefore, to combine strength and lightness in the ideal compromise. In the past there has been an element of the dictum 'If it breaks it was not strong enough, if it doesn't it was too heavy'. In a way this holds good – one must get as near to the limit as possible and yet take no risk of crossing it. Fortunately, not only are modern materials improving rapidly (see Chapter 9) but the knowledge of their use is also keeping pace.

The problems and dangers of a heavy multihull are well illustrated by the following hypothetical case. A 54ft trimaran is designed to weigh four tons. Her underwater shape is semicircular in cross-section and then parallel-sided for the few inches above the water-line. Her water-line length is 45ft and her maximum water-line beam is 3ft 6in. When launched she floats perfectly to her marks but later on in her career, owing to weakness and lack of stiffness, she is considerably strengthened. The result is, fully loaded for her last race, she weighs 5 tons. Let us examine the damage this has done:

1. Her power-to-weight ratio is down by a disastrous 20 per cent.

2. To displace the extra ton our trimaran will have sunk over 6ins. This not only increases wetted surface area, it also lowers the crossbeams nearer the water thus exposing them to the slowing-down effect of striking wave tops.

3. The trimaran was probably designed with both floats just touching the water when at rest. Now, instead of resting lightly on one float in light airs, our boat will have both floats planted firmly in the water.

4. It may appear that the extra weight at least contributes to safety, in this case it could be quite the opposite. If the tri had been designed with floats of 120 per cent buoyancy at four tons displacement, that float will now, with her extra weight, represent only 84 per cent buoyancy. The effect of this reduction could be capsize (see the section on floats for more detail on percentage buoyancy).

*Sail area.* The fourth and final part of the stability and potential speed equation is the sail area. More sail means greater speed and less stability for a given multihull. The designer has to consider a number of factors when deciding on the amount and distribution of this area. In terms of out-and-out speed the more the better, but there are several limitations. The first is safety, which is closely allied to the practicalities of sail changing; if the sail area is so large that the trimaran will start to capsize in 10 knots of breeze it would be necessary to reef and reduce jib size each time the wind rose to force 2! Aside from this crazy situation the disadvantages of all that sail changing would far outweigh the advantages in very light airs. Second, one would be carrying a large amount of mast way up in the air where it is detrimental to the pitching moment of the boat and when the sail was reefed (which would be nearly always) it would create severe drag through windage. The third practical limitation would be the difficulty in handling such an oversized rig: this, plus the cost factor, tend to keep the sail area to sensible proportions not unlike that of monohulls of a similar size.

Having decided, then, on a given maximum sail area the next question is how to distribute it – masthead, fractional, high aspect or low aspect. These matters are discussed in chapter 10.

# Hull shape

*Underwater shape.* The fast trimaran will have a main hull water-line with a length-to-beam ratio greater than 10:1, i.e. a long narrow shape with a shallow draft, to ensure little distortion in the water-line plane or along the keel line. The immersed canoe body can therefore be drawn with almost parallel sides. The major decision in this area is how fine to make the bow and stern. A fine bow will knife through the waves well and will help windward performance yet it may lack buoyancy, causing the bow to drive under on a dead run. It will therefore need a flared topside as a buoyancy reserve. As well as this a yacht with very fine ends tends to pitch excessively, although this can be alleviated by float positioning. A full bow, on the other hand, will be hard to drive through the water. Fig. 23 shows a typical water-line plane and keel profile.

The section of the hull at any point could be V- or U-shaped. Early Polynesian catamarans were built with V sections from bow to stern as having no centreboard, they relied on an immersed V to provide lateral resistance while sailing. Early modern multihulls tended to follow this pattern even after the addition of centreboards. It is now recognized that the V section is far from ideal for performance craft as its wetted surface is high for a given displacement (see fig. 24). So why not make all multihull underwater shapes semicircular? The advantage of a V shape is that it won't pound when slamming into the water, and also the low resistance and fine forward section it can provide. So it makes sense to have a V-shape forward turning into a semicircular section which is then held all the way to the stern.

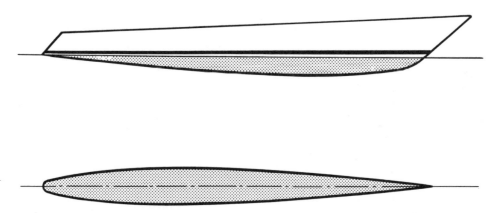

**Fig 23** *Typical main hull underwater shape*

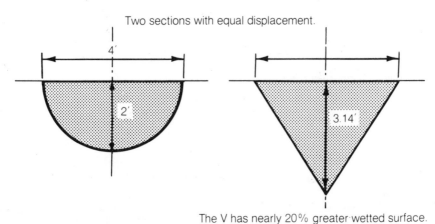

**Fig 24** *Circular against V'd sections*

*Above water shape.* The profile of the main hull above water will only effect the trimaran's speed through windage. The higher the free-board of the yacht the greater the windage – and also the weight of skin material. But if the free-board is too small not only will accommodation space be lost, but the crossbeams will also be lower and nearer the water. Different designers have compromised the two in different ways. In general English and American designers favour higher-sided trimarans than other European designers. A large trimaran from Dick Newick, Derek Kelsall, John Shuttleworth or Ron Holland will normally be high enough to have standing headroom below. Another option is to go for low freeboard and then place the crossbeams on top of the main hull. While this configuration is ugly and plays havoc with the deck layout, it is probably the best way of reducing weight and windage.

The profile of the bow and stern are only of interest in the way they effect water-line length as the vessel is loaded. If the water-line is drawn as in fig.25 (i.e. from the knuckle of the bow to the tip of the transom), then on overloading the boat will need to pick up depth (sink) to provide the extra displacement. To counteract this my recent co-design with Ron Holland, the 60ft *Colt Cars GB*, was drawn to pick up length and less depth when loaded. This means the design can have a wider range of total displacement without detracting from performance (see fig. 26).

The sections above water are controlled by two requirements: deck layout and accommodation. It is safe to assume that in all racing boats the former is far more important. For instance, with *Colt Cars GB* (deck layout in fig. 27) we decided on the optimum sheet-lead positions and this controlled the maximum deck beam. Drawing the cross section then became a simple exercise in joining the underwater shape to the deck-line, using a minimum of material. Each designer has his own way of flaring out from a narrow water-line to a minimum deck requirement. Four typical examples are shown in fig. 28. The accommodation then has to be squeezed into the resulting interior shape. An example is shown in fig. 29.

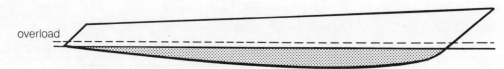

**Fig 25** *Detrimental overloaded waterline*

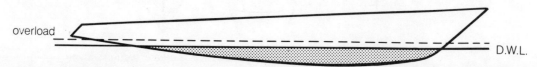

**Fig 26** *Acceptable overloaded waterline*

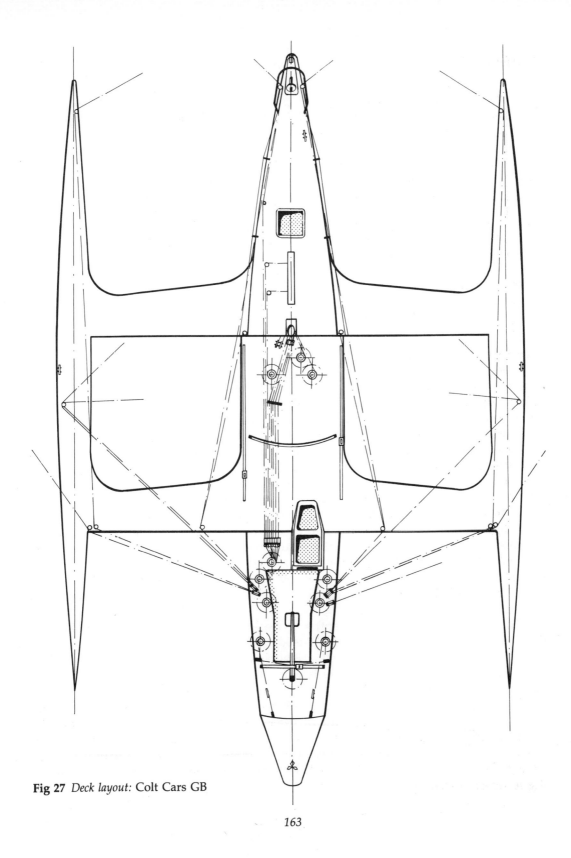

**Fig 27** *Deck layout:* Colt Cars GB

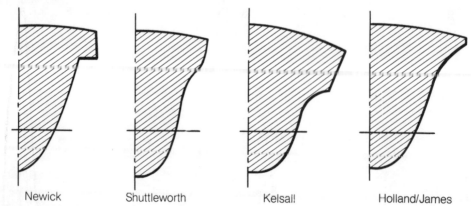

| Newick | Shuttleworth | Kelsall | Holland/James |

**Fig 28** *Flare treatment*

## Floats

The variables to be considered are the size, shape and position relative to the main hull.

*Float size.* If a single float, when fully immersed, displaces the same volume of water as the whole trimaran at rest (i.e. it equals the design displacement of the boat), it is said to be of 100 per cent buoyancy. If it displaces 10 per cent more than the whole, it has 110 per cent buoyancy and if 10 per cent less, then 90 per cent, and so on. The buoyancy percentage of the floats is probably the biggest design decision to be made.

For a long time the argument for more than 100 per cent buoyancy and that for less than 100 per cent buoyancy was fought out both on the water and in the design office. The relative merits of each were considered on two grounds: speed and safety.

The small floats seen on *Kriter IV* and now found on *Jacques Ribourel* (both trimarans were designed for De Kersauson by Allegre) have the advantage of low weight and windage. The windward float is totally redundant on a trimaran and simply has to be dragged through the air. However the leeward float is pressed into the water and a unit of less than 100 per cent will have its deck and beam/float junctions awash when driven hard. This creates terrible turbulence and considerable drag as the ends of the crossbeams immerse themselves.

A large float (more than 100 per cent) will create higher windage to windward but less drag to leeward as it is never fully immersed.

It is my belief that a high-buoyancy float is superior as it keeps the crossbeams well clear of the wave tops. The extra windage is worth the penalty. If one is going for a high buoyancy, then, a figure of 140–150 per cent appears to be fastest.

From the safety aspect it is necessary to contemplate the results of a trimaran being driven to the extreme. A float of less than 100 per cent will be driven right under before the main hull lifts (see fig. 30); if the yacht is still sailing the float which is dug in will trip her rapidly round to leeward and on to a dead run. If she were stationary, beam on to the sea, either hove-to or lying a hull, and was forced sideways by a wave the lee float would again dig in and a capsize could result (see Chapter 15). The trimaran with larger floats will show

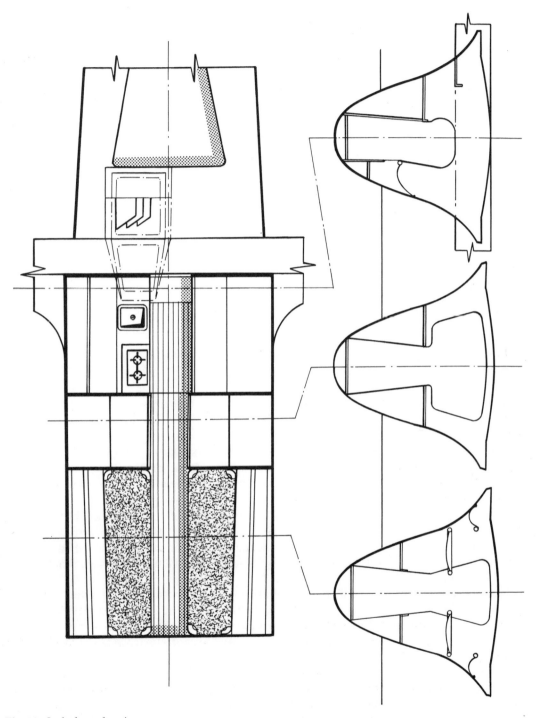

**Fig 29** *Scale from drawing*

Multihulls Offshore

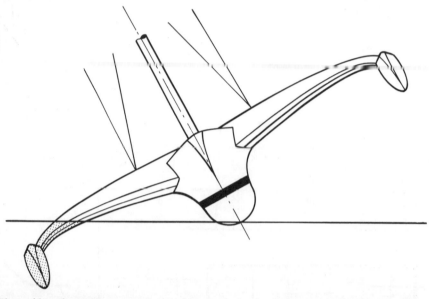

**Fig 30** *Float of less than 100 per cent bouyancy*

a different pattern of behaviour; the main hull will lift *before* the lee float is fully submerged (see fig.31).

*Float shape and position.* Again there are two aspects to float shape: speed and safety. The safety requirement dictates that the float be fairly long in order to create diagonal stability, because a trimaran could quite easily, while beating to windward in a gale, fail to surmount a wave and fall backwards on to her leeward quarter. In this case the lack of stability in a diagonal direction could cause a capsize. A trimaran such as Eric Tabarly's *Paul Ricard* with her very short floats would be a dangerous boat in any but the most experienced hands.

As far as speed is concerned a float needs to provide high lift for low drag. The first point to bear in mind is the submarine characteristics of the float; it can be driven well under water and should therefore be looked upon as an underwater shape. It should have either a canoe or pointed stern for the best possible results, and not a transom as was common in the 1970s (see fig. 32).

In section the float needs to be more V-shaped than the main hull as it is succeptible to pounding along its entire length, for instance when rolling in a beam sea. The V-shaped section gives a fairly high narrow float, ideal for keeping the crossbeams clear of the water and it also gives good lateral resistance thus allowing the centreboard area to reduce as the wind rises.

For good heavy-weather performance the centre of buoyancy of the float should be well forward. When the trimaran is sailing to windward in a reasonable breeze the displacement is shared between the float to leeward and the main hull. Placing the buoyancy of the float forward of that of the main hull has the effect of markedly reducing

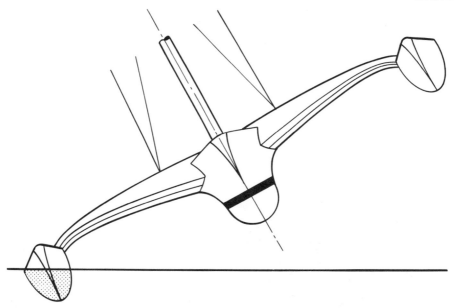

**Fig 31** *Floats of greater than 100 per cent bouyancy*

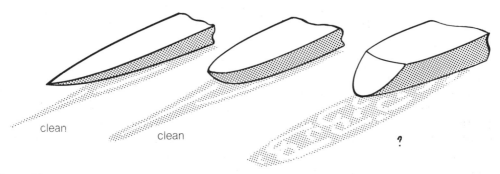

clean

clean

?

**Fig 32** *Float sterns*

the boat's tendency to pitch. One can achieve the good combination with weight near the centre (in a fore and aft plane) and yet good buoyancy at each end.

For good light-airs performance the float should be fine at the forward end. It was noticeable when racing *Colt Cars GB* in the Solent against *Livery Dole* (Shuttleworth-design) that *Colt Cars'* finer floats were much cleaner through the water than *Livery Dole'*s wider floats.

A compromise would be to make the float fine forward with a high freeboard for extra buoyancy. This, of course, will increase windage, but that can be reduced by rounding the hull-to-deck join over at least a 3in radius.

It is important to position the floats correctly in all directions, particularly the up or down aspect of the bows. If the float is set bows up – which looks correct on a drawing –

Triple Fantasy. *Note the transoms on the floats which cause drag.*

the main hull takes on a bows *down* attitude as the displacement of the whole trimaran transfers from the hull to the float (see fig. 33). The final insult to this undesirable situation arises when the rudder lifts out of the water. To a slight degree this happened to *GB IV*. If the float is set bows down the opposite happens: as the vessel becomes more pressed so the bow of the main hull lifts while the float takes up the displacement. The centre of the float's buoyancy, placed well forward, helps to produce this effect (see fig. 34). *Brittany Ferries GB* was a perfect example of this phenomenon. The ideal geometry would be to have the stern leaving the water last, i.e. the main hull, as it lifts out of the water, rotates around the rudder.

The float should be attached with a slight 'foot out' angle so that it becomes upright as the trimaran heels onto it (see fig. 35).

## Crossbeams

There are as many crossbeam shapes and sizes as there are trimaran designs. The options available fall into three basic categories: straight, curved, or compound. The designer has to compromise between beam strength and water clearance and yet also has to keep the hull free-board within sensible limits.

*Straight beams.* This system was used by nearly all early trimarans and was dictated by the

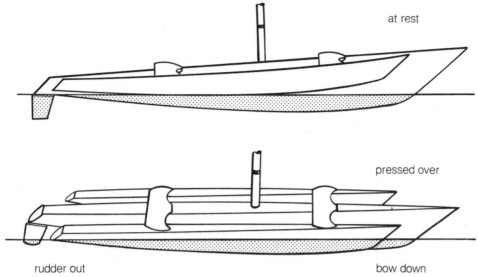

at rest

pressed over

rudder out                    bow down

**Fig 33** *Incorrectly positioned float*

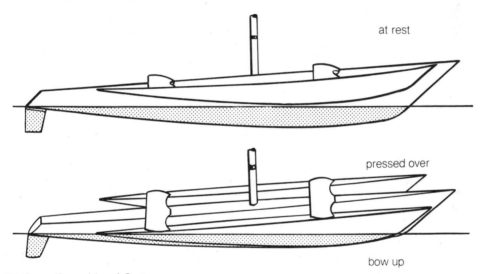

at rest

pressed over

bow up

**Fig 34** *Correctly positioned float*

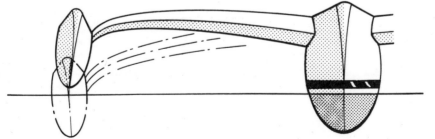

**Fig 35** *Float fitted 'toe out'*

materials then available – aluminium spars or girders (see fig. 36). There were problems involved; not only was the lower strut continually driving into the water, there was also the difficulty of fixing the beams to the hull and floats. Nowadays, nearly every trimaran crossbeam is constructed from composite materials, (Kevlar, carbon, glass and resin) or wood laminated with resin. In either case constructing compound shapes is simple and hence, with rare exceptions, straight beams are no longer used.

*Curved beams*. Dick Newick and Walter Green, the American designers, favour this approach for all their small and medium sized multihulls (up to 45ft). It has the big advantage in allowing the centre hull to have plenty of free-board which keeps the beams well clear of the sea (see fig. 37). This extra height also gives better accommodation in smaller tris. With larger vessels the system would mean an unnecessarily large hull and therefore it is never used. A beam set-up of this type has a potential weakness in the beam-to-main-hull join as there is no inherent knee shape at that point. This can be overcome by the addition of a wire from near the beam end to the main hull under the water-line. The wire will also take a great deal of the load from the beam, supporting especially any rigging forces at the beam ends.

*Compound shape beams*. A beam combining straight and curved parts is good for any sized trimaran. Some of the earliest compound beams resemble giant moustaches (see fig. 38) and good water clearance was achieved. These beams, when made of composite

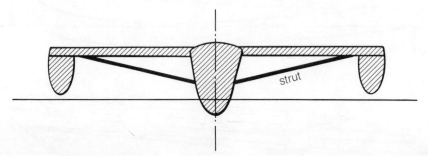

**Fig 36** *Possible crossbeam configurations*

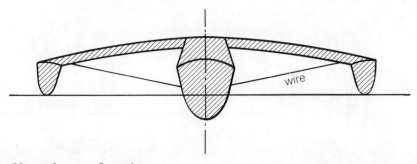

**Fig 37** *Possible crossbeam configurations*

materials, can be built to varying depths to allow for the loads on them. Thus a typical beam is deeper near the main hull end than at the float. For instance, a 60ft trimaran with a 40ft width would have had, up until 1980, crossbeams with depths of 2ft 6ins at the hull tapering to 9ins at the float. With improvements in modern composites and laminating techniques (see Chapter 14) it is now possible to achieve the required strength with a beam depth of 18ins tapering to 6ins for a similar sized boat. The results are improved water clearance and an improved top profile of the yacht thus reducing windage (see fig 39). It is now common practice to construct the beam in a box shape with the later addition of an aerodynamic fairing (fairings are discussed later).

*Crossbeam position and number*. The beams must support the lift from the floats and their position fore and aft must be arranged accordingly. At the same time a crossbeam makes an excellent support for the mast and associated rigging strains.

In the early 1970s racing trimarans were usually of two-beam configuration with the mast stepped between the two. There was a weakness in this system though: the beams were well able to support the lift from the float but the rig had somehow to be supported between them, which meant the stiffness of the rig depended not only on the stiffness of the beams but also on the part of float between the beams. As this was not very satisfactory, especially for larger craft, a third beam was tried. The centre beam could now take the rigging loads, and a high percentage of the float lift, and weight could be contained nearer the centre of the boat by making the forward and aft beams lighter. The disadvantage is the extra weight of a third beam plus its fairing. Still, two of the most successful trimarans of the day were built along these lines – *Rogue Wave* and *Brittany Ferries GB*, designed respectively by Dick Newick and John Shuttleworth.

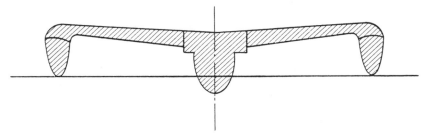

**Fig 38** *Possible crossbeam configurations*

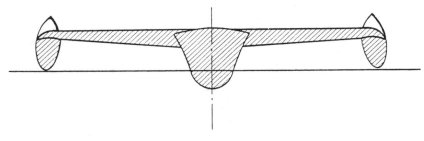

**Fig 39** *Possible crossbeam configurations*

*High curved beams on the Newick-designed VAL 31. The strengthening wires can be seen under the beam.*

*The wing beam on the Newick-designed 40 footer* Downtown Flyer.

172

Another school of thought is to have only two beams and move the mast forward so that it stands on or near the forward beam. This usually means adopting a fractional rig – a perfectly viable option on a large multihull. The drawings of *Great Britain IV*, *Brittany Ferries GB* and *Colt Cars GB* illustrate these three types (figs. 3, 7, 13).

There is a further option – to use only one beam. Trimarans fitted with hydrofoils, such as *Paul Ricard, Gautier and Gautier II* obtain all their stabilizing lift from one point – the foils – and hence need only one beam. In this case the end of the beam has to be braced to the main hull fore and aft with wires or struts. For a while Newick designed an alternative single-beam system incorporating conventional full-length floats connected to the main hull with a wing-like beam (see fig. 40). The advantage was mainly a gain in internal space, as bunks could be built into the wing. Their configuration is now confined mostly to cruising multihulls. More about beam strength can be found in Chapter 14.

## Beam fairing

The purpose of the fairing is to convert a strong box shape into a reasonably streamlined section. Initially, the major concern was wind resistance and fairings were designed to point straight forward into the wind (see fig. 41). This created a problem in that the waves between the hull and lee float hit the beams – not from straight ahead but up at an angle. A forward facing fairing presented a surface flat on to the sea; *GB IV* was a particularly good (or bad) example. Today fairings are given a droop-nose altitude to alleviate wave slamming (see fig. 42).

The longer the fairing (i.e. the more pointed) the more efficient and yet the more heavily constructed it must be to resist water impact. A compromise has to be reached. On *Colt Cars GB* we built the fairings too light and fixed them weakly, with the result that they broke. Fairings must be strong!

Fairings should be put on all beams. Although the aft beam is protected slightly by the one in front, it is nearer the water when the yacht is pressed and will be hitting the waves. One of the few problems with *Brittany Ferries* was the slamming of occasional waves on the unfaired, leading edge of her aft beam. This slamming not only slows a yacht down, it tends also to trip her to leeward which is detrimental to windward performance.

## Centreboard

A trimaran with its long narrow hulls has quite a good resistance to sideways drift or leeway. However, for any degree of performance some sort of fin keel is needed – especially in light airs and just after tacking. This keel does not need to be ballasted, for reasons discussed earlier; indeed, like the rest of the trimaran, the lighter the better. The size and shape of the board may vary from yacht to yacht, but in general they will be parallel-sided with an aspect-ratio underwater of about 2:1. Some designers, notably Green, favour deeper, narrower boards but these are difficult to make strong enough and breakages have been known. In cross-section the board should be a good aerofoil shape. A typical board is shown in fig. 43.

All modern multihulls have boards of the dagger variety, i.e. they are raised and lowered along their own axes rather than pivoted aft. The advantage of the former is that

*The three beam configuration on* Brittany Ferries GB. *This picture shows how the centre beam takes all rigging loads.*

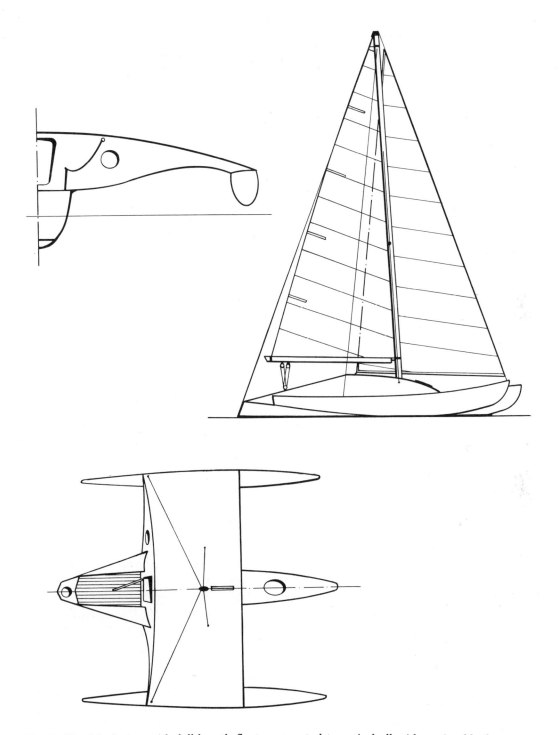

**Fig 40** Newick design with full length floats connected to main hull with a wing-like beam.

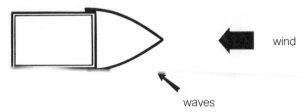

wind

waves

**Fig 41** *Old type beam fairings*

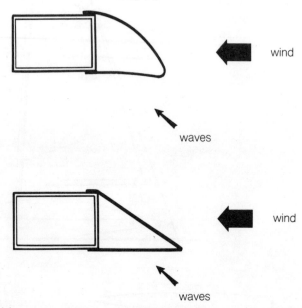

wind

waves

wind

waves

**Fig 42** *New type beam fairings*

the box, into which the unit retracts, is small and always full of board. On *Great Britain III* Kelsall tried a pivoting centreboard, which was intended it to fold up neatly in the event of it striking an underwater object; unfortunately there was no effective way of sealing the empty box when the board was down and the resulting turbulence created enough pressure to blow off the lid of the box. Several remedies were tried including air bags pumped up to displace the water which filled the box after lowering the board. These failed as they were destroyed by the turbulence before they were ever correctly employed. Eventually the yacht was converted to carry a straight dagger.

For raising and lowering the daggerboard, the best system is the most common. It consists of an uphaul line leading over a sleeve at the side of the box, down and through a sleeve set athwartships in the board and up to a dead-eye on deck. The downhaul line is dead-eyed on the side of the box near its base, passes up and over a sleeve set athwartships in the board, down again and round a sleeve set fore and aft into the box side and then up to the deck. Both lines are led through stoppers to a winch (see fig. 43).

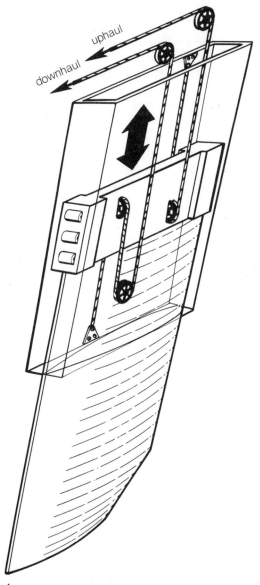

**Fig 43** *Centreboard controls*

Even more critical than its shape is the position of the board and therein lies one of the fundamental differences in the geometry of any multihull relative to a monohull. When a monohull heels the centre of effort of the sails moves to leeward of the hull. The drive of the rig and the drag of the hull form a moment that tends to turn the yacht to windward, i.e. weather-helm. Taking this factor into account a designer places the keel a certain distance *aft* of the centre of effort of the sails and in this way counteracts the weather-helm. With a trimaran the matter is quite different.

When the trimaran is pressed it heels slightly (say 10 degrees) and the rig, as above, moves to leeward of the main hull. However, while this is going on the displacement of the vessel transfers towards the lee float, until, in extremes, all the displacement is provided by that float. As this occurs the centre of resistance to forward motion also moves to leeward; in fact, it moves further outboard than the drive of the rig and the ensuing moment tries to turn the trimaran to leeward – i.e. lee helm (see fig. 44). To counteract this tendency the centreboard must be placed *forward* of the centre of effort of the sails, thus inducing sufficient weather-helm to neutralize the dynamic effect described.

*Trimaran drawings.* The drawings of *Great Britain III, Great Britain IV, Boatfile, Brittany Ferries GB* and *Colt Cars GB* in Part I show different approaches by different designers. They also illustrate quite well the development of multihulls from 1974 to 1982.

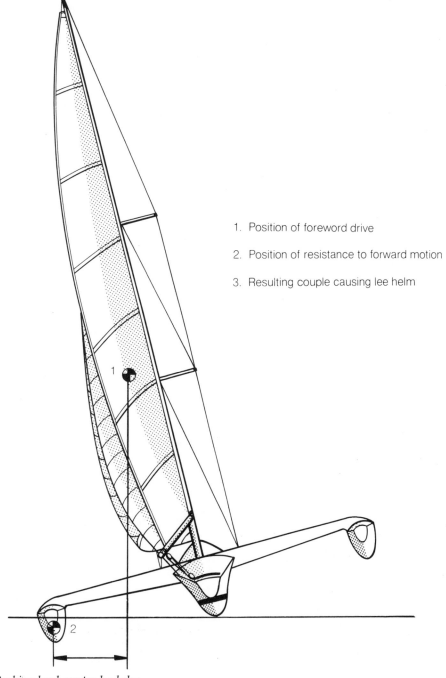

1. Position of foreword drive

2. Position of resistance to forward motion

3. Resulting couple causing lee helm

**Fig 44** *Pushing hard creates lee helm*

# 7

# *Catamaran Design*

All early multihulls were catamarans or proas, and yet, in the 1970's, all successful racing multihulls were trimarans. Only in 1981 did catamarans begin to reassert their performance potential and in 1982 they provided the winners and runners up of two of the three big races. A few comparisons will explain this development.

When catamarans were first raced, the exceptional difficulty of holding the hulls together, and the rig stiff, became apparent; unless the boat was built very much overweight it would be too flexible. The problem is illustrated in fig. 45. The 70ft *British Oxygen*, designed by MacAlpine-Downie was the first modern ocean going cat. However, problems were encountered with the structure. The aluminium mast sections employed as crossbeams were barely strong enough to support the rig. The yacht proved fast and successful in the 1974 Round Britain Race, narrowly beating a much smaller trimaran, but she broke up in her first ocean race, the 1976 OSTAR. The lessons were there for all to learn – if catamarans could be made strong enough *and* light enough they would be a force to be reckoned with. Meanwhile, most multihull racers continued to choose trimarans with their much simplified engineering problems (mainly because there is a centre hull to support the mast on).

It was hard, though, to ignore the stunning performance of small catamarans and

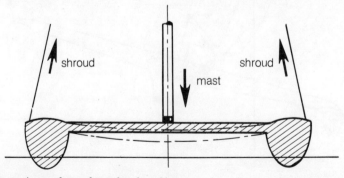

**Fig 45** *Early mast staying and crossbeam bend problems*

before long designers, aided by better understanding of the difficulties and by far superior construction materials, were having another go at giant cats. *Sea Falcon* was built in 1981, a direct descendant of *British Oxygen* but with far more advanced crossbeam technology; she was strong and fast in most conditions. The French were simultaneously at work on *Elf Aquitaine,* designed by Sylvester Langevin. She proved to be very fast – especially off the wind. Neither of these cats could match *Brittany Ferries* in the tough windward slog during the first half of the 1981 Two-handed Transatlantic Race, nevertheless, they heralded the return of the cats to ocean racing. Since then there have been several more successful racing designs. It is interesting to compare various aspects of current catamaran design with the modern trimarans.

## Overall dimensions

*Speed.* The arguments are exactly those explained in this section in the chapter on trimarans. Like tris, a catamaran achieves its stability from the length of the lever arm in the righting moment rather than the magnitude of the force, i.e. given sufficient beam the cat does not need weight to achieve stability. Therefore the hulls can be narrow as they do not have to support the excessive weight of a keel. The wider and lighter the boat, the better the potential speed.

*Length.* As with trimarans, overall length does not restrict maximum speed. The absence of wave making resistance means that there is no theoretical speed limit. Yet, in general, larger cats do beat smaller ones in offshore races. Why?

Firstly, one should look carefully at the results of the various international speed weeks. During these meetings craft of all shapes and sizes are timed over a 500 metre course, preferably in flat water. At nearly every meeting there have been several of the Tornado class catamaran competing and their results over the years in all weather conditions do tend to indicate that there *is* a speed barrier related to overall length. For the Tornado, this barrier is 20 to 21 knots. The only way this speed has been bettered by similar sized craft is with the help of hydrofoils or kite sails – both options lift the hulls as well as drive them. One comes to the conclusion that even a very narrow hull will eventually "stick" and therefore greater length will be required to extend the barrier.

Secondly, smaller catamarans tend to be slowed down by head seas more than larger vessels, regardless of their top speed potential. Off the wind the difference is negligible – in some conditions the small boat will surf more readily; but in average offshore weather, greater length does pay off.

*Beam and weight.* As already shown, the wider and lighter a catamaran the faster it will go. There are, though, still a few practical limitations.

The stability of any multihull depends on its weight and overall beam. The righting moment for a catamaran is created in the same way as for a trimaran. The weight acts down through the centre of gravity and the buoyancy acts up through the lee hull (assuming the windward hull comes clear of the water). Thus, for a catamaran to have the equal stability – and hence power – of a similar weight trimaran it must have the same beam. This means that its cross beams would have to be the same length, without the help of a main hull to support them in the centre. This is practically impossible and no modern catamarans have gone to this extreme. For instance, a 60ft trimaran may have a beam of 40 to 41ft and a cat of the same length will have a beam of 35 to 36ft. If the cat were made any beamier the weight of the crossbeams – to achieve sufficient strength and stiffness – would negate all power gain achieved. (See fig. 46.)

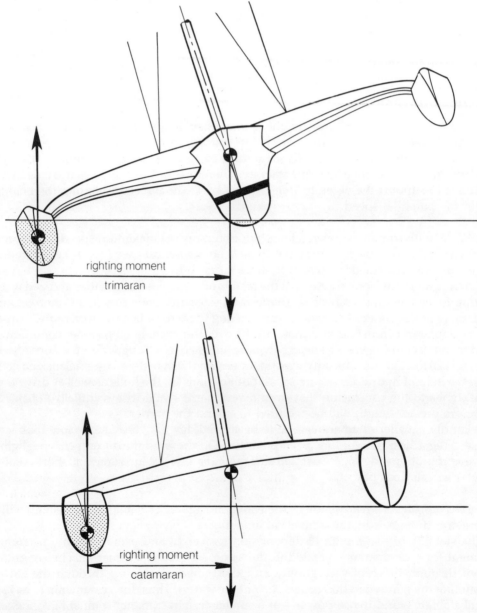

**Fig 46** *Righting moments of trimaran and catamaran*

*Sail area.* The direct result of the catamaran's narrower beam is a loss of stability compared to a trimaran. If the catamaran is given the same sail area, it must therefore become overpowered sooner. It is obviously necessary, then, to give the cat a slightly smaller rig. This need not mean a reduction in power-to-weight ratio, provided weight is kept down.

The rig is dealt with in detail in later chapters, but it is worth pointing out now a particular problem related to catamarans. Headstay tension, and hence straightness of jib luff, depends on the fore and aft stiffness of the yacht. On a cat it also depends on the athwartships stiffness of the forward cross beam (which takes the jib tack). Rather than make this beam massively strong and heavy the trend is to rig catamarans with small jibs and large mainsails – i.e. a pronounced fractional rig, see chapter 5 and 6.

## Hull shape

*Underwater shape.* The static displacement of a trimaran is borne only by the main hull, while a catamaran splits it equally between the two hulls. So at rest, each hull may have a waterline length to beam ratio greater than that of the trimaran's main hull (figures of 18 to 1 for the cat and 13 to 1 for the tri are feasible). The pay off, of course, is that there are two of them to push through the water. As the cat is pressed one hull will have to support its total displacement. This can be allowed for by increasing the waterline beam of each hull above the static waterline (to a ratio of 16 to 1, for instance).

The actual cross-sectional shape of a catamaran's hull should be semicircular over most of its length. It will obviously need to be V'd forward to provide a fine entry and to avoid slamming in a sea way. Towards the stern the shape can be treated in two ways; either leaving it full size and abruptly 'cut-off' at the transom, or it can be narrowed to a fine stern. The latter solution seems better, especially in light and medium airs where a square transom will create tremendous drag if depressed into the water. It is interesting to note that *Elf Aquitaine* – see drawing – has had her sterns lengthened (since this drawing was made) for just this reason.

The radius of the semicircle will, for a given weight, dictate the underwater shape both at rest and when pressed onto one float. At one extreme the shape of each hull can be made a full semicircle under water when the vessel is at rest, and then when sailing hard on only one hull the shape will become U'd. As an example, lets say the waterline beam of each hull is 3 feet and hence the static draft is 1ft 6in. When sailing on one hull, if the waterline beam stays at 3 feet the draft will increase by 1ft 2in to 2ft 8in. In the other extreme the cross section shape is designed so that one hull takes up the exact semicircular shape when it supports the whole weight of the vessel. In this case, assuming the same displacement as the above example, the figures would be; static condition water line beam of each hull 3ft 10in and draft 1ft 3½in. When on one hull the beam increases to 4ft 3in and the draft by only 10in to 2ft 1½in. The first extreme would be ideal for light airs as there would be less wetted surface at rest but less suitable for a breeze, as the wetted surface would be more than the second option, and the greater increase in draft will necessitate a higher initial freeboard – with associated weight and windage penalties. As usual a compromise between the two would probably be the best solution.

*The successful Langevin-designed cat* Elf Aquitaine. *Note the efficient solent jib.*

*Above water shape.* Unlike a trimaran, where the deck of the main hull is the deck of the vessel, the cats 'deck' is the space between the two hulls, thereby obviating the need to flare the topsides of the hulls for deck space or sheeting angles.

The amount of freeboard required will depend on the crossbeam shape – curved or straight – and the cockpit arrangement used – centre pod, or two cockpits, one in each hull. (See Deck Layout.)

## Crossbeams

The crossbeams are the most important feature of the catamaran design. The development in this area has made the difference in competitiveness and reliability in recent offshore races. The beams must be designed to achieve five major objectives.

1. To hold the hulls together. The beam strength required for this purpose is more than adequately covered by that required for the other objectives.

2. To support the mast. Fig. 47 illustrates the problem and shows two ways of solving it. In both cases the central crossbeam supporting the mast must be massively stiff and strong.

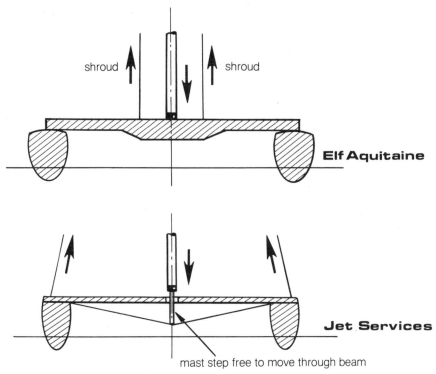

shroud

shroud

**Elf Aquitaine**

**Jet Services**

mast step free to move through beam

**Fig 47** Elf Aquitaine *(Langevin) and* Jet Services *(Olivier) Mast step arrangements*

3. To hold down the forestay. A beam is required forward to provide a chain plate for the base of the forestay and the jib tack. Again, this beam has to be very stiff to resist the pull of the forestay. However, as this forward beam is not so vital to the structural integrity of the boat this strength is best achieved by incorporating a diamond wire and vertical spreader arrangement (commonly called the dolphin striker because a similar set up used to be incorporated under the main beam to provide mast support).

4. To provide a mainsail sheeting base. The main could be sheeted to a wire traveller between the two hulls but it is better to bolt a track onto the aft beam – which is required anyway for objective 5.

5. To stop the two hulls twisting. This is the critical area. If the three beams described were strong enough to eliminate twisting they would easily be strong enough to meet objectives 1 to 4. They would also be very heavy. What the designer will do is try to save weight by allowing the vessel to twist. The question is, by how much? Any flexing will be detrimental to windward performance – see later – but will not affect offwind speed. There is also a construction point to consider here. It is safer to allow a composite or wooden crossbeam to bend than an alloy one. The latter will eventually develop fatigue cracks. However, as nearly all multihull crossbeams are now of composite construction it is safe to allow a diagonal twist of 8in or more in a 60ft catamaran. Two examples – Nigel Irens' design *Vital* (50ft) and David Barker's design *Stratosphere* (61ft) – both flex this amount.

Making them stiffer would improve windward performance but reduce downwind speed (due to the extra weight).

## Centreboards and rudders

*Centreboards.* The centreboards on a catamaran would normally be placed in each hull. As only one is in use at a time they can be assymetrical in shape in order to develop more lift. Their size and position is similar to that of a trimaran but perhaps not as far forward relative to the centre of effort of the sails. A cat has a smaller half beam than a tri and hence the 'heel induced' leehelm is less.

*Rudders.* A problem peculiar to catamarans is their need for two rudders. The two have to be linked very accurately indeed. It would be possible to connect the two units – by rod or wires – several degrees out of true and yet still feel a balanced helm. The resulting drag from such a situation would be considerable. There are several steering options – wheel or tiller – and with either one central or two separate steering positions. This will depend on the deck layout.

## Deck layout

The major decision in any catamaran design is whether to arrange the vessel with a central control pod or with a cockpit in each hull.

*The centre pod.* This system is used by the 70ft *Sea Falcon* (Mac Alpine-Downie) and the 67ft *Chatrent Maritime* (Joubert/Nivelt). Steering and all control lines are led to a cockpit built between the hulls and between the centre and aft crossbeams. The effect on deck layout is not unlike that of a trimaran. The advantage of this system is that the two hulls do not need built-in cockpits and need not support steering arrangements. Tacking and gybing is easier as running across netting between the hulls is not part of the operation. The big disadvantage of the centre pod is simply its weight. It has to be strong and heavy enough to take sheet tracks and winches.

*Twin cockpits.* This alternative means that the area between the two hulls is empty except for a net. Sheet tracks are replaced by wires running fore and aft between the centre and aft beams. All sheets and control lines have to be duplicated so that they can be adjusted from each cockpit. The advantage of this system is weight saving, the disadvantages, miles of control lines, duplicated winching systems and athletic tacking. Within this system there are two sub-options. One is to keep all halyards and reefing lines at the base of the mast – for example *Elf Aquitaine* (Langevin). The other is to duplicate everything, including halyards and reefing lines – like *Vital* (Irens). Both systems have proved successful.

Finally, there is a further possibility that complicates the deck layout yet again. This is the unique, but fast, rig used on the 56ft catamaran *Jaz*. She used two conventional sloop rigs – one on each hull – directly abeam of each other. The advantages are: no problem with beam stiffness to support the mast and forestay, small, easily handled sails and

Charante Maritime: *Note central pod for control and living.*

massive sail area on a broad reach and run. The only disadvantage is interaction between the two rigs when the apparent wind is near the beam. This remains an interesting development especially for short handed racing – or indeed cruising.

## Performance comparisons cats v tris

The arguments about the relative speeds of cats and tris will go on forever. The picture is clouded by the all too familiar laments, 'if this had not broken' or 'if we hadn't gone so far North' etc. Up to 1981 results pointed to the trimarans as being consistently faster than the catamarans. But now, with catamaran development rapidly catching up a different picture begins to emerge. In order to compare their relative performances it will be necessary to look at the differences in varying wind conditions.

*Light airs*. We assume, in light airs, that both cats and tris will be carrying full sail. Despite the fact that a cat has one less hull it will, due to the weight requirement to make the structure sufficiently strong, weigh in at about the same as a tri of similar length. We can assume similar power-to-weight ratios. So, if the driving forces are the same, how do the respective drags compare?

A trimaran in ideal light wind conditions will sail with its total displacement in the centre hull. For the sake of comparison we will take it that her underwater shape is the same as the two catamaran hulls. If we use as our example a trimaran of 10,000lbs displacement, a waterline length of 45ft, a prismatic coefficient of 55 per cent (i.e. average tapering of the underwater section towards each end of the hull) and of basically semicircular section, we find that the maximum waterline beam is 4ft 2ins, the maximum draft 2ft 1in and the skin distance around the underwater section is 6ft 6in.

*The old fashioned* Sea Falcon. *Big and heavy but fast in a breeze.*

For a similar sized catamaran we have in effect two hulls of 5,000lbs displacement each: the same calculation produces these results; maximum waterline beam 2ft 11in, maximum draft 1ft 5½in and the skin distance around the underwater section is 4ft 7in. Of course, as there are two hulls the total for this last figure is 9ft 2in.

We find then, that the relative surface areas are in a ratio of; trimaran 6ft 6in to catamaran 9ft 2in or, more simply put, the catamaran has just over 40 per cent more wetted surface than the trimaran (see fig. 48). In practice this percentage difference will be slightly reduced as the trimaran will always have some float area touching the water.

*Medium airs.* When the trimaran is heeling in medium airs we can make a comparison at the point where her displacement is split evenly between the lee float and the main hull. At this junction a catamaran, if it experiences the same heeling force, will reach equilibrium when 75 per cent of the displacement is on the lee hull and 25 per cent on the windward hull. The calculations now become complicated as the exact shape of the hulls and floats becomes more important, but it is safe to assume that the two types will be suffering almost identical wetted surface area and hence equal resistance due to skin friction. The catamaran in these conditions will have a slight advantage; it doesn't have a third hull flying out to windward creating significant windage.

Wave making resistance will also be similar as both vessels are dragging two hulls.

*Heavy airs.* Both vessels are now sailing nearly 100 per cent on their lee hull or float. The catamaran has the advantage in that one of her hulls is better able to support her whole displacement than is the lee float of a trimaran. Allied to this is the greater likelihood of a trimaran float/beam joint becoming immersed. The windage advantage again goes in favour of the catamaran.

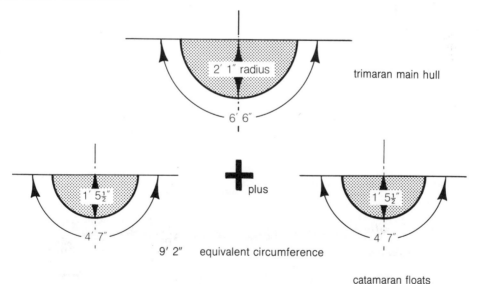

**Fig 48** *Immersed sections and wetted surface areas in light airs*

# Summary

In theory, it would appear that the trimaran has the advantage in light airs but as soon as it starts to blow the catamaran overtakes her. This should apply to all points of sailing. However, it has been consistently shown that a trimaran outsails a catamaran when beating into a seaway. Why is this so? I believe the answer lies in the relatively greater flexibility of the catamaran. When beating a yacht meets the waves diagonally – as a wave hits, the bows of the catamaran's windward hull lifts. As this occurs, the diagonal flex causes the bow of the leeward hull to move downwards just in time for it to punch into the passing wave. This motion must slow the vessel down and could only be overcome by sailing freer. So the cat sails freer and faster in a breeze, but makes less ground to windward.

In my view the evidence of the race course is inconclusive and it is impossible to choose between the two types of boat for race winning potential. There is, too, the matter of personal preference, and a sailor who prefers one type will only change his mind when there is sufficient proof of greater speed potential with the other type.

## Future trends – cats or tris?

In May 1982 there was a fully crewed race from La Rochelles to New Orleans a distance of 5,000 miles. The favourite multihulls were:

### TRIMARANS

| | | | | | | |
|---|---|---|---|---|---|---|
| Jacques Ribourel | designed by | Joubert | skippered by | de Kersauson | size | 80' |
| Gautier III | ,, | Langevin | ,,, | Terlain | ,, | 60' |
| Royale | ,, | Graal | ,, | Caradec | ,, | 60' |
| Fleury Michon | ,, | Shuttleworth | ,, | Poupon | ,, | 56' |
| Umupro Jardin | ,, | Green | ,, | Birch | ,, | 53' |
| Lois | ,, | Green | ,, | Vallin | ,, | 53' |

### CATAMARANS

| | | | | | | |
|---|---|---|---|---|---|---|
| Elf Aquitaine | ,, | Langevin | ,, | Pajot | ,, | 67' |
| Charente Maritime | ,, | Joubert/Nivelt | ,, | Fountain | ,, | 67' |
| Jet Services | ,, | Ollier | ,, | Morvan | ,, | 50' |

(Elf was lengthened after 1981)

### PROAS

| | | | | | | |
|---|---|---|---|---|---|---|
| Lestra Sport | ,, | Ollier | ,, | Delage | ,, | 56' |

(ex *Sudinox*)

The results were largely due to the capriciousness of the weather. The skippers who chose the southerly – trade wind – route gained at least two and one half days by doing so. The results were as follows:

| | | |
|---|---|---|
| Charente Maritime | (cat) | (Southerly route) |
| Elf Aquitaine | (cat) | (Northerly route) |

| Lestra Sport | (proa) | 2 hours later | (Southerly route) |
| Jet Services | (cat) | 1 day 10 hours later | ,, |
| Gautier III | (tri) | 3 hours later | (Northerly route) |
| Lois | (tri) | 1 day 12 hours later | ,, |
| Umupro Jardin | (tri) | 1 hour later | ,, |

Even allowing for the fact that the varying routes affected the results enormously, and taking into account the absence of the top British multihulls (*Brittany Ferries* has beaten *Elf Aquitaine* and *Colt Cars GB* has beaten *Brittany Ferries*) this was quite a convincing argument for catamarans.

In November 1982 the singlehanded Route du Rhum took place. The course, St Malo to Guadeloupe, consisted of 5 days of strong to gale force headwinds followed by trade wind running and reaching for a further 2 weeks.

The favourite multihulls were:

## TRIMARANS

| William Saurin | designed by | Kelsall | sailed by | Riguidel | size | 88' |
| Jacques Ribourel | ,, | Shuttleworth | ,, | de Kersausaon | ,, | 80' |
| Brittany Ferries GB | ,, | Joubert | ,, | Blyth | ,, | 65' |
| Royale | ,, | Graal | ,, | Caradec | ,, | 60' |
| Charles Heidsieck | ,, | Shuttleworth | ,, | Gabbay | ,, | 60' |
| Colt Cars GB | ,, | Holland/James | ,, | James | ,, | 60' |
| Gautier III | ,, | Langevin | ,, | Terlain | ,, | 60' |
| Biotherm | ,, | — | ,, | Arthaud | ,, | 60' |
| Paul Ricard | ,, | — | ,, | Tabarly | ,, | 56' |
| Fleury Michon | ,, | Shuttleworth | ,, | Poupon | ,, | 56' |
| Umupro Jardin | ,, | Morrison | ,, | Fauconnier | ,, | 54' |
| (ex *Exmouth Challenge*) | | | | | | |
| Gauloise IV | ,, | Green | ,, | Loiseau | ,, | 44' |

## CATAMARANS

| Olympus III | ,, | MacAlpine-Downie | ,, | Knox-Johnston | ,, | 70' |
| Elf Aquitaine | ,, | Langevin | ,, | Pajot | ,, | 67' |
| Charente Maritime | ,, | Joubert/Nivelt | ,, | Follenfant | ,, | 67' |
| Vital | ,, | Irens | ,, | Birch | ,, | 50' |

In the early stages of the race – the strong headwinds – the leaders were *Gauloise IV*, *Brittany Ferries*, myself on *Colt Cars GB* and *Elf Aquitaine*. *Elf* was the only cat in the leading group. However, one by one, the trimarans dropped out or fell back until at the end of the race the finishing order was:

1. *Elf Aquitaine* (cat)
2. *Jaz* (cat)
3. *Vital* (cat)
4. *Gauloise IV* (tri)

On the surface this result should be enough to kill trimarans for life. But a closer examination of what happened does mitigate the tri's bad performances. Nearly all the large tris suffered problems such as electrical, self steering, rigging, etc, which were not related to their number of hulls. My own *Colt Cars GB* (retired day 5 with rigging damage) was faster than the eventual winner in all conditions between calm and force 7 – I led in the gale force headwinds, I overtook *Elf* in force 7 tail winds four hours after the start and *Colt Cars GB*'s light airs performance is exceptional. The same arguments go for *Brittany Ferries* (retired day 5 with self steering problems) – she is as fast if not faster than *Elf*, and so on. So is it coincidence that the cats won through? Not really, but I do not believe the battle is over yet.

It is interesting to note that, other than engineering improvements, cats are not changing a great deal in appearance: tris, on the other hand, with their ever increasing float size, are slowly progressing towards the catamaran theme. I think one can safely predict that by the end of the 80's the top racing boats will either be cats or they will be tris with hydrofoil stablization (see Chapter 13).

# 8

## *Proas*

Proas or Praus (the word comes from the Malaysian *prau*, denoting a fast rowing or sailing boat) have had, to say the least, a chequered career in long distance sailing. The first result that could in any way be called successful was that of the Newick-designed 40ft *Cheers*, sailed by the American Tom Follet into third place in the 1968 OSTAR. Her crossing time of 27 days was good for the day, although slow by modern standards. Her high overall placing was the result of excellent seamanship (i.e. she did not capsize), and the choice of the southerly route. The most significant aspect of her position was that she was the only modern multihull in the fleet and she heralded the arrival of her designer in the offshore, multihull world.

Since *Cheers* the only other successful proa has been the 56ft *Sudinox Funambule/Lestra Sport* designed by Ollier. In the 1981 Two Star she retired with sail problems but later redeemed herself by making the return trip from New York to the Lizard in under 11 days, one day and 11 hours behind *Elf Aquitaine*'s record. In 1982, as has just been recorded, she came a creditable third in the La Rochelle to New Orleans race. Other than in these two races, the history of proas is a very sorry one indeed, with a capsize rate of nearly 100 per cent. It is beyond my comprehension why anyone should want to risk his life in an offshore proa. Why do they do it? The answer, of course, is speed. A proa has all the advantages of a trimaran but without the windage of a windward float. But it does list a few disadvantages of its own: first, the rig and hulls have to be able to sail in both directions; and second, the boat has stability to resist a capsize in one direction only.

While the proa is under control and sailing normally she will be potentially faster than any other multihull. For a given size she will weigh 10 to 20 per cent less than a trimaran. The great difficulty is keeping her under control.

## Proa design

If a proa only had to sail on one tack it would look like a trimaran with only one float. But, as it has to go both ways there is a need for symmetry, i.e. two bows, two rudders, etc. As far as the hull and outriggers are concerned, they are designed with a bow at each end. The bow not in use becomes a neat, canoe stern. There must be two rudders, each set well

Lestra Sport – *A successful proa. Two mains and a jib each end.*

in from their respective bow/stern and both retractable, as it would be impossible to sail with a reversed rudder in the bow. The centreboard may be formed by these rudders or it may be separate.

The cockpit also has to work both ways, which is easy to arrange. The rig is slightly more difficult to organize. There are two popular proa rigs, the first is the one favoured by designers as it is stronger and safer, the second is preferred by the more extreme proa sailors as it is faster.

The first rig, shown in fig. 49(a), consists of two masts with a mainsail on each that can be sheeted to either end of the boat. Although the resulting sail plan looks unbalanced it is in fact not too bad in that it counteracts the lee helm tendency caused by the tripping effect of the float, and in light airs a loose-luffed genoa can be set at the front bow. The second, more modern approach is to have one central mast with a mainsail capable of sheeting either way, as in the former, and to add two furler genoas from the masthead to each end of the boat. Employing this method the forward jib can be in use and the aft one furled away (see fig. 49(b)). Dick Newick favours the former of these two rig options. He believes that a design such as that shown in fig. 50 represents the fastest possible single-handed yacht. On this concept Newick says: 'This is a modification of a design I did for Jean Marie Vidal who then altered the rig without my approval so that I had to disavow the result before she was launched. She was lost when her rig failed. Neither of the other two proas I designed at that time were rigged according to my specification'.

Some proas are designed with a small float or buoyancy device tacked on to the windward side of the hull at deck level. This may prevent the proa turning upside down if it falls over to windward but it will never stop a capsize in real life – such as being caught with the sails aback.

## Pacific proa

A proa with the outrigger to windward – and nothing to leeward – may sound pretty outrageous. Such designs have proved successful but only in the context of outrigger canoes, or inshore craft aimed at sailing speed records.

The Pacific proa relies on the weight of the windward float for stability. The stability can be increased by using body weight or incorporating water ballast. Not exactly an offshore vessel. Yet in 1982 Guy Delarge entered *Rosier*, a 60ft Pacific proa with an 80ft beam, in the Route du Rhum single-handed transatlantic race. Delarge is unique in having sailed the Atlantic four times in a 'conventional' proa. *Rosier* was anything but conventional. The single crossbeam with its small windward float could be angled aft – rather like a swing wing aeroplane, to encourage the bows to lift. After tacking the arm could be swept the other way . . . combine all this with a wing mast, four furler genoas and a windward float that pivots (and occasionally turned sideways on, causing a violent luff, or rather preventing any forward motion) and you have quite a handful!

*Rosier* actually made it to the start of the race. Delarge was busy sweeping back the crossarm (achieved with two guys led to winches) when he inadvertently let go the forward guy. The crossarm and float folded dramatically aft and the vessel promptly fell over. That was the end of his race.

There were a lot of good ideas in *Rosier* and we may see more like her yet.

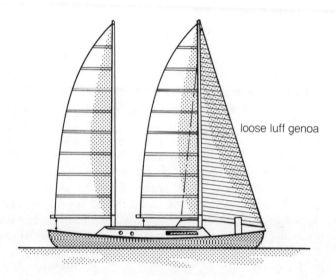

**Fig 44(a)** *Proa rigged with two masts and loose luff genoa*

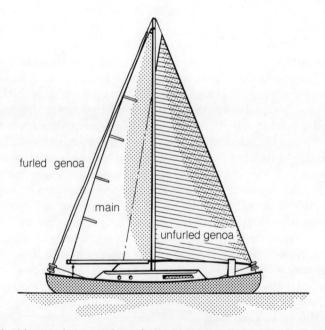

**Fig 49(b)** *Proa rigged with central mast and two furling genoas*

196

**Fig 50** *Newick-designed proa*

## Proa sailing

The major difference in sailing a proa is in the way one tacks and gybes. In both cases the secret is to get on to a beam reach and then slow down to a stop, with the mainsail(s) flapping and the jibs (if applicable) furled. Having lost way and lying beam on to the sea, lower the new rudder, raise the old rudder, sheet in the mainsail(s) for the new direction, unfurl the new forward jib and away you go.

It is an irony of proa sailing that the tacking and gyying manoeuvres take a significant time. This loss of progress is negligible in a trans-ocean race where one seldom tacks, yet it is crucial while racing inshore where the tacking-time to racing-time ratio is higher. Because of this a proa only becomes a potential racing machine offshore – the one place where they are totally unsafe. Inshore, where they should be of interest, they are impractical.

Proas are still being built for short-handed races. A vessel that is inherently unsafe becomes doubly so when raced single-handed as the chances of being caught aback are very high indeed. In the 1980 OSTAR, despite hardly sleeping at all, I woke at least once every other day to find my trimaran with her sails backed. What chance has a proa?

Other than *Cheers* and *Lestra Sport* not one proa has finished an ocean race. In the last two transatlantic races, out of a total of seven proas entered, two capsized on the way to the start, two capsized during the races and one retired as a result of damage.

The results speak for themselves.

# 9

# Multihull Construction

As in all forms of yacht building the last few years have brought about a vast improvement in the materials and techniques available to the boat builder. The goal aimed for most by a builder, whether he uses wood, aluminium or composite materials is to achieve maximum strength and stiffness for minimum weight.

## Structural strength and stiffness

The designer can employ several useful ways to achieve the best compromise between lightness and strength. Each part of the boat is treated in different ways.

*Main hull.* As the athwartships rigging loads are taken by the crossbeams the main hull of a trimaran, or the two hulls of a catamaran, need only support the strains from the fore and aft rigging, the centreboard, the rudder and the impact of the sea. The impact resistance of the skin will be automatically taken care of by designing a structure stiff enough to withstand the fore and aft bending from the forestay, backstay and mast compression forces (see fig. 51).

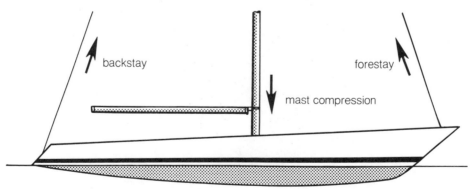

**Fig 51** *Fore and aft bending*

Fortunately, a multihull hull, with its narrow beam and nearly vertical sides, is well able to resist vertical bending. John Shuttleworth employs a bulkhead running fore and aft down the centre of all his designs, which runs from the bow back to the middle of the boat and adds stiffness where needed. When Ron Holland and I were designing our first 60ft trimaran, *Colt Cars GB*, I set a breaking limit on each component part and also a limit to bending under certain loads. For the main hull I specified a maximum of half an inch of fore and aft bend under normal rigging loads. The engineering calculation showed that this could easily be achieved by building material into the hull sides themselves rather than employing a centre-line bulkhead. Whichever system is used it is important to ensure that the hull is stiff in a fore and aft plane. Building a very strong deck will help; either build the deck specifically to strengthen the hull, rather than simply to support the crew above, or take the latter course and add an additional space frame underneath.

The centreboard will generate considerable forces when sailing. For instance, if the yacht makes 4 degrees of leeway at 20 knots the side force on a 28sq ft centreboard will be over 6,000lbs. As well as the board, the centreboard box must be strong enough to take this force. The box should be supported by a horizontal floor across the hull at about mid-hull height – the purpose being to take the point loading created by the top edge of the board when in its fully down position (fig. 52).

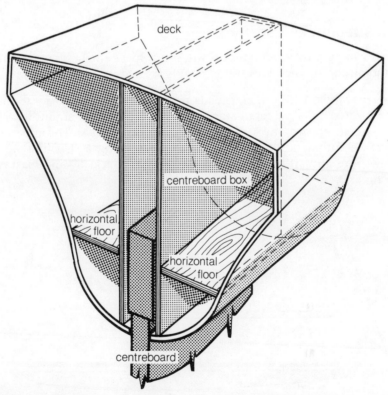

**Fig 52** *Centreboard box detail*

The forces on the rudder are even larger. For example, if one could put the helm of a 7sq ft rudder hard over at 24 knots the force would be 15,000lbs (more detail is given later in this chapter under rudder construction). Suffice to say that the mounting of the rudder bearings must be extremely strong. The practical limit to the force from the rudder is dictated by the helmsman's physical strength at the steering gear. However, this could be superseded by the force generated when making stern way in a heavy sea and falling back on the rudder – a situation to be avoided if at all possible.

*Trimaran floats.* The impulsive forces generated by wave impact dictate the need to build a float strongly. The most vulnerable part is that forward of the forward crossbeam; there have been several cases of floats breaking off just forward of the beam. A high-sided, narrow bow is ideally shaped to withstand the upward forces produced by its impact into a wave, but if the trimaran falls sideways off a wave and on to the large exposed side of a float bow the power of such a fall could do extensive damage. Unfortunately, it is necessary to have quite a length of bow forward of, and hence unsupported by, the forward beam in order to obtain the correct distribution of float buoyancy. The most effective way of strengthening this section is to build a horizontal floor halfway up the float and running from the bow aft to the forward beam (fig. 53).

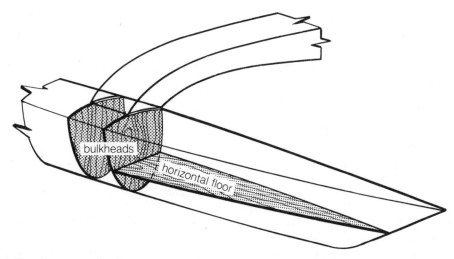

**Fig 53** *Float bow strengthening*

*Crossbeams.* Probably these are the most critical part of the structure. How strong do they have to be? Consider first a trimaran. The strength required can be looked at in two ways, static and dynamic. Statically, the point to look at is that shown in fig. 54. Here the trimaran is pivoting about the lee float and the power in the sails, transmitted through the windward rigging, is enough to hold the main hull clear of the water. Assume the leeward rigging has gone slack; assume, also, for ease of calculation, that all the rigging force is through a cap-shroud to the float or beam end. Our trimaran weighs Dlb,

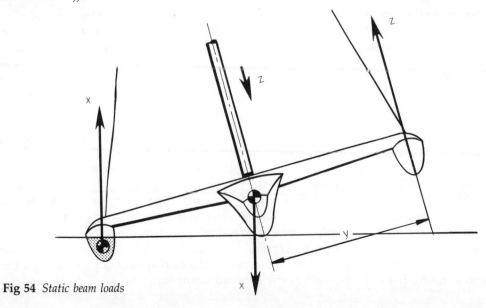

**Fig 54** *Static beam loads*

it has a beam of 2y feet from centre-line of one float to the centre-line of the other; the vertical component of the force in the weather rigging is z pounds. The main hull lifts clear at 17 degrees of heel.

If the trimaran in Fig 54 is in equilibrium, the capsizing moment is exactly balanced by the righting moment.

The capsizing moment = z × y (ft lbs)

And this is transmitted into the hull as a bending moment in the weather crossbeam, ANTICLOCKWISE in our diagram.

The righting moment = z × D × y (cosine heel angle)

And this is transmitted into the hull as a bending moment in the leeward crossbeam, CLOCKWISE in our diagram. Since the two are equal, z = cos 17 × D, so the static load on each crossbeam is 0.96Dy ft lb, or just under the full weight of the boat (hull, floats, crossbeams and rig) times half the beam.

This is the largest static load, and the crossbeams should be engineered accordingly, not only to be strong enough ultimately, but also, if the rigging is indeed taken out to the float or beam end, to ensure that the rigging does not become dangerously slack, i.e. with no more than about 1 inch of beam bend. As can be seen in the equation, if z becomes equal to D, the trimaran will capsize. If the rigging is either totally, or in part, to the main hull similar calculations will give the identical beam strength required. Incidentally these calculations also show the maximum static rigging and mast compression loads obtainable, assuming the lee rigging has gone slack before the main hull lifts clear of the water.

Dynamically, the problem is much more complex and depends on how extreme a sea condition the vessel is built to take. The calculations are easy enough but the input is a matter of judgment. For instance, if the trimaran takes off over a wave, drops 10ft, lands only on her floats with the main hull over a trough and comes to rest after sinking two feet into the water, the resulting calculations show a beam strength required that is similar to the static tests just done. But should one assume a fall of 12ft or more? Unfortunately, a trimaran built to take *any* conditions will be too heavy to win any races. As always a designer must choose a level of compromise. The forward beam certainly needs to be stronger than the aft one, as it carries not only the rigging loads but also – assuming normal float buoyancy distribution – two-thirds of the lift generated.

The calculations for a catamaran are exactly the same. In practice, though, there are still further difficulties; the mast compression acts at a point on the beam, which means the load is not spread in the same way as on a trimaran with her main hull.

## Materials

In multihull construction as in monohull, there is a very large range of possible building systems. The main ingredients are alloy, wood, composite (GRP., kevlar, carbon fibre, cores and resins) or even a combination of any of these materials.

*Alloy.* Although still used by the majority of French multihull manufacturers, alloy is not used in either England or the USA, where the designers favour wood or a composite construction. In order to achieve the light weights required it is necessary to use a plate thickness of 4mm or less and this is really too weak in panel stiffness to withstand strains and impacts at sea. Even with heavy space frames tying the major stress points together the skin still has to be strong enough to withstand the severe wave impacts. It is also difficult, if not impossible, to produce a fair hull as distortion at the welds is bad with thin plate. Riveting and gluing the panels is a good alternative but in any case an alloy multihull is unlikely to have the strength-to-weight characteristics of alternative construction methods.

If alloy is used it is likely to be used throughout, including in the crossbeam construction. The results are in general unattractive and although alloy multis have had their successes (*Manureva/Pen Duick IV, Paul Ricard, Kriter IV*) they are becoming outclassed by more modern construction techniques. An interesting exception is *Elf Aquitaine* which was built in alloy. Her designer, Langevin, says, 'The choice of light alloy guaranteed the easy assembly of the structure. We chose dismountable crossbeams to allow, among other things, the building of units in one place and assembly in another. Moreover, it is a material we are well used to in France and I have been designing boats built of it for the last 15 years. Finally, any necessary modifications or repairs are simple'.

The penalty of this argument is a catamaran displacing over 15,000lbs (7,000kg) for 62ft overall, before she was lengthened, which in turn requires a massive sail area to make her competitive. It is also interesting to note that the bolts holding the parts together only just survived her dash to a new transatlantic record in 1981, and the centre beam cracked in the 1982 Route du Rhun.

*Wood.* The original, and to some, the only boat building material. In fact wood is experiencing a resurgence in popularity in its use with epoxy resins. Wood has the advantages of relatively low cost, availability, and ease of use. Its mechanical properties are also very good: stiffness, strength-to-weight ratio and fatigue resistance can only be matched by 'exotic' materials (see later).

Unfortunately wood has one enemy – moisture – and this causes several problems. It will swell and shrink with changes in temperature and humidity; it will lose strength as it absorbs moisture and in the long term it will rot. The secret to overcoming these disadvantages is to eliminate them by sealing the wood with epoxy resin. If each piece of wood in a yacht is completely covered in resin the moisture content is stabilized. The structure will then not change with the conditions and hence the wood won't crack, the paint won't peel and maintenance problems are generally eased. Of even more importance from the structural point of view is the effect of stabilizing the wood's properties, making structural engineering easier. The actual construction of the hulls can be done in one of two ways:

(i) *Mould method*. A male mould or plug is made from frames set up on the floor and covered either with longitudinal battens or with planks. The frames obviously have to be cut to allow not only for the eventual hull thickness but also for the ribond or plank thickness. The mould then becomes the form over which veneers of wood may be formed. As wood is a uni-directional material (i.e. it has strength in one direction only) the veneers are layed in different directions to produce the desired overall strength. The first layer is stapled down on to the mould and subsequent layers are stapled and epoxy glued. The staples can be removed from the previous layer, area by area, as the next is added. When the hull is finished it is turned up the correct way and the mould removed. The interior can now be completed.

This system is suitable for smaller hulls – especially if more than one is being made, for example two floats or symmetrical catamaran hulls – but it is not as common as the following system.

(ii) *Frames, stringers and planks*. This is the most widely used method of constructing a wooden hull and is suitable for one-off construction of any size.

Essentially the hull is built from the inside out. The frames and bulkheads are set up, deck downwards, and notched to accept fore and aft stringers. The first veneer is difficult to apply as it has limited support from the stringers, unlike the mould method. For this reason this first veneer may be plywood, thus forming an adequate mould for further veneers to be added as before.

The crossbeams can be box sections laminated in a similar way, or I beams made up from larger pieces of wood. The success in wood construction is ensured by completely covering each piece in epoxy as it is used, and in the correct choice of wood. Cedar or spruce skins with douglas fir crossbeams is a good combination.

*Composite*. Composite construction is a term employed to encompass all types of fibre reinforced plastic construction. The fibres may be glass, Kevlar or carbon; the plastic may be epoxy, vynlester or polyester resin and the hull may be made with or without a mould and with or without a sandwich core. There are too many possibilities to analyse them all in this book. Instead, I will look at two ends of the scale (of cost and performance), a glass/polyester-skinned foam sandwich for low coast and ease of building and an ultimately exotic construction such as that used in *Colt Cars GB*.

(i) *Glass reinforced plastics (GRP) foam sandwich*. This system is used extensively for multihulls as it is cheap, easy to use and has a good strength-to-weight ratio. The result typically is a skin consisting of 4mm of glass and resin on either side of a 20mm foam sheet core. The purpose of this core is twofold. It creates a stiffer skin than would 8mm of solid glass and, in respect of the foam, it provides an easy building method as no mould is required.

First, temporary frames are set up and these are covered with longitudinal battens (1in × 1in at 6in centres for example). The sheets of foam are bent over this plug and secured by screws from the inside. Once the core hull has been completed the outer skin of glass and resin is applied. The outside is then filled, faired and painted before the whole is turned the right way up. The frames and battens can now be removed and the inner skin of glass applied, followed by the bulkheads and interior. The resulting hulls are somewhat crude in the context of a fast offshore multihull, especially as considerable weight is needed to attain the required strength.

(ii) *Exotics.* Before looking at the construction of *Colt Cars GB* let us consider what is meant by exotic materials and what their advantages are. There are several alternatives to the use of glass as the reinforcing fibre. They can be used on their own or in any combination with each other and/or glass.

Kevlar is an aramid fibre that has several advantages over glass. It is lighter (by half), it has good tensile strength and excellent impact resistance. Therefore it won't shatter when hit by a wave. It has one major disadvantage in that it is not good in compression. It costs, at present, five times as much as glass.

Carbon fibre is a form of graphite which, like Kevlar, has good tensile strength and has in addition excellent strength in compression. However it is non ductile (brittle) and hence is ideal for use in conjunction with Kevlar. It costs ten times as much as glass (approximately £25 a kilo, unwoven, in 1982).

Most modern composite multihulls have a considerable percentage of Kevlar cloth and a small percentage of carbon. The former is usually added to the glass skin while the latter is employed in reinforcing areas of stress such as the rigging loads and especially in the crossbeams (see later). When using exotic fibres it is sensible to use epoxy or vynlester rather than polyester resin. Epoxy has better adhesion, less shrinkage and better elongation than polyester. But it is nearly three times as expensive. Vynlester resin is a bastardized epoxy that has been diluted with styreen. It is twice as expensive as polyester.

The core can be improved by using Nomex, a honeycomb material considerably lighter than foam or balsa (it weighs ¾lb for a cubic foot) and is much stronger in compression. At £4 a sq ft for a 2cm thick sheet it is, however, very expensive indeed. It also cannot be secured like foam so a different building method is required, see *Colt Cars GB*.

(iii) *Colt Cars GB.* For this trimaran we elected to use a material system that at the time, and for some time to come, was about as far as one could go in terms of achieving strength and stiffness for minimum weight.

Nomex was chosen as the core material. The fibre used was an omni-directional cloth made up of Kevlar and carbon in a 50:50 ratio by weight. The cloth weighed 22.5gm (.05lb) per sq ft and ten layers were used, five either side of the core, laminated with epoxy resin. The resulting skin weight comprised ¼lb carbon, ¼lb of Kevlar, ½lb of resin and a negligible weight of Nomex in each square foot. 1lb a sq ft is very light (approx 3mm alloy plate) and yet very strong.

The main hull was built over a fully planked plug. The five inner cloths were laid together, a difficult job when one remembers that the resins must be mixed in small loads, a kilo at a time, as one only has 20 minutes or so before it starts to cure. (In fact, if the resin is left in the pot its own generated heat will start the cure sooner and it will be unworkable in a little over five minutes). Immediately after the five layers were laid the precut Nomex was added and a vacuum bag spread over the whole. This vacuum pulls all the air out of the lay-up and also ensures a good bond between the Nomex and skin. After an initial cure (six to eight hours) the vacuum was removed. The outer five skins were then applied – again simultaneously. Filling and fairing followed; in this case the filling and sanding took only four days because of the accuracy of the initial plug and of the building process. The hull was turned over and a minimum interior fitted. The cabin furniture was made with light 'home-made' sandwich panels.

The deck was constructed in a similar way, but in a concave mould, and then bonded to the hull.

The two floats created a problem as we wanted a heavily curved hull to deck join to reduce windage. This meant that it would be impossible to remove an intact plug from one float for use on the second as the sides of the float skin curved inwards at the top. Because of this limitation a plug was made and from it a split mould taken; the two floats were moulded in four halves and glassed down the centre. The fine bow prohibited laying up a whole float together.

*A fine bow on a trimaran float, while excellent in light airs, will, when pressed in a breeze, sink to such an extent that wave tops strike the crossbeams.*

The float decks were made in from a female mould and then glued and riveted to the float hulls.

The crossbeams were designed to bend only 1in over 40ft when exposed to normal working rigging loads. The two beams were made in four parts from a female mould – two front halves and two aft halves which were then glued and screwed together. The lay-up was mainly carbon.

All the parts were then bonded together and beam fairings added. The completed trimaran of 60ft LOA and 40ft 6in beam displaces 11,000lbs of which only 6,000lbs is in the skins, floors, bulkheads, floats, decks and crossbeams. A remarkable boat building achievement by Tim Gurr and S.P. Composites Ltd.

## Future building trends

There is a possible way of improving the strength and reducing the weight of a composite boat still further. This can be done by using what is known as 'pre-preg' cloth. The cloth to be used for the lay-up is passed through a bath of resin and solvent. It is then hung in a drying tower for a few minutes, which effects a part cure and burns off the solvent. The pre-preg cloth is then stored in a fridge ready for use. The boat builder buys it in this form. The hull is laid up in much the same way as was *Colt Cars* except that no wetting out is required as the cloth is prepared. The cloth can be used at room temperature for several days. Thus the whole hull can be layed up (core included), and a vacuum applied. Now comes the clever part: heat is applied in stages at first to get the resin to flow and a few minutes later full heat (100 degrees centigrade plus) to cook the whole hull and effect the cure.

The advantages are not only ease and clean use of the cloths but also a controlled resin-to-cloth ratio (less than 50 per cent) and an excellent mechanical result after cure.

The disadvantages lie in the pre-preg organization which is time consuming and costly to set up and of course the whole yacht has to be cooked to a very high temperature. This causes all sorts of practical complications with a big structure.

When the time comes for boat builders to be able to accommodate such facilities, 'pre-pregging' will find a ready outlet in multihulls where lightweight and high strength count for everything.

## Appendages

*Rudder.* Constructing a rudder capable of accepting the loads described earlier in this chapter is complicated because of its small size and the fact that ideally, it is thin as well. Even a 60ft multihull cannot afford a rudder stock wider than 3ins. Taking this dimension as a limiting size the only means of obtaining the required strength (a rudder 3ft 6ins deep and 2ft fore and aft exerts a bending load of 300,000 ft lbs on the stock if put hard over at 24 knots) is to use a stainless steel or solid titanium stock. The latter, at two-thirds of the weight of the former, is preferable, if a trifle expensive at the present time.

The stock is machined to fit the bearings in the hull and here weight can be saved by tapering the stock towards the top bearing. Below the hull it should be fixed by a series of webs to a blade constructed out of a combination of composite materials. Carbon fibre is ideal. Incidentally, all the carbon fibre rudders that broke in the 1979 monohull offshore racing season were constructed with carbon fibre rudder stocks. It was the rudder stocks that broke. The trend now in all top racing boats is towards titanium stocks although carbon fibre will re-emerge as lay-up techniques improve.

*Centreboard.* As the wind rises the centreboard can be reduced in area (by raising it into its box). The side force on the board per unit area increases with the wind, but because the board can be retracted the total load on the board remains about the same. However, this load, acting at the centre of the board's area, exerts a greater bending moment on a full board than on a partly retracted one. Thus the board can be constructed with less strength, and hence less weight, towards its tip.

Early centreboards were made of solid wood and although this gave more than adequate strength, they were unnecessarily heavy. Even though any board will float (and needs to be winched down against its buoyancy) the lighter the better. In fact, as a really light centreboard is lowered it *reduces* the displacement of the hull and you are actually winching the boat out of the water.

Aluminium can be used for centreboards. A construction of webs and frames is covered with aluminium plates. A problem, though, is how to fix the plates to the frames from the outside. This caused difficulties for *Brittany Ferries GB* when the alloy plates split at the trailing edge. The result was a hollow board filled with water.

Wood can be used to produce a very light, strong board. This is currently achieved by laminating plywood (preferably birch 'aircraft' spec.), with epoxy resin, over a central box member. Fore and aft of the box, shaped frames are fixed and are covered with the plywood skin. This system is a direct copy of the construction of wooden aircraft wings of several years ago. It has the advantage of zero 'fatigue'.

Composites can also be used in board construction; there are three ways: either laying-up over a foam core (most common), laying up over a contoured honeycomb core (most expensive) or laid up in a mould and then the two skins joined together.

When designing *Colt Cars GB* we looked exhaustively at all the possibilities and chose laminated wood as the best material. I would have chosen a heat-cured carbon/Kevlar lay-up over contoured honeycomb core except that the core material came to the same price as a no.1 genoa! This particular board has a total volume of 11cu ft of which 8.5cu ft is underwater when fully lowered. This represents a buoyancy of 500lbs. The total board weight could have been as follows:

| Construction material | Weight |
|---|---|
| 1. Solid teak | 600lbs |
| 2. Solid pine | 450lbs |
| 3. Solid cedar | 340lbs |
| 4. Laminated birch plywood (hollow) | 190lbs |
| 5. Aluminium fabrication | 200lbs approx |
| 6. Composite over honeycomb core | 100lbs approx |

By choosing option 4 we achieved a net gain of 310lbs of buoyancy (500−190).

# 10

## *Rigging Systems*

For the purpose of this chapter – and in the interests of speed and efficiency at sea – I am disregarding unusual rigs such as ketches, schooners, masts in each hull and all other variants. This leaves us with a sloop rig, either masthead or fractional. Wing masts will be discussed later in Chapter 18.

A few rather unusual rigging systems have appeared on multihulls over the past few years. There is no doubt that trimaran and catamaran designers have lagged far behind their monohull contemporaries when it comes to rig design. It was not until 1980 that 'state-of-the-art' rigs appeared on the scene and even then they were in the minority. It is extraordinary how multihull designers were quite prepared to try some outrageous ideas in hull design and yet remained ultra conservative in the rig. Now, though, the realization has finally struck home that winning means having good windward ability in a multihull and for that a modern rig is essential.

There are obviously slight differences in staying a multihull mast. First a multihull's motion in a seaway demands greater stiffness or support fore and aft than on a similar sized monohull. Second, the beam of a multi provides a broader athwartships staying base that may be utilized if so desired. The mast section itself should be as stiff as possible in the fore and aft plane. Athwartships stiffness is not as critical owing to the facility of a broad, staying base. The compressive strength of the section should exceed the maximum total rigging load as the main hull lifts clear of the water at the start of a capsize. This load will depend on the staying base, as will be seen shortly.

## Masthead rig

*Fore and aft staying.* There need be no rig difference from a conventional monohull in the fore and aft plane. In the past, jumper struts have been used to stiffen certain mast panels; this is not necessary and is better done by more controllable running backstays. A typical rig is shown in fig. 55. The double running backstay, inner forestay and babystay hold the mast in column while the backstay holds the rig up and provides tension to the headstay. The backstay should be adjusted hydraulically so that this tension can be controlled. Mast bend can be effected by adjustment of the running backstays and inner and babystays. A

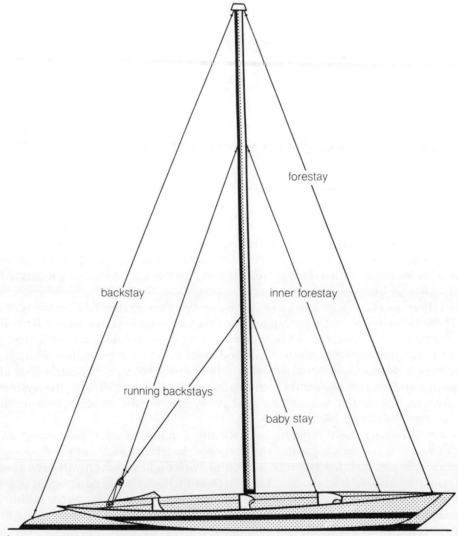

**Fig 55** *Fore and aft rigging. Masthead rig*

reasonable question to ask is whether to bend the mast at all. The theory is well-known: a mainsail is cut with a rounded luff which induces fullness in the mainsail when set on a straight mast. By easing the running backstays and taking in on the babystay and inner forestay the mast bows forward in the centre, takes up the sail's luff curve and flattens it off for stronger winds. While it is quite normal, and safe, to have a bendy rig offshore with a full crew, it is a fairly risky business short-handed. As nearly all offshore, multihull races are single- or two-handed a sensible compromise would be to limit the amount of bend, to, for example, 1in over 10ft of mast height. This amount can be controlled on the running backstays and main backstay without the need for continual adjustment on the inner forestays. For a race such as the OSTAR – to windward across the Atlantic single-handed – I would have the mast locked in the same shape with the runners tight (giving the minimum bend required to suit the mainsail) for the whole race. But when racing with a full crew the rig should be carefully tuned to give the fullest benefit the many varying wind strengths.

*Athwartships staying.* When designing the athwartships rig on a multihull the major decision is whether or not to use the full beam of the boat to support the rig. The argument for doing so is the benefit of the wider cap-shroud angle; the argument against is the difficulty of tuning the cap-shroud relative to the rest of the rigging (lowers and intermediates) which must stay close in to the mast to facilitate genoa sheeting. There are three basic possibilities with a masthead rig:
  1. All stays in near the mast (fig. 56).
  2. All rigging loads on the cap-shroud at maximum beam (fig. 57).
  3. A combination of cap-shroud at maximum beam and intermediates and lowers near the mast (fig. 58).
The first system has the advantage that the rig does not have to rely on crossbeam stiffness to remain tight. This set-up is particularly suited to catamarans where the bending load from cap-shrouds to the two hulls may be unacceptable over the length of the crossbeam. However it is essential to keep the rigging in as close to the mast as possible in order to get a narrow sheeting angle. There is a minimum limit to the shroud to mast angle which is 10 to 11 degrees and this, combined with spreader length, controls the staying base.

The second system requires the mast to be held rigidly in a straight line while all the support load is on the cap-shrouds to the floats. This is achieved by treating the lowers and intermediates as diamond shrouds – in other words they terminate at their lower end actually on the mast. This system has the advantage of no tuning problem between intermediates and cap-shrouds, but the big disadvantage of having 100 per cent of the sideways force of the sails held by one wire – a possible failure would mean certain dismasting.

A combination of the two is probably best, sheeting the genoas inside the cap-shrouds, which go out to the maximum beam, and outside the conventional intermediates. Having the cap-shroud in the correct tension relative to the intermediates is vital; this means it must be set up not only correctly but the crossbeam itself must not bend more than the absolute minimum ($\frac{1}{2}$in in 20ft) while under load. If the cap-shroud is too loose the masthead will fall off to leeward; too tight and it will cause the masthead tip to bend to windward, which would be very bad. A diamond shroud as shown in fig. 58 will help to reconcile the balance between the shrouds.

## Fractional rig

Because they allow smaller, more easily handled genoas, and they provide the facility for carrying enormous masthead genoas and spinnakers in light airs, fractional rigs are becoming more popular. In a breeze the extra mast height will contribute adversely to pitching, but then that applies to any high/low aspect ratio argument. In most cases it is a small price to pay for a large, efficient rig.

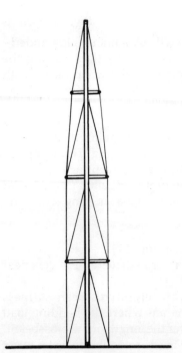

**Fig 56** *Alternative athwartships masthead rig. All stays in near mast*

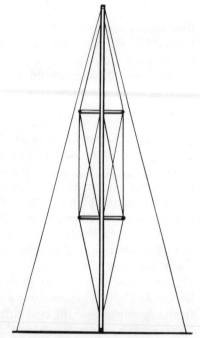

**Fig 57** *Alternative athwartships masthead rig. All rigging loads on the cap-shroud at maximum beam*

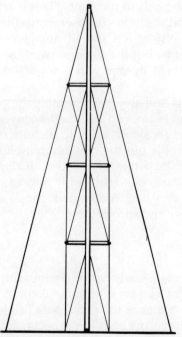

**Fig 58** *Alternative athwartships masthead rig. Combination of cap-shroud at maximum beam with intermediates and liners near the mast*

*Fore and aft staying.* Typical fore and aft staying for a fractional rig is shown in fig. 59. The double running backstay supports the mast and provides headstay tension. Whether or not the top section is supported by a combination diamond/jumper strut depends on the rigidity of the section used. The sideways component of this diamond may not be needed if the cap-shrouds are led to the maximum beam as will be seen in the next section. The fore and aft component will prevent the top section of the mast bending aft. This means that application of main backstay tension will have the effect of pulling the mast top section aft as a solid girder which will in turn contribute to headstay tension *and* induce bend in the lower section of the mast. As for mast bend, the same arguments used to describe the masthead rig apply. Again, the recommendation for short-handed offshore events is to limit and fix the amount of mast bend and to then most definitely leave it alone for all conditions.

*Athwartships staying.* The three basic options as described for masthead rig also apply to fractionals and they are shown in figs. 60, 61 and 62. The most interesting case is the third, combining maximum beam, cap-shroud, and conventional intermediate and lower staying. One of the problems of a fractional rig on a monohull is to get sufficient sideways support to the masthead and yet keep the cap-shrouds reasonably low down so they do not interfere with the set of the genoa on the wind. On a multihull we can attach the inner cap-shrouds to the mast just below the forestay attachment point and the outer cap-shrouds to the mast well *above* the forestay point. This provides a nice spread of support, clear genoa sheeting, and reduces the need for diamonds at the masthead. Also illustrated is the best way to combine minimum staying angles with a very narrow shroud base and hence tight genoa sheeting positions. The angles between the inner cap-shrouds and intermediate shroud, and the mast, are controlled by the length of the spreaders. A good lower shroud angle is achieved by crossing it over the other shrouds to a chain plate further outboard. This system provides good support and yet allows the foot of the genoa to be brought right in to the position shown. If masthead sails are to be used in light airs then the sideways support of masthead diamonds will be needed.

## Rigging Details

Having chosen the mast and rigging system one now has to decide between rod and wire rigging. The advantages of rod are a smaller diameter for the equivalent breaking strain of wire and much less stretch under load. The disadvantages are fatigue and susceptibility to badly aligned end terminals. Rod rigging will last longer if it is linked at the spreader ends rather than bent round them. Although it is hard to persuade a rigger to state catagorically that wire is more reliable – and there are undoubtedly cases of safely rigged, rod-stayed, ocean-going yachts – there is no doubt in my mind that rod not only has to be replaced often (about every 20,000 miles) but is is also more prone to failure, especially if it is allowed to go slack and snatch to leeward. Continual dismastings bear this out. However, the advantages of rod justify the risks.

*Running backstays.* The tails on the running backstays should be wire to minimize stretch, and the blocks, especially on a fractional rig, should be of large diameter and very strong. Their safe working load must be in excess of the maximum backstay load.

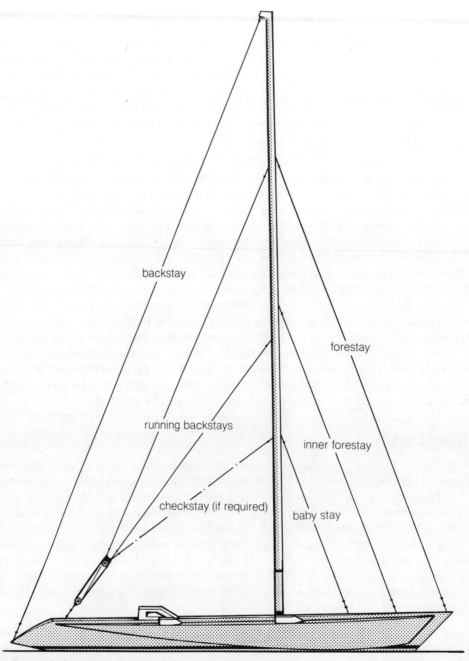

backstay

forestay

running backstays

inner forestay

checkstay (if required)

baby stay

**Fig 59** *Fore and aft rigging. Fractional rig*

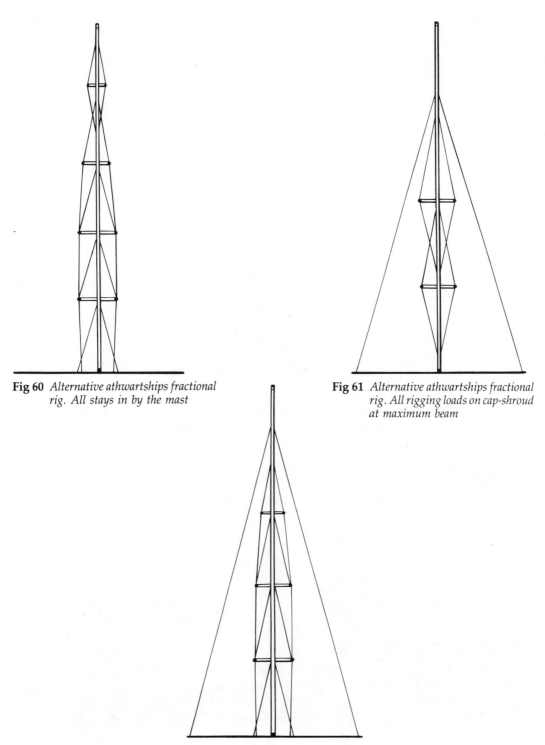

**Fig 60** *Alternative athwartships fractional rig. All stays in by the mast*

**Fig 61** *Alternative athwartships fractional rig. All rigging loads on cap-shroud at maximum beam*

**Fig 62** *Alternative athwartships fractional rig. Combination of above two*

*A modern fractional rig. Three spreaders, diamonds and an extra cap-shroud to the float. The latter allows the inner cap-shroud to be lower on the mast, facilitating genoa sheeting.*

216

*Forestay*. The type of forestay will depend on the genoa system to be used (see next chapter). If one intends to change jibs reguarly while sailing short-handed there is no more secure or reliable system than good, old-fashioned hanks. However, as the narrow bow of a trimaran is notoriously difficult to work on when sailing to windward a hanked system often means having to stop to change sails. Life is easier on a catamaran but in general, on any multihull over 45ft long, the advantages of a furler jib outway its disadvantages; sail changes are quicker and safer and although a partly furled jib does not set that well one would probably lose more mileage by stopping to change sail.

The type of furler to choose is a system which allows for ordinary changing of genoas, which one will certainly want to do sometimes. Two systems are shown in fig. 63. System A incorporates a conventional non-rotating wire forestay. Around the stay is an aluminium extrusion made up of 6ft sections which form a groove for the genoa luff. Each

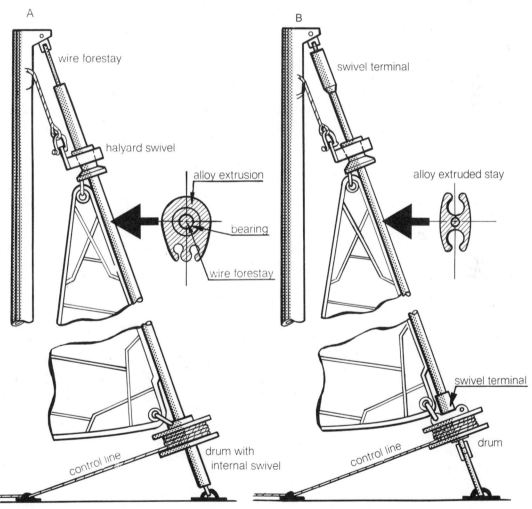

**Fig 63** *Two types of roller forestay*

*Multihulls Offshore*

section is joined to the next by an inner sleeve which acts as a bearing on to the stay. The whole sleeve thus formed is fixed to a drum at the base of the stay: as the drum is rotated (by a line to a winch) the sleeve rotates round the forestay, taking the jib luff with it and thereby furling the sail. The halyard is fixed, via a swivel round the extrusion, to the head of the sail. This allows the sail to be raised and lowered conventionally or raised and furled.

System B, which is much neater, is different in that the *whole forestay* is a rotating aluminium extrusion, achieved by pressure bearings on each end. The drum and halyard system work as above. The line from the drum needs to be quite strong and led through blocks aft to avoid chafe. In order to reduce stretch a wire with a rope tail is advisable.

Neither of the two systems is 100 per cent reliable and many short-handed yachtsmen have encountered problems with them. Yet, on balance, they are totally necessary.

*Halyards.* Halyards can be made effectively from stainless or galvanized wire. Galvanized wire is still best as it does not suffer from stranding (nasty on the hands) or work hardening.

The tendency inshore, especially for racing, is to reduce windage at the masthead by having three halyards emerging from sheaves in the mast; these halyyards double as spinnaker and genoa hoists. This is not suitable for long ocean races because of chafe. It is better to use the old system of two genoa halyards, which exit over sheaves in the mast, and two rope or wire spinnaker halyards which exit from the mast through double sheaves or some other chafe-free exit, and then pass over swivel blocks hung on cranes at the masthead. This traditional set-up is almost chafe free.

While discussing spinnaker halyards it should be remembered that if you use snap-shackles to fix the halyard to the head of the sail, the pin should be taped to prevent it shaking undone. An alternative is to tie the halyard to the sail with a bowline. Although it takes time it is infinitely more secure.

*Mast and boom fittings.* There are several possible failure areas needing attention. The attachment of the mainsail clew to the boom is a point often underbuilt by spar makers. As was observed in the 1981 TwoSTAR the clew slide pulled clean out of the boom on *Brittany Ferries GB*. In that case the fitting was simply not designed to take even half the leech load of a 1,000 sq ft mainsail.

The mainsheet attachment has to be strong, and unless the boom is a really stiff, deep section, it is a good idea to spread this load so that it adequately covers the forward movement of the leech load as the mainsail is reefed. This will avoid damage through the bending moment on the boom caused by the leech and sheet position.

The track or groove on the mast which takes the mainsail luff should have considerable local reinforcing at the point where the head of the sail sets when it is reefed. This is especially relevant when the track is an extrusion riveted on to the back of the mast. The sail should be tried with one, two, three and then four reefs and the head position marked in each case. Each point on the track should then be beefed up. If this is not done you can expect the track to peel off at a most critical or inconvenient moment – like mid-ocean or mid-race.

A boom vang or kicking strap is absolutely essential to limit the mainsail twist. One of the problems of a kicking strap is that it has to work at an angle which puts a large

218

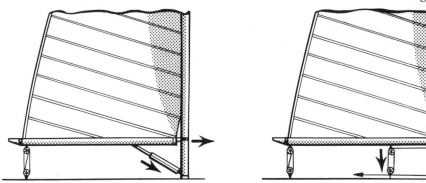

**Fig 64** *Alternative vanging systems*

compression load on the boom, mast attachment and hence into the mast itself. The problem is alleviated by raising the boom further above the deck but this may not be desirable. An alternative is a vang tackle to a circular track (see fig. 64). In general the spar manufacturer should be aware that multihulls place severe loads on their rigs. This should be borne in mind not only when selecting the mast extrusion, but also when designing and building all fittings.

# 11

## Sail Plan

Most monohulls race under the International Offshore Rule, which applies overall and handicap limits to the dimensions and shapes of all sails. Offshore multihulls, however, are nearly always raced under completely open rules. Although the multihull IOMR measures sail area, the rule is used for so few of the prestigious races that it is totally ignored at the design stage. Racing multihulls are all designed for line honours, possibly within a class (defined by overall length), and not to achieve as low a rating as possible as is the case with monohulls.

The result of this free hand is that the modern multihull is designed with as much sail area as can be

1. Handled in a short-handed race;
2. Afforded if there are budget limitations; and
3. Capable of maintaining a safe stability limit bearing in mind the weight and beam of the vessel.

There is also the consideration of sheer weight on a multihull and this restricts the sail wardrobe in size and number of individual sails. For instance a 60ft multi will carry only seven of the 20 or so sails carried by the same sized monohull.

In this chapter each sail is examined in turn, and we shall see how they combine to form an efficient, low weight, cost-effective wardrobe.

## Mainsail

In both open and IOMR racing there is no limit on mainsail shape, specifically; the sail can be made with a large roach (fig. 65). The IOMR only measures the triangular area, so any roach is 'free'. As this extra part of the sail will not stand up on its own or even with the help of short battens, full battens are necessary. These have to be particularly stiff (carbon fibre over honeycomb or kevlar/glass over wood core are common) as the tension of the mainsheet and vang try to pull the leech of the sail into a straight line. This would push unwanted fullness into the sail unless restricted by stiff battens. I sailed with a high roach mainsail on *Boatfile* in the 1980 OSTAR but the battens were too flexible. This resulted in too full a main if I sheeted it in correctly, and a flat one only if it was not sheeted right in, but then I had to suffer an undesirable amount of twist.

*Fully battened main with medium roach, combined with a very small jib on* Charante Maritime.

A subsidiary advantage to full-length battens is that the mainsail doesn't flog when it's eased in a breeze; instead, it takes up a wavy S-bend profile that is easier on the nerves and there is less likelihood of damage during reefing.

When using full-length battens it must be remembered to ensure that the aft end of the batten remains inside the leech, otherwise it forms a sure snag for halyards, spinnakers, running backstays etc.

There have always been two schools of thought on whether a fully battened low-aspect main is better than a high-aspect triangular sail of similar area. Certainly, for a given mast height a fully battened main gives more area, or, for a given area it keeps the centre of effort as low as possible. Still, the higher aspect medium roach sail is probably more efficient. The answer is perhaps to go for a fully battened main with a reasonable roach but not too extreme.

The major disadvantage of the current crop of extreme roach mainsails on masthead rigs is that one has to partly lower them each time the boat tacks in order to clear the backstay.

221

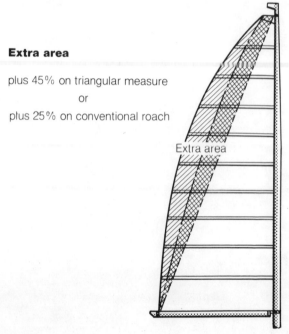

**Extra area**

plus 45% on triangular measure

or

plus 25% on conventional roach

Extra area

**Fig 65** *A high roach mainsail*

On fractional boats the problem is how to avoid breaking the battens on the running backstays – when gybing!

## Jibs

As mentioned earlier the sail wardrobe must be kept as light and as easily handled as possible. Three sails will furnish this end; a specialist, light-weather genoa, a specialist, heavy-weather jib and a furler genoa for all other conditions.

*Furler genoa.* Such limitations as there are in the design and use of a furling genoa may prejudice a multihull owner against them. My memories of the 1978 Round the Island Race ensure this will never happen to me. We lost a full 20 minutes in a two-hour beat through our ineptitude on the foredeck of a pitching trimaran. Our crew had experience of foredeck work in the most severe conditions but on this occasion we were all beaten by our inability to work quickly and efficiently. The time lost would have been the same if we had stopped completely for the two headsail changes. While this pantomime was going on Phil Weld was powering past us on *Rogue Wave*, quietly and efficiently furling his genoa in and out to suit the conditions.

In this instance, *Rogue Wave* could have been beaten only if our speed loss due to the badly set, partly furled jib had been 17 per cent (ten minutes in an hour), in other words if *GB IV* could beat to windward at 9 knots *Rogue Wave*'s speed would have to be only 7½ knots for us to get the better of her. Alternatively, if we assume she moved at the same

*A low-cut furler genoa combined with a recessed furler drum gives an efficient deck sweeping foot. The car and track for fore and aft sheet lead adjustment can be seen.*

speed she would be able to sail 9 degrees freer and she would *still* be able to pass us as we changed sails!

The above example was an extreme case but it shows the viability of the furler set up in the context of winning a race.

Even if other jibs are carried to augment a furler genoa, it is necessary to ensure that this sail can be used at any stage of furling, including when it has been reduced down to the minutest, storm jib size. To this end it must not be too large – about no. 2 genoa size; also, it should be cut fairly flat which will improve its shape when furled. If the sail is too full when partly furled it will have a very tight leech and luff and a baggy body. A fat bolt rope, tapered at top and bottom, sewn just inside the luff of the sail will improve the part furled shape considerably. Also the leech and foot line must be adjustable at the clew, not at the tack as has become fashionable.

Until recently furling genoas have been cut with a high clew (see fig. 66). The main reason for this was the limited, or complete lack of, need to move the sheet lead forward as the sail furls. The sheet lead of any genoa is found by taking an imaginary line from the mid-luff point of the sail, down through the clew and continuing on till it reaches the track. As the sail furls the clew moves towards the forestay along a line perpendicular to the stay. The sheet must be kept parallel to its original lead. Therefore a sail with equal foot and leech dimensions will need no sheet lead adjustments. Unfortunately, such a shape is

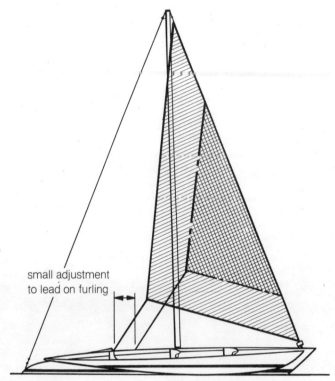

small adjustment
to lead on furling

**Fig 66** *High-cut furler genoa*

not very efficient and also lacks area. A conventional, low-cut genoa will suit better (see fig. 67).

The advantage of a conventional genoa shape is its much higher efficiency to windward, which can be further improved by lowering the foot close to the deck. This was accomplished on *Colt Cars GB* by neatly recessing the furler drum into a well in the foredeck. As this cut of sail will need considerable sheet adjustment it is a good idea to incorporate a fore and aft track for the sheet fairlead so that quick and accurate adjustment can be made.

Any furler jib must be made from a cloth sufficiently heavy to be used as a storm sail – even though this means the full sail is a cloth weight heavier than is normally considered ideal for light winds.

*Light genoa.* An excellent strategy is to combine a furler genoa with a light genoa. Because sail changing is relatively easy in light airs and on flat water, it makes sense to change to a light genoa when the wind drops below 16 knots apparent. This sail should be hoisted up the forestay in the conventional way if the rig is masthead or, if the mast is fractionally rigged, an option could be to hoist the sail to the masthead on a special halyard, and once it is setting loose-luffed, the furler can be rolled up out of the way. In the latter case the sail can only be used in up to 10 knots apparent wind. Above this strength the luff will fall off to leeward, and maybe the masthead with it.

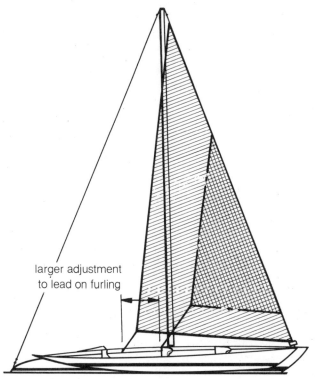

larger adjustment
to lead on furling

**Fig 67** *Low-cut furler genoa*

The light genoa should be cut with a low deck-sweeping foot and to a size of approximately 150 per cent J (J = base of foretriangle). Although, unlike in the IOR, there is no maximum limit to genoa size, any genoa larger than 150 per cent J will be useless in very light airs as the trailing edge will collapse and destroy what little air flow there might have been. The cloth used should be the latest from the sailmaker's art; a laminate of plastic film and dacron, for example.

*Solent jib.* The name Solent jib has been given to the full-luff, short-foot, high-aspect ratio jibs that have recently become mandatory on all racing monohulls. The great value of this sail is the way in which it develops tremendous power from its luff length, and yet its area is small enough to allow the sail to be carried in winds of up to 30 knots and more. It is also easy to tack which is not so important offshore but a good point all the same.

Adding this jib to the wardrobe provides an alternative to the partly furled genoa but is only effective if there is crew available to make the change when the wind rises to 25 knots. Ideally, because of the difficulties of changing, it would be preferable to know that the wind was going to stay between 25 and 35 knots for some time. A particular occasion was the start of the 1981 Two-handed Transatlantic Race when the wind blew 30 knots at the start and was forecast to remain that strength for several days. The decision to carry a Solent jib would have been correct.

The sail should be made from a heavy cloth, probably with a reinforced leech or indeed

100% 2 ply. The low stretch characteristics of Kevlar cloth – used for this sail by racing monohulls – are an advantage, rather outweighed on long races, by handling difficulties and possible failure after continual use. Normal dacron is safer for offshore racing.

*Staysails.* The staysail is a particularly useful sail on a trimaran – although no longer used for its initial function, that of the second half of a cutter rig. Cutter rigs were used on multihulls for two reasons that are now both totally out of date. First it was thought that multihulls couldn't point well to windward so an efficient offwind cutter rig was adopted and, second, as the furler had to be cut with a high clew to avoid sheet lead problems it conveniently formed the jib top, or yankee, part of the cutter combination. However we now know that a multihull can and must point well and to this end a low cut genoa must be used.

A staysail can of course be used to good effect slightly free of the wind but it really earns its keep as a storm sail. An almost fully rolled furler also makes an effective storm jib but, as I explained in the section on centreboards in Chapter 6, it has the effect of putting the centre of effort too far forward which may raise lee helm. Using the staysail on its own stay as the storm jib will effectively counteract this tendency.

There are two possible staysail arrangements. The first is to use a full sized staysail in conjunction with a genoa for close reaching and another smaller, tougher sail as a storm jib; the alternative is to have the large staysail designed so that it can be reefed down into storm jib size.

In both instances see that the staysail gear is very strong indeed. This will be the key sail for taking the multihull to windward in storm conditions.

Ideally the tack of the staysail should be 30 per cent of the distance down the foredeck from the headstay to the mast. This is not possible in a catamaran as the tack on any sail has to be on a heavily reinforced crossbeam; in this case the staysail has to be tacked down by the forestay and is not used in conjunction with a genoa but only by itself as a storm jib.

*Spinnakers.* Conventional spinnakers form an essential part of any racing multihull's wardrobe. A number of compromise reaching sails, resembling what are now termed cruising spinnakers, have been tried. The reasoning behind these asymmetrical sails was that they could be tacked down to the bow of the windward float and would set around the forestay like a gigantic reaching genoa. The idea is reasonable but, in practice, it makes no sense, for the following reasons:

1. If the apparent wind is on or forward of the beam the sail cannot be set as it would have to sheet inside the forestay in order to get the right angle of attack on the luff.
2. If the apparent wind is aft of the beam a normal spinnaker, with much greater area, will set perfectly.

There used to be a feeling that multihulls didn't need real spinnakers at all; because of their super high speeds tacking down wind was thought to be the way to go. This misconception arose with the inflated ideas the multihull owners had of their boats actual speed, and the owners' inability to set spinnakers except when the wind was near the stern. It is now deemed necessary to carry a spinnaker whenever the apparent wind is 60 degrees or more on the bow. Admittedly, the true wind will need to be well aft of the beam for this angle to be reached, but even so this is quite a high proportion of the time. For example, if one tacks down wind, even gybing through 70 to 80 degrees, a spinnaker should still be carried. A fractional rig permits a light spinnaker to be carried from the masthead in very light airs. The sail should not be too full or large – if it is, it won't set in a near calm.

Two spinnakers are required: a light radial head for light airs and running and a flatter (but not too flat) medium weight, tri-radial for heavier airs and reaching. Both sails should be equipped with a spi-squeezer system if short-handed sailing is anticipated. Spinnaker setting is discussed in the next chapter so it is sufficient to say here that no spinnaker poles and attendant fittings are required.

The sail plans shown in figs. 68 and 69 summarize two possible sail wardrobes.

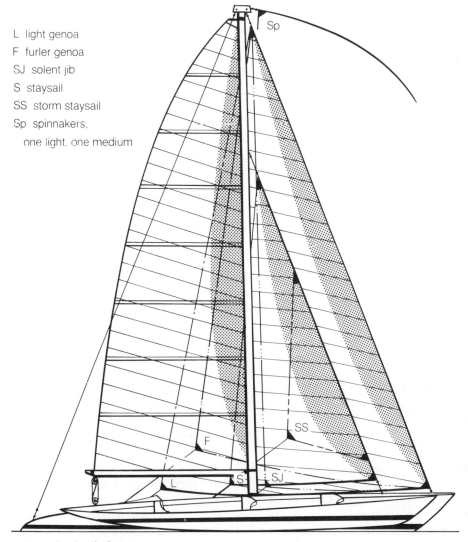

L  light genoa
F  furler genoa
SJ  solent jib
S  staysail
SS  storm staysail
Sp  spinnakers,
    one light, one medium

**Fig 68** *A masthead sail plan*

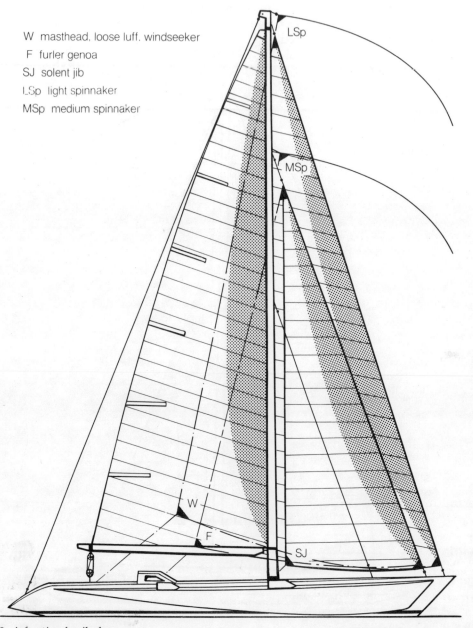

W masthead, loose luff, windseeker
F furler genoa
SJ solent jib
LSp light spinnaker
MSp medium spinnaker

**Fig 69** *A fractional sail plan*

# 12

## Sail Handling and Setting

### Mainsail

*Shape control.* Fullness is built into a mainsail in two ways, by panel contouring and luff round. The horizontal panels forming the sail are individually shaped by tapering slightly towards the ends, so that, when sown together, a bag or fullness is induced into the sail. Once the panels have been sown together the sail luff is cut with a convex curve.

If the mainsail is set on a straight mast with little or no tension on the luff, leech or foot, it will set with all the fullness that has been cut into it. Tensioning the edges of the sail will have the effect of flattening it off by drawing the fullness out of the centre. The luff is tensioned by tightening either the halyard or cunningham control – the latter is easier as the halyard has to pull against gravity, luff, and leech loads. The foot is controlled by the clew outhaul which should be hooked up to a very powerful adjustment system, such as the hydraulic cylinder in the boom. The flattening reef system common on racing monohulls is not needed on a multihull as there is no, 'black band' limitation as on IOR boats. Instead the clew can be pulled out as far as required to produce the desired foot tension. The leech is tensioned by the mainsheet and/or vang gear.

Care must be taken to keep the leech and luff tension in reasonable balance. Too much luff and the fullness moves forward in the sail, thereby destroying pointing ability; too much leech and the fullness moves aft, where it tries to pull the yacht backwards. Ideally, the point of maximum fullness should be 45 degrees back from the luff.

The mainsail fullness caused by the cut of the luff can only be reduced by mast bend. As pointed out earlier it is not always desirable or safe to play with a bendy spar offshore. If the intention is to keep the mast straight, or nearly so, the mainsail should be cut accordingly.

To whatever degree one wishes to tune up the mainsail, there is always a good point to remember. If it looks right it probably is right.

*Setting.* There is no major difference between monohulls and multihulls regarding sail set. One aspect, though, which should be given considerable regard is control of the twist. Obviously the object, is to have the luff in line with the apparent wind all the way from tack to head. Two factors effect the direction of the apparent wind:

229

*Sailhandling made easy on* Colt Cars GB *by leading lines to the cockpit. The group forward are mainsheet, reefing lines, jib furler line and centreboard controls. Those led by way of the crossbeams are spinnaker controls and genoa car control.*

1. The jib has more of a backing effect lower down – especially on a fractional rig; and
2. The true wind is stronger higher up.

Both these phenomena have the effect of increasing the apparent wind angle towards the top of the mainsail, indicating the need for a small amount of twist (see fig. 70). Mainsheet tension close-hauled and vang or kicking-strap tension free of the wind should be used carefully to allow an accurate degree of twist.

Boom preventers are an essential control offshore on any kind of yacht. On a multihull they are easy to rig out to the floats and back to the cockpit.

*Reefing.* Slab reefing is by far the most superior system to use on any yacht and multis are no exception. With a fully battened main it is the only option. Once reefing becomes necessary it will be greatly speeded up by leading the reefing leech line back to a powerful winch near the mainsheet control (fig. 71). As a crewman must go forward to hook in the luff it is not so necessary to have the halyard led aft – in fact it can be a hindrance.

Below is the reefing sequence for a fully battened mainsail:

1. The leech line is already led (fig. 71). *Leave* the main sheeted *in.*
2. Ease the halyard and pull down on the luff by hand till the eye is near the boom.

230

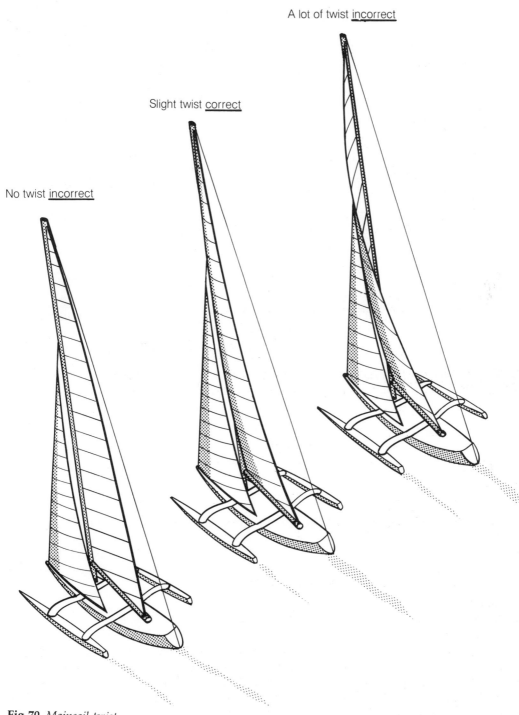

A lot of twist <u>incorrect</u>

Slight twist <u>correct</u>

No twist <u>incorrect</u>

**Fig 70** *Mainsail twist*

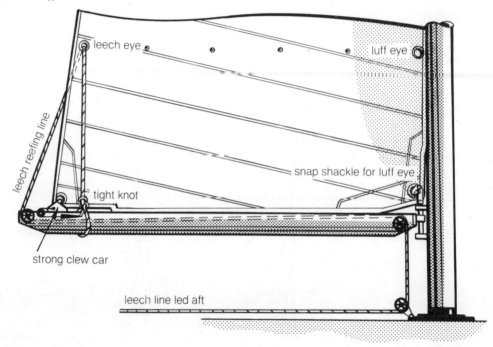

**Fig 71** *Slab reefing set-up*

3. Make the halyard fast and secure the luff eye.

4. Winch up maximum halyard tension.

5. Take in the leech line and ease the mainsheet at the same time. Don't over ease the sheet too soon or it will flog unnecessarily.

6. Once the clew is down *tight* to the boom resheet the main.

## Genoas and staysails

Assuming we have the sail wardrobe discussed in the previous chapter we have at our disposal the following:

    light genoa
    furler genoa
    solent jib
    staysail
    storm staysail

The basic situation when short-handed is to rely on the furler genoa from zero knots to storm conditions – not exactly ideal at the higher and lower ends of the wind scale. A stage better would be to set the storm staysail when the wind reached 40–50 knots and roll up the furler completely. Despite our good intentions on *Brittany Ferries GB* we found that the time lost changing to the light genoa was unacceptable owing to a problem we had with the furler forestay, hence we just used the furler and staysail. On *Colt Cars GB* we used the furler jib for the whole race round Britain, only using the other jibs when fully crewed.

Ideally, of course, the whole wardrobe should be employed. The sequence with full crew for close-hauled work could be:

0–16 knots of wind  light genoa
16–24 knots of wind  furler
24–34 knots of wind  solent jib
34–42 knots of wind  staysail, no jib
42–60 knots of wind  storm staysail, no jib

*Furler genoa trim.* The fore and aft sheet lead position for any jib is most conveniently found ashore by taking a line from mid-luff to clew, and marking this angle on the sail. This is especially helpful with the furler when the lead is continually changing. The best method of lead control is a traveller on a fore and aft track; the traveller should be free to run, especially under load, and can be controlled by a line back to the cockpit. (Releasing the line takes the traveller aft, winching in the line brings it forward, see fig. 72). Without the track, adjusting the lead on a furler is time consuming, and dangerous with the genoa sheet flogging nearby.

The athwartship position of the sheet lead is a much more complex problem and depends very much on the design of the rig, especially on the position of the cap-shrouds. With a multihull there is the advantage of the broad beam which allows the lead to be barberhauled outboard in freer winds. Close-hauled it is imperative to keep the sheet lead very narrow, owing to a multihull's good windward speed the apparent wind is drawn so far ahead of the true wind that the boat must point very high to achieve an acceptable

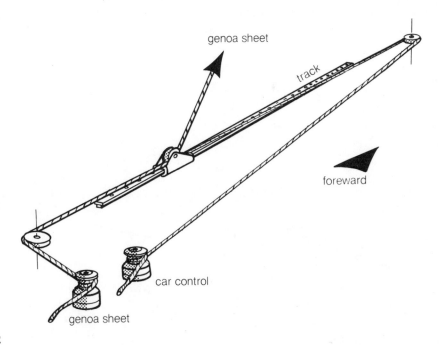

**Fig 72**

tacking angle (see next chapter, Racing performance). Or looking at it another way, because of a multihull's low resistance to forward motion it may be sailed at a closer angle to the wind and still maintain a forward component of drive from the sails sufficient to make good progress. Of course to do this the sails must be sheeted accordingly.

*Brittany Ferries* was designed with a genoa sheeting angle of 10 degrees. This was later reduced to 7.5 degrees and the windward performance was improved enormously. Unfortunately, because the rig had not been designed for such narrow angles, the genoa was always tight up against the cap-shrouds.

The genoa track position should be arranged so that the aft end makes an angle of 7.5 degrees at the bow and at the forward end 9 degrees. Alternatively two tracks on each side can be fitted to achieve these angles. The cap-shrouds should then be brought in close enough to the mast to facilitate this sheet lead. (See fig. 73.)

There should be a line permanently rigged through a block on the float (or hull on a cat) at its mid-point to use as a barberhauler, but care must be taken not to overdo it or the sail will end up too flat (see fig. 74).

*Furling.* The procedure for rolling up the furler is as follows:
1. Ease the leeward sheet until the sail starts to flog;
2. Winch in on the drum line;
3. Ease more sheet if it starts to take any weight;
4. Winch in more drum until the sail is the required size; and
5. Move the sheetlead forward and sheet in again.

Stage 5 is no problem if the lead is on a track. If not it is inadvisable to alter the lead while the sail is flogging. Instead it will be necessary to sheet back to the old position, take a bight of the windward sheet round to leeward and make it up on a winch, then alter the lead. Unfurling is done in the same way. In light airs the sheet will have to be pulled in to encourage the sail to unwind.

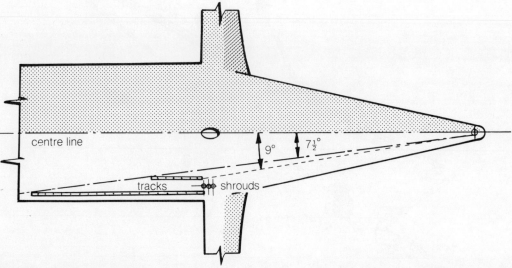

**Fig 73** *Genoa sheeting angles*

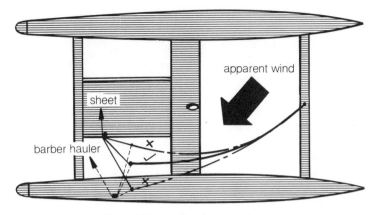

apparent wind

sheet

barber hauler

x

✓

x

The middle position is correct

**Fig 74** *Barber hauling the sheet outboard off the wind*

*Narrow sheeting angle on* Colt Cars GB. *A narrow shroud base with the caps and intermediates crossing* inside *the lower facilitates this.*

## Spinnakers

The greatest innovation in recent times for short-handed racing is the spinnaker squeezer. The spinnaker is stowed, hoisted and lowered wrapped in a cloth tube almost the same length as the spinnaker. In case the reader has never used one I will explain its intricacies. At the bottom of the tube (1 oz spinnaker cloth) is a fibreglass, bell-shaped cylinder with a line tied to it. This line goes up inside the tube, out through a fitting at the head and down outside in a long loop back to the bell (see fig. 75). The line is pulled at deck level to raise and lower the bell which unstops and restops the spinnaker. The tube concertinas the squeezer above the head of the sail when it is set.

Before hoisting the spinnaker check that the guys and sheets are correctly led. Because of the wide beam good use can be made of a set-up that will preclude the need for a pole. On each side three lines are joined in the normal way to a snap-shackle; the first (the sheet) is led to the aft end of the float (or cat hull), the second (the guy) is led to the bow of the float, and the third (the foreguy) is led to the base of the forestay. Thus weight on the guy will hold the windward clew forward and out just as a pole would (see fig. 76).

*Hoisting the spinnaker.*
1. Lay out the spinnaker in its squeezer on the foredeck ensuring there are no twists in the tube;
2. Slide the bell about 10ft up the sail; take one clew to leeward of the genoa and up around the forestay from leeward to windward;
3. Attach the windward snap-shackle with its three lines to the clew by the forestay;
4. Attach the leeward snap-shackle with its three lines to the other clew, leaving a lot of slack in the foreguy.
5. Take the halyard to leeward of the genoa, in under its foot and attach it to the head of the sail; and
6. Make sure the endless line is not tangled. A good tip here is to untie the bottom of the line from the bell when the sail is stowed below. Then at the present stage of the operation flake out the line and retie it.
7. Hoist, making sure you don't lose hold of the line. The position is now as shown in fig. 75.
8. Tension the windward guy to hold the windward clew just to windward of the forestay.
9. Hoist the bell by the endless line and sheet in (if crew numbers allow) at the same time.
10. Having adjusted the sheets and guys for the best set make up the endless line to a point at the base of the mast.
11. Lower or furl the headsail.

*Spinnaker trim.* The sail is setting with a guy, foreguy and sheet on each side as shown in fig. 76. With the apparent wind on the beam, set the windward clew with weight on the foreguy and the guy; this will stop it rising, and will hold it off the forestay. The leeward side is controlled by the sheet only.

For a wind on the quarter the windward clew should be set with weight on the foreguy,

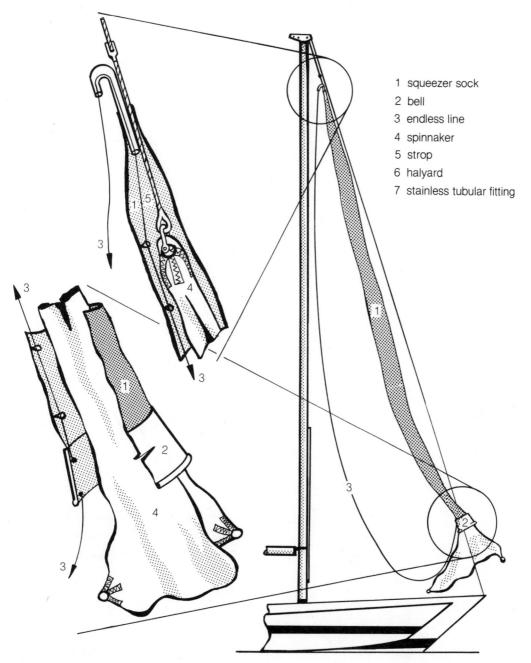

1 squeezer sock
2 bell
3 endless line
4 spinnaker
5 strop
6 halyard
7 stainless tubular fitting

**Fig 75** *Spinnaker squeezer system*

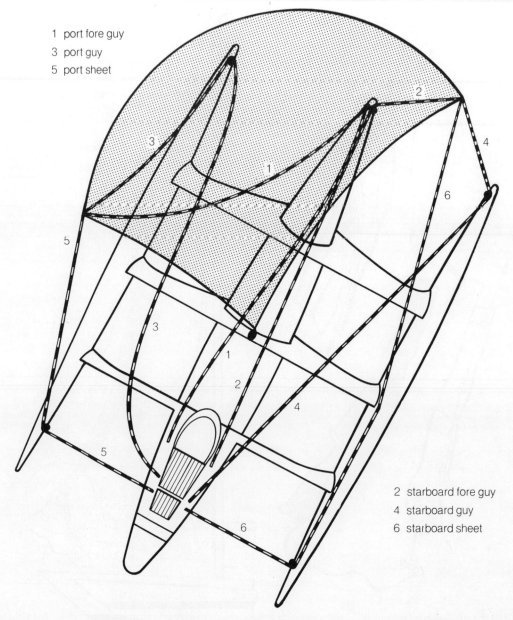

1  port fore guy
3  port guy
5  port sheet

2  starboard fore guy
4  starboard guy
6  starboard sheet

With the wind on the starboard quarter weight will be on 2, 4, 6 and 5

**Fig 76** *Spinnaker controls*

*A spinnaker hoisted in its squeezer ready for breaking out.*

*The spinnaker set with three lines on each clew.*

guy and sheet. This will hold it out from the centreline and well forward. By taking more weight on the sheet and less on the guy the clew will be allowed to lift nicely. Again, the leeward side is controlled by the sheet.

For dead running the sail is set using the sheets on either side and, in a breeze, a bit of weight on the guys to prevent the sail rising too high.

On a smaller multihull the foreguy is not needed. If necessary the windward clew can be held down for a reach by taking a bight of the windward (lazy) sheet straight down to a cleat near the base of the forestay.

In very light winds the spinnaker is obviously reluctant to fill. When it collapses the windward clew can drift in towards the mast, from where it is unlikely to rise; tension on the guy will hold the clew out to windward but overdoing it will stop it rising when the sail fills. In these conditions fix the staysail halyard onto the windward clew to hold it up.

*Lowering the spinnaker.*
1. Unfurl or hoist the headsail.
2. Having made sure that the endless line is free, ease the windward guy and sheet so that the windward clew is near the forestay.
3. Let go the leeward sheet.
3. Standing up in the bow, haul down the bell.
4. When the bell is within a few feet of the foot of the sail, release both clews from their controls.
5. Haul down the bell completely to the foot of the sail and on to the foredeck.
6. Lower the halyard and gather in the tube.
The jib can be hoisted after step 6. This makes it easier to haul down the bell but means sailing bare-headed for a while.

*Gybing.* Gybing the spinnaker on a multihull is simplicity itself. Because of the absence of a pole the procedure is this:
1. Bear away on to a dead run.
2. Ease the leeward sheet and take in the windward sheet.
3. With little or no weight on the guys gybe the mainsail.
4. Ease the new windward sheet, taking some weight on the windward guy and foreguy.
5. Let off the leeward guy and foreguy. Sheet in.
6. Alter course on the new gybe as required.

# 13

## *Racing Performance*

Multihulls, even more so than monohulls, have the ability to go faster on some points of sailing than others. Will it pay, navigation considerations aside, to sail a few degrees away from the planned course if, as a result, the boat obtains a greater speed? This will nearly always be the case when the required course is dead downwind, but also to a lesser extent on reaching and, very occasionally, to windward.

### VMG to windward

Velocity made good is the term used to describe a yacht's speed made good towards its objective. To windward VMG indicates how quickly the vessel is making ground into the eye of the wind. The age-old beating dilemma – sail free and fast or slow and close – is simple to analyse. The objective is to maximize the VMG. Fig. 77 shows an example of two multihulls racing from A to B; one sails at 45 degrees to the true wind at 8 knots, arriving at B after tacking through 90 degrees. The second sails at 60 degrees to the true wind at 11 knots, believing the greater speed will pay. Either by calculation or geometry it can be seen that the first yacht's VMG is 2.8 per cent higher.

The formula VMG =

yacht speed $x$ cosine (angle sailed to the true wind) produces table 11:

### TABLE 11
### *BOAT SPEED AND ANGLE TO TRUE WIND GIVES VMG*

| Speed | 3 | 4 | 5 | 6 | 7 | 8 | 9 | 10 | 11 | 12 | 13 | 14 | 15 |
|---|---|---|---|---|---|---|---|---|---|---|---|---|---|
| **Angle to true wind**<br>(½ tacking angle) | | | | | | | **VMG** | | | | | | |
| **35°** | 2·5 | 3·3 | 4·1 | 4·9 | 5·7 | 6·5 | 7·4 | 8·2 | | | | | |
| **40°** | 2·3 | 3·1 | 3·8 | 4·6 | 5·4 | 6·1 | 6·9 | 7·7 | 8·4 | | | | |
| **45°** | 2·1 | 2·8 | 3·5 | 4·2 | 4·9 | 5·7 | 6·4 | 7·1 | 7·8 | 8·5 | | | |
| **50°** | 1·9 | 2·6 | 3·2 | 3·9 | 4·5 | 5·1 | 5·8 | 6·4 | 7·1 | 7·7 | 8·4 | | |
| **55°** | 1·7 | 2·3 | 2·9 | 3·4 | 4·0 | 4·6 | 5·2 | 5·7 | 6·3 | 6·9 | 7·5 | 8·0 | |
| **60°** | 1·5 | 2·0 | 2·5 | 3·0 | 3·5 | 4·0 | 4·5 | 5·0 | 5·5 | 6·0 | 6·5 | 7·0 | 7·5 |

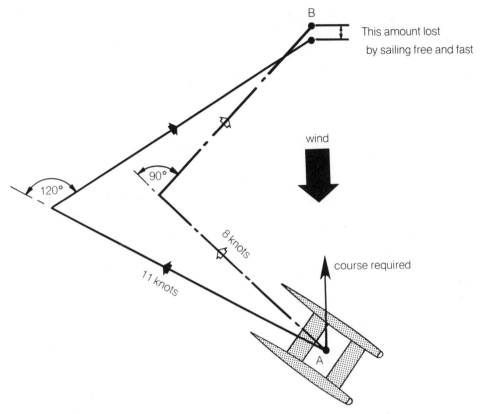

**Fig 77** *VMG upwind*

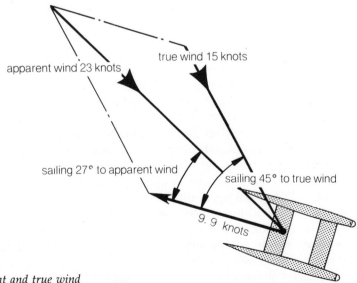

**Fig 78** *Apparent and true wind*

A quick glance at the table may convince one that sailing free and fast is always going to pay. It may look as though the extra speed required can easily be obtained by freeing off the number of degrees indicated. This is *not* so because the wind angles in the table are *true*. Bearing away from 45 degrees to 60 degrees true will only alter the apparent wind 7 degrees or so, not enough to give the increase in speed sufficient to make it pay off. Fig. 78 shows the vector created by the boat's forward motion and the true wind, forming the apparent wind.

Table 12 demonstrates the possible combinations of boat speed and angle required to arrive at a very high VMG of 7 knots in 15 knots of true wind.

**TABLE 12**

*COMBINATIONS OF BOAT SPEED AND WIND ANGLE TO ACHIEVE 7 KNOTS VMG IN 15 KNOTS OF TRUE WIND*

| Sailing at this angle to the true wind | One would need this boat speed | Which would give this angle to the apparent wind |
|---|---|---|
| 35° | 8·5 knots | 22·5° |
| 40° | 9·1 | 25·4° |
| 45° | 9·9 | 27·2° |
| 50° | 10·9 | 29·5° |
| 55° | 12·2 | 30·7° |
| 60° | 14·0 | 31·0° |

An interesting, and quite realistic, result of studying VMG is to observe an unwary multihull sailor. It's a fine day with 15 knots of breeze and a flat sea; with full sail up, he sees he is making 7 knots at 31 degrees to the apparent wind and the wind gauge registers 20 knots. He perhaps doesn't realize that he is sailing 45 degrees to the true wind (tacking through 90 degrees) and his VMG is 5 knots. Looking for improvement he frees off to 40° apparent and his boat speed goes to 10 knots. (He is now sailing at 65 degrees to the true wind and his VMG is down to 4¼ knots). Mistakenly encouraged, he tries 45 degrees apparent and makes 13 knots; great speed, not too free, this is the way to take a multihull to windward! Of course, speed is his enemy and he's actually sailing at 83 degrees to the true wind, with a VMG of 1½ knots and getting nowhere.

Because a multihull draws the wind so far ahead steering to windward is difficult, especially at night when the true wind direction cannot be observed by eye. The best approach on such occasions is to sail on boat speed; if it drops below what you have come to expect for given conditions, bear away a little and, more importantly, if the speed goes up, sail closer. In very light airs, in order to make any windward progress at all, it is necessary to pinch up to 20 degrees apparent. For example 34 degrees apparent in 2 knots of wind with a boat speed of 3 knots, would mean tacking through 180 degrees!

While on the subject of tacking I will explain the most efficient way of accomplishing this manoeuvre without bother. A multihull, being a good deal lighter than a monohull, will not carry its way once drive is lost. A tack must be started from a close-hauled course; trying to tack from a reach will most likely result in complete loss of speed by the time the boat is head to wind and then she will stop. The aim is to get the boat round slowing it down as little as possible. In flat water don't put the helm right over but rather start with 10 degrees or so, increasing it to hard over as the vessel passes through the eye of the wind. Don't back the jib as this will stop the boat in its tracks; instead, ensure that the mainsail is right in, and then let the jib fly. On the new tack ease the mainsail while the jib is sheeted in as this will help the boat bear away. If all way has been lost before the tack is completed back the jib as a last resort. In waves it is better to use full helm immediately thus hoping for a quick tack. The breaking effect of the helm is less than that of hitting a wave while head to wind.

## VMG downwind

Off the wind it is nearly always better to make a series of broad reaches instead of keeping the wind dead astern. Fig. 79 shows two multihulls racing from A to B: The course is to

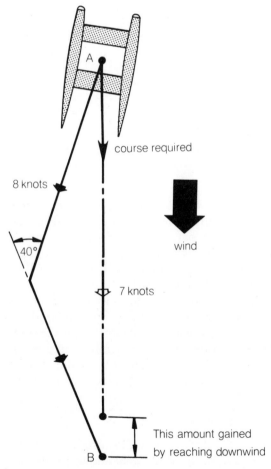

**Fig 79** *VMG downwind*

leeward; one has the wind right aft and makes 7 knots along the shortest route. The other reaches a substantial 20 degrees off course, gybes through 40 degrees and reaches back to the finish. Her speed is 8 knots. She finishes first as the extra distance covered is made up for by the 1 knot speed advantage. One factor particularly helpful to the reaching boat is the fact that he has brought the apparent wind direction more than 30 degrees off the stern, which will have improved the efficiency of his rig enormously.

The formula VMG = yacht speed x cos (angle off course) gives a table which will tell at a glance the best tactics to adopt (see table 13). It is interesting to note that a deviation of up to 20 degrees will always be a better bet if there is any noticeable increase in speed.

TABLE 13

## SPEEDS REQUIRED WHEN TACKING DOWNWIND

| | Speeds obtainable on course | | | | | | | | | | | | |
|---|---|---|---|---|---|---|---|---|---|---|---|---|---|
| | 3 | 4 | 5 | 6 | 7 | 8 | 9 | 10 | 11 | 12 | 13 | 14 | 15 |
| **Angle off course** ($\frac{1}{2}$ **gybing angle**) | **At angles off course-speeds required to equal above** | | | | | | | | | | | | |
| 10° | 3·0 | 4·1 | 5·1 | 6·1 | 7·1 | 8·1 | 9·1 | 10·2 | 11·2 | 12·2 | 13·2 | 14·2 | 15·2 |
| 15° | 3·1 | 4·1 | 5·2 | 6·2 | 7·2 | 8·3 | 9·3 | 10·4 | 11·3 | 12·4 | 13·5 | 14·5 | 15·5 |
| 20° | 3·2 | 4·3 | 5·3 | 6·4 | 7·4 | 8·5 | 9·6 | 10·6 | 11·7 | 12·8 | 13·8 | 14·9 | 16·0 |
| 25° | 3·3 | 4·4 | 5·5 | 6·6 | 7·7 | 8·8 | 9·9 | 11·0 | 12·1 | 13·2 | 14·3 | 15·4 | 16·6 |
| 30° | 3·5 | 4·6 | 5·8 | 6·9 | 8·1 | 9·2 | 10·4 | 11·5 | 12·7 | 13·9 | 15·0 | 16·2 | 17·3 |
| 35° | 3·7 | 4·9 | 6·1 | 7·3 | 8·5 | 9·8 | 11·0 | 12·2 | 13·4 | 14·6 | 15·9 | 17·1 | 18·3 |
| 40° | 3·9 | 5·2 | 6·5 | 7·8 | 9·1 | 10·4 | 11·7 | 13·0 | 14·4 | 15·7 | 17·0 | 18·3 | 19·6 |
| 45° | 4·2 | 5·7 | 7·1 | 8·5 | 9·9 | 11·3 | 12·7 | 14·1 | 15·6 | 17·0 | 18·4 | 19·8 | 21·6 |

On *Colt Cars GB* the lighter the wind the more it pays to reach downwind. In a true wind of 7 knots we may make 4 knots on a dead run. By reaching 45 degrees off dead downwind we make 6½ knots easily. In this particular case we gybe through 90 degrees yet the apparent wind goes from 15 degrees forward of one beam to 15 degrees forward of the other. In a strong breeze we gybe through 60°. The start of the 1982 Route du Rhum illustrated the effect of gybing angle on VMG.

The first 40 miles of the race were dead downwind in a force 6 to 7 with short steep waves. *Elf Aquitaine* reached downwind gybing through 90° thus keeping the apparent wind on the beam and going very fast. On *Colt Cars* I ran square for the first 4 miles and lost ¼ mile to *Elf* in the process. I then started reaching, but gybing through less than 50°. After a further 30 miles I was back level with the catamaran. The lesson learnt here is that the stronger the wind the less the necessity to reach downwind.

## VMG reaching

This final VMG case is fairly complex. When beating or running, any course variation relative to the wind can be followed by an equal and opposite variation (after tacking or gybing) to arrive at one's destination. When reaching this is not the case. For instance,

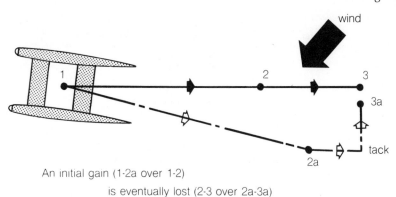

An initial gain (1-2a over 1-2)

is eventually lost (2-3 over 2a-3a)

**Fig 80** *VMG reaching*

sailing with the wind abeam in a blow, it might seem a good idea to free off 20 degrees, increase speed and hence improve VMG. However, as to make the finish it will eventually be necessary to come close-hauled, or even to tack, and the VMG advantage will probably have been wiped out (see fig. 80). An accurate forecast of the wind direction will decide your tactics for reaching.

# 14

## *Heavy Weather*

Handling a multihull in light and medium airs, when everything is behaving as normal and as expected, has been covered in Chapter 12. However, when the going gets rough a number of new problems arise. The fact that all multihulls are inherently unsafe (they can capsize) makes it essential not to make a mistake. Although all yachts behave in different ways there are a lot of advisable and inadvisable actions to follow when attempting to get the best out of a multihull in heavy weather.

### Heavy weather to windward

As the wind increases, so the sail area must be reduced in the normal way. Take care to recognize when a multihull is overpowered; because it sails upright it is harder to judge when sail reductions are needed. Watching the lee float and developing a feel for the boat will soon enable you to develop the right degree of prudence and judgment on a trimaran. In a catamaran the leeward hull will still have a massive reserve of buoyancy when the windward hull lifts so that in itself is not a very good indication of overpowering. A useful rule that applies to sail changing on any yacht is 'if you are thinking about doing it – do it, a potential sail change will not have occurred to you unless it was already needed. Experience and common sense will eventually be your best rule of thumb.

Steering a multihull to windward in a gale is one of the wettest, most unpleasant pastimes yet invented. Disregarding that, a good helmsman can make an enormous difference to forward progress. The trick is to get the boat through the waves as cleanly as possible without deviating from the course more than a few degrees. As I mentioned before, the most important instrument in these conditions is the knotmeter. That, combined with visual observation of true wind direction, are your main assets.

The danger of sailing too close to the wind is twofold: if a wave stops the boat or, worse, she goes aback, she could sail backwards down the wave and put an intolerable strain on the rudder. This could lead to a capsize (see next chapter). Beware of a fall in speed from, say, 8 knots to 6 knots. At that point speed loss can be very rapid so a prudent bearing away is called for.

The opposite problem occurs when the bows are knocked off the wind by a wave.

Immediately speed picks up, the lee float digs in and a bit of lee helm can quickly bring the multihull on to a close reach. By now the speed could be up to 15 or even 20 knots. The difficulty is getting the boat back close-hauled without hitting a wave at high speed, which would probably result in several seconds airborne and inevitable damage. What one has to do is to stay on a reach for a few seconds looking for a gap in the wave crests through which you can luff up and get under complete control again. This can be especially hard on the nerves.

The helmsman works through the waves in much the same way as he would on a monohull, luffing slightly up the face of the wave and bearing away down its back. This not only reduces slamming but maintains a steady wind angle. In a monohull it is sometimes necessary to reduce sail to windward simply to slow down and minimize the slamming. In trimarans this is not always a good idea because in their case the V-shaped float slams less than the rounded, main hull; keeping more sail on will put even more displacement on the float and actually hold the main hull up from the very worst of the slams.

The centreboard requires critical attention in a strong wind. The forces on it become very high as the wind increases and as it is designed to be of the area required for light winds it should be lifted progressively to 80% of its area in 20 knots, to 70% when the first reef goes in, to 60% for the second reef and to 50% for three reefs. The area is reduced in this way for two reasons: the remaining board area generates more lift and hence resistance to leeway as speed increases; and the lee hull or float provides extra lift itself as it is depressed into the water.

Tacking must be undertaken with great care in rough seas. Try to pick a hole in the wave tops through which to poke the bows in the tack. If all way is lost and it is necessary to back the jib remember to reverse the helm and hold it very tight. As stern way is made the forces on the rudder are immense and losing control of the helm could be bad news.

In general, there is no doubt that multihulls must be kept sailing, even to windward, as long as possible. If it becomes totally impossible to continue then survival tactics must be adopted (see later section).

## Heavy weather off the wind

To sail a multihull beam on to a large sea is very difficult. It is an unnerving experience as speed is very high and the wave crests hit the boat from abeam. There is little margin for error. In fact it is psychologically impossible to keep it up for very long – all helmsmen will naturally put the waves either just forward of the beam or well aft of the beam. Not only are these options safer, but they seem to happen automatically.

Once the waves are aft of the beam the fun starts. Provided the yacht is well designed and the bows do not drive under there is no limit to how hard and fast a multihull can be pushed. Average speeds of over 17 knots for periods as long as 24 hours have been proved. To achieve this, bursts of 30 knots are likely to be reached. Luckily, there is an excellent safety measure in this situation; turning on to a dead run will reduce the apparent wind speed dramatically and any problem or potential problem, such as a torn sail, can be sorted out. Because of a multihull's speed, a dead run is her safest direction of sailing. With the true wind (and waves) forward of the beam the safest action in a squall is to luff up and feather the sails. But if the true wind is aft of the beam the correct procedure is to bear away.

When running or broad reaching in a rising wind beware of the problems of reefing. It is obviously impossible to luff up to reef (an apparent wind of 20 knots on the run may be as much as 45 knots if you turn into it). Fighting the sail down while it is pressed up against the rigging is the only thing to do and this can be helped by rigging a line through the reefing luff eye and taking it to a winch. The chafe on the sail during this performance is considerable.

The centreboard should be raised almost completely. This will improve speed by reducing drag and act as a safety valve in the event of a broach (discussed in Chapter 6). The action of the wind alone will never cause a multihull to round up but a breaking wave on the quarter could easily turn her beam on. If this happens with the centreboard up she will skid safely sideways rather than tripping over it.

## Survival conditions

When sailing is no longer possible because of crew fatigue, damage or sheer wind strength some action must be taken. It is obviously possible to hide from the wind by reducing sail but it is impossible to hide from the sea. The basic options open to a multihull are:

1. Keep sailing;
2. Heave to or lie ahull;
3. Lie to a sea anchor; or
4. Run off.

*Keep sailing.* I have included this as the no. 1 survival tactic as I am firm in the belief that it is the correct thing to do, even to windward. But it does need very good organization and a very determined helmsman.

The storm staysail must be small and the fourth reef (or third in a smaller multihull) must reduce the mainsail to less than a quarter of its full size. With this combination one should keep going for as long as one dares.

The most likely event that may cause one to give up the effort is damage. Therefore it is imperative to take care that nothing breaks. Particular points to look at are chafing of the sheets (check the leads) and chafing of the reefing leech line (a regular occurrence and extremely annoying if it breaks). First make quite sure the reefing line is strong enough for the job. Remember it has to take the complete leech load of the sail – the same load that requires a multi-part main sheet. It should have a diameter bigger than that of the main sheet and with sheaves in the boom large enough to take it. If there is any sign of chafe (which there will be) cut off the end of the line when the reef is next out. Also make a habit of tying a strong strop through the reefing eye and round the end of the boom as a preventer. This preventer could save your mainsail, and allow you to keep sailing.

*Heaving-to or lying ahull.* Heaving-to and lying ahull, in multihull terms, mean the same thing; that is, lying beam on to the sea with possibly a minimum of sail to hold the bows slightly to windward. Heaving-to in the normal sense, i.e. simply with the jib backed and the main sheet eased, is a fine tactic while waiting for a race to start or eating your dinner on a cruising boat but it is no survival tactic; if there is too much wind to sail there is too much for the amount of sail required to heave-to. The windage on the sails would encourage a capsize.

There are two distinctly different ways of lying beam on to the sea, one is to remain stationary with no forward motion and the other is to keep moving slowly forward. The first option requires lowering all sail, raising the centreboard and lashing the helm to leeward. The boat will lie beam on, making a lot of leeway and perhaps a knot forward. The centreboard is completely up so that there is no resistance to sideways motion. For the second option a small sail is left up, as far aft as possible, the helm is lashed amidships and a small amount of board is left down (an example of the success of these tactics will be given shortly).

If the boat is a modern catamaran, because of the high-buoyancy, hulls and shallow draft (probably as little as 12ins, even on a 60 footer) she will be readily pushed sideways by a wave. First the approaching wave will lift her windward hull rather alarmingly. The amount it lifts will depend on the height and angle of the wave and the beam of the vessel. The wave crest quickly passes under the catamaran and hits the leeward hull from the inside. This has the effect of cancelling out the capsize movement and also shoving the whole boat hard to leeward. A momentary sideways surf will result before the crest passes away and leaves the yacht in the trough waiting for the next wave. There is the danger of the windward hull being lifted over the top of the leeward one – if the breaking crest is large enough – before the sideways surf starts. But this is fairly unlikely with large catamarans, which are the only type of multihull that would be suitable for this lying ahull procedure. Even so the strains on a large structure are enormous when lying beam on to a sea in this way and that in itself may be the limiting factor. Old-fashioned catamarans have laid beam on with safety, but in 1976 *Kriter III* (ex *British Oxygen*) broke up while lying ahull in an Atlantic gale. Her crossbeam-to-hull join simply could not take the strain. Today's catamarans are stronger yet beamier. The beam will make lying ahull safer, but it also presents bigger engineering problems in holding everything together. On balance, if progress to windward is impossible and running off is ruled out because of ground lost to leeward, lie ahull.

In a trimaran the situation will be slightly different. A tri with high-buoyancy floats will behave similarly to a cat. However, the geometry is different and not quite as safe. The approaching wave lifts the windward float and the trimaran heels. Displacement is immediately taken almost 100 per cent on the leeward float which will dig in to the water. All being well the wave crest passes under the vessel, striking the main hull, then the lee float, and the danger is past. What *may* happen though is this: although the lee float is not driven under, its shape (more V-shaped and narrower than a cat's hull) means that it will have a draft of almost 4ft (for a 60 footer) when pressed over and this may act as a brake to the safety valve of sideways surfing. A trip over could result. Therefore, while lying ahull is possible, it is not recommended.

A trimaran with low-buoyancy floats is the worst case. Here, as before, the wave lifts the windward float and immediately the leeward float digs underwater and a perfect tripping moment is created. A capsize is a strong possibility. Do not lie ahull in a low-buoyancy float trimaran. (See fig. 81.)

The alternative to lying ahull is running before the sea. In a racing situation, desperate

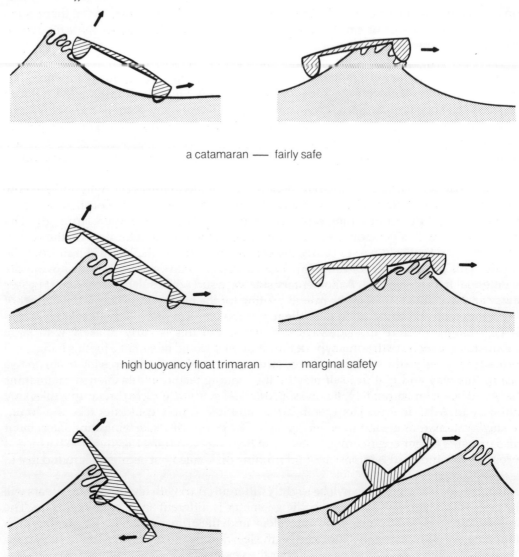

a catamaran — fairly safe

high buoyancy float trimaran — marginal safety

low buoyancy float trimaran — unsafe

**Fig 81** *Lying ahull*

to make ground to windward, it is heart-breaking to lose perhaps 200 miles in 24 hours by running off. A compromise between safety and throwing the race away must be made. How can lying ahull be made safer? The answer is to try leaving a little sail up so that a minimum of way is maintained, preferably with a slight bows upwind aspect.

On *Brittany Ferries GB* we lay ahull once when a broken reefing leech line forced us to lower the mainsail. This left us with just the storm staysail set and we remained like that for six hours. It was a big mistake. The sail area was too far forward and held our bows below beam on to the seas. Just after each wave the bows would fall off, she would reach forward, the helm would take effect and we would turn back to exactly beam on for the next wave – all wrong! Unfortunately we were finding it difficult to rig a new reefing line so we accepted the risk of the status quo. It would have been better to have left up a really deep-reefed mainsail and lashed the helm amidships. I did exactly this in the 1980 OSTAR on the 31ft trimaran *Boatfile*.

*Boatfile* was a sister ship to the three Val 31s which had all taken part in the stormy 1976 OSTAR. Of the three, two survived (with spells of lying ahull) and the third capsized. With a ratio of 2 to 1 I was not altogether happy about lying ahull myself. There seemed to me to be, when I tried it, a danger of tripping over the V-shaped lee float even though it was not driven under. So I hoisted a small amount of mainsail, sheeted in hard but with the traveller 3ft down the track and found that *Boatfile* was happy to make about 2.5 knots forward at an angle of 60 to 70 degrees to the wind and sea. There was no need to touch the helm: there was enough forward speed to climb over the waves and at an angle of 60 degrees there was no danger of being stopped or put aback. Also, as the waves were no longer on the beam, the danger of rolling over was lessened. With 30 per cent of the centreboard down I even made some small progress to windward.

In summary then:

Catamarans – fairly safe to lie ahull;

High-buoyancy float trimarans – only safe to lie ahull with some mainsail;

Low-buoyancy float trimarans – never safe to lie ahull.

*Lying to a sea anchor.* The theory behind riding to a sea anchor is that it is safer than lying ahull and loses less ground than running off. Rather than lie ahull a yacht is expected to stream a sea anchor over its bow to hold the vessel's head to wind and sea. Alternatively, instead of running off fast, the theory states that a sea anchor, or warps, should be trailed to stop the boat surfing.

As an alternative to lying ahull, lying to a sea anchor is not much better. There are all sorts of practical problems involved in deploying and recovering the anchor which itself must be very large to be of any use at all. There are several possibilities which have been tried with varying degrees of success. If the sea anchor is small, it may hold the trimaran's bows up but it will not stop her progression sharply backwards on each wave. Stern way is not only dangerous to the rudder but can cause a diagonal bows-over-quarter capsize. Nigel Irens sailing his own design *Gordano Goose* retired from the 1981 Atlantic race when he suffered rudder damage in just this way. Alternatively, if the sea anchor is very large – a standard parachute has been employed with success – it will stop stern way but put intolerable strain on to the point of the boat to which it is fixed. In 1980 I carried an army surplus parachute, with an arrangement of lines to keep it open when streamed, on two nylon warps from the bows of each float. But it never crossed my mind to use it, mainly because the weather was not bad enough and partly because there was no way I could have worked on the floats to rig it, even if I'd wanted to.

Lying bows on to a sea anchor should be discounted completely on a multihull as a safety measure.

Lying stern on to a sea anchor is a much better bet because at least the vessel is moving forward and the sea anchor is serving to slow down the boat's progress to leeward. Any anchor deployed in this fashion will need to be extremely strong, made probably of tyres and chain streamed on a long and stretchy warp. Even so, it could well break. The problem again is one of size; for the anchor to reduce downwind drift sufficiently it will have to be large and heavy – the last thing you want on a multihull. If you are going to use one make it fast to a very strong point, such as the base of the mast, and then secure its direction by two lines as it leads over the quarter. Even so, I don't like the idea (see fig. 82).

Lying beam on to a sea anchor is a way of holding the windward hull down while lying

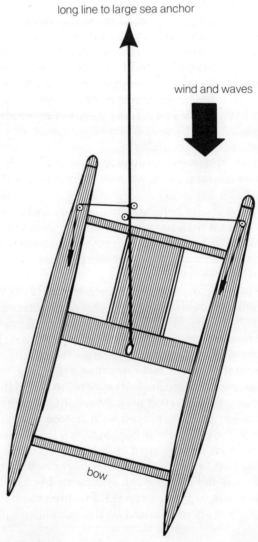

long line to large sea anchor

wind and waves

bow

**Fig 82** *The only way to try a sea anchor*

ahull. Unfortunately it also closes the door on sideways slide which is desirable to prevent capsize. Not to be recommended.

In general, it is my belief that a sea anchor will cause more problems than it cures. It holds the vessel on to the waves and this in turn puts great stress on the structure. It is like walking into a punch from a heavy-weight boxer rather than being carried away with it; neither option is particularly desirable but the second will cause less damage.

*Running before.* Running before a storm is, in a modern multihull, the best survival tactic. Needless to say there are several qualifications to this statement. When running off, even under bare poles, it must be accepted that any multihull will make a lot of ground to leeward. This can present a problem if there is land in the way. Moreover, moving fast with the storm will make it last longer as the relative speed of the weather pattern to the yacht is reduced. Even so, I favour this approach if allowable. I don't mean to say that one should immediately give up a windward race as soon as a gale develops. The racing man must try to balance progress against safety and many will try anything to hold ground to windward. However, no capsized boat has won a race yet so even running off in the wrong direction could be the correct race tactic.

Streaming warps when running will slow progress down and reduce the chance of the bows digging in after a surf; a distinct possibility in smaller craft. The biggest snag of this kind of survival tactic is the need for a constant, alert helmsman – a lot to ask of a short-handed sailor. A self-steering arrangement will be invaluable here but it may need a bit of assistance to keep the bows downwind, such as a storm staysail or a very small amount of furler sheeted flat fore and aft and a few warps trailed behind. A broach must be avoided at all cost.

If conditions are ultimately bad move all loose gear as far aft as possible – especially wet sails – to keep the bows out and the rudder in. Provided the structure of the hull can take it and there is sea room, running off is now generally accepted to be the safest survival tactic – not *safe,* but safer than the other options.

*Survival summary.* As a general guide the order of preference in survival tactics is:
1 Keep sailing
2 Run off, using warps as necessary
3 Lie ahull (cats and high buoyancy float tris)
4 Lie to a sea anchor
5 Lie ahull (low buoyancy float tris)

# 15

## *Capsizes and Losses*

Accidents will happen at sea and there is no way to prevent them completely other than stopping all sailing, especially racing. As this is undoubtedly out of the question we should look at the most effective ways of reducing the number of accidents, and, in case they do occur, examine the severity of their consequences.

As long as there are offshore multihull races there will be capsizes. Yachtsmen, when racing, will take chances they wouldn't dream of taking normally. The capsize, when it arrives, will have many contributing factors: human error, wind, sea, design fault and structural failures are just a few. Most likely it will be a combination of several of these, but let us look at each in turn and illustrate them with a few case histories.

## Wind action alone

This is a fairly rare occurrence but has happened. It is caused by driving a multihull hard in squally conditions, probably with an offshore wind and being unable to release sheets or steer the boat out of trouble. Provided that the sheets can be released before the windward hull of a catamaran or the mainhull of a tri lifts clear of the water the accident can be averted. The danger is jamming instead of running free. If hit by a squall I would let go both main *and* genoa sheets as quickly, and as completely, as possible. The recorded cases of capsize from wind action alone all involve old-fashioned designs, that is, cruiser-oriented catamarans, and low-buoyancy float trimarans.

*Tripple Arrow. Tripple Arrow* was a trimaran with an overall length of 49ft, a beam of 30ft and a displacement of 7,300lbs. She was designed by Simpson Wild and sailed by Brian Cooke in the 1974 Round Britain and Ireland Race. She was moderately rigged by today's standards with a 50ft tall sloop rig and floats of low (less than 100 per cent) buoyancy. The crossbeams were modern box section with very low volume, and hence with little reserve of buoyancy.

Cooke had almost completed the third leg of the race. He had run down from Muckle Flugga, the Northern tip of the Shetland Islands, towards Lerwick in a north-north-easterly force 5, carrying full sail and spinnaker. Rounding the tip of Bressay Island, a sheer cliff promontory, Cooke came hard on the wind and set a no. 2 genoa with full main.

He considered his boat at this stage undercanvassed. The wind, coming off the hills less than a half a mile away, was alternately lulls and squalls. Immediately after a lull, when the trimaran had stopped, a squall hit without warning, not coming across the water but down on to the boat at an estimated 45 degrees angle. With no way on, and the sails sheeted in tight the capsize moment was enormous; the boat turned over in less than 10 seconds. Neither Cooke nor his crew had time to reach the sheets, let alone ease them. Both crew ended up in the water but they, along with their trimaran, were soon rescued.

This incident may not have happened if the tri had had full buoyancy floats. The speed of capsize would have been slower, perhaps allowing time for the sheets to be eased. All the other leaders experienced severe squalls at this spot and one other nearly suffered the same fate. After the first squall the crew kept the sheets in their hands.

*Tripple Arrow* capsized again in 1976. She was found 450 miles from the Canary Islands and her solo skipper, again Brian Cooke, was missing. The trimaran may have turned over before or after Cooke was lost.

*A cruising catamaran.* There is no documented evidence of an ocean-racing catamaran turning over from wind action alone. However, it has happened to cruiser racers. One such was *Golden Cockerel* which was reaching fast down the English Channel in 1968 with a lot of sail up. The skipper, Bill Howell, was on the foredeck hanking on a smaller jib when the catamaran simply sailed over. The crew in the cockpit released the main sheet but the genoa sheet jammed with a riding turn on the winch. At the last moment, with the vessel almost on her side, the helmsman luffed up – which may or may not have contributed to the accident. Again the crew and boat were picked up.

To avoid capsize in this sort of squally weather when the boat is being driven hard it would be necessary to sail with the sheets in your hand all the time; but this is not really practical. Still, on several occasions, especially in an offshore wind, I have sailed with all the sheets uncleated ready to release.

## By wave action while lying ahull, or to a sea anchor

The prime candidates for this sort of capsize are the small (because this makes the wave relatively larger), and low-buoyancy float trimarans. As has been demonstrated earlier, lying ahull in a low-buoyancy float trimaran is a risky game. The lee float can so easily be pushed underwater and act as a hinge around which the vessel turns until it is upside down (see fig. 81, lower example). While lying ahull watch the lee float and if there is any danger of it being driven under, it is time to start sailing again – probably running off.

An overweight and overloaded trimaran will be in even more danger as the percentage buoyancy of the floats will be thereby reduced. This factor may have contributed to the capsize of *GB IV*.

*Great Britain IV.* This 54ft Kelsall-design is the same trimaran as the one described in chapter 4. After Chay Blyth and I had won the Round Britain Race, *GB IV* was considerably strengthened for the 1978 Route du Rhum. Even so, the improvements were inadequate. She was further strengthened and yet the same problems occurred in the next race, the 1979 Transat-en-double. After that the chain plates were finally sorted out properly and *GB IV* became a pretty sound vessel, but with a displacement very much above that of her original design.

In 1981 she was bought by Alan Toone, who took her across the Bay of Biscay to qualify for the 1981 Two-handed Transatlantic Race. Alan relates what happened:

'I left on the qualifying trip for the TwoSTAR with my crewman Laurie Cambell who had about 20,000 miles sailing experience as a skipper but limited multihull experience. We left the Channel heading for Tenerife making good speed on course. 100 miles north-west of Finistère a severe gale blew up, with the wind rising rapidly from 15 knots to 55–60 knots. We ran off under storm jib and I steered. It was pitch dark. On the front of the waves *GB IV* was touching 18–20 knots – the waves were probably 20–30ft high. Unfortunately my crewman wasn't experienced enough to helm under these conditions so I continued till I started to suffer lapses of concentration. It then seemed like a good idea to round up and lay to a sea anchor. We came round between waves, stopped and streamed the sea anchor (about 6ft across) from the bows on about 300ft of 2in warp. *GB IV* settled down quite comfortably, taking the seas well, bow on. Occasionally she would yaw but I wasn't over concerned. I was on listening watch while Laurie was asleep below and I was about to wake him when I heard a large breaking sea approaching from forward on the port side. The boat heeled to starboard about 25 degrees. The wave passed under the main hull as we made some stern way and then, I believe, the lee float buried, causing a slow capsize. The whole flip took about 30 seconds with a pause at the half way point, which gave me sufficient time to consider whether to go below or not; I decided it would be safer below. I knew we wouldn't sink so we stayed quite calm and organized the boat below as we'd prearranged for such an eventuality. The lighting continued to work and we rigged a platform above water level. Although wet we were fairly warm and decided to stay as we were until dawn. We managed about five hours sleep by which time it was getting light so we dug a hole in the bottom of the hull and made a lookout hatch. The wind had gone down to about 30 knots but the waves were still large. On inspection of the sea anchor later, we found it ripped to shreds which probably explained our stern way.

'I would never again heave-to or lie ahull in a multihull and would probably try instead to keep going to windward under heavily reduced sail, but sufficient to make a little headway into the seas. Also, I think, that if I'd stayed on deck I would have been washed off the hull and not have been able to cling on for any length of time to the slippery surface.'

It is interesting to note that Alan felt certain that the lee float was driven under. Here is a classic example of a trimaran designed with floats of greater than 100 per cent buoyancy but, because of an increase in overall displacement, she ended up with floats of a lot less than 100 per cent.

*Jan of Santa Cruz/Boatfile.* Yet again this story relates to another vessel I raced in. She was one of the rare breed of multihull that lived to capsize twice.

The first occasion was the 1976 OSTAR when she was sailed by Hamilton Ferris. She was the third of three sister Val 31s – the one that didn't make it. She was rolled over while lying ahull with the centreboard raised. After rescue and a distinguished couple of years under the ownership of Nigel Irens she came into my hands. The story of our entry in the 1980 OSTAR has already been told. I left *Boatfile* in Newport, Rhode Island, and sailed back on another yacht. Eventually I sold the trimaran to a new owner in the UK and engaged deliverers to bring her back across the Atlantic in April 1981. Nick Hallam and his crew enjoyed a trouble-free passage until they hit a gale 300 miles west of Land's End. They lay ahull comfortably for 24 hours. Hallam was prepared to employ a sea anchor if necessary but was reluctant to run off as this would bring him nearer the centre of the depression and hence into bad weather for longer. Anyway, with the daggerboard right up and the helm lashed to leeward, *Boatfile* was lying quietly and slipping sideways downwind quite safely. The wind speed was force 8 and the waves approximately 20ft. The wave that capsized them must have been much larger. Being safely down below the crew didn't see it, and the yacht was very rapidly rolled over.

The problems experienced after a capsize are detailed shortly. This particular case was a classic rescue at the very limit of air-sea rescue range; but more of that later.

Need the capsize have happened? It is impossible for us to judge as we were not there. My belief is that they may have avoided the incident by running off – they had sea room and were not racing. However, at the time she was lying ahull happily so the decision to remain as they were, while in retrospect wrong, was probably what anyone else would have done. The lesson must be, if in any doubt, run off as soon as sailing is no longer considered possible.

*Bucks Fizz.* A modern 38ft Newick-designed trimaran; she was lost with all hands while sailing in company with the 1979 Fastnet fleet.

I was sailing on *Condor of Bermuda* (a 77ft monohull) in this race and we sighted *Bucks Fizz* close reaching into the Fastnet Rock as we passed in the other direction. The time was 20.00 on Monday August 13, the wind was south-south-west 25 knots and rising as predicted in the forecast two hours earlier. At this point *Bucks Fizz* was 50 miles from the rock. By midnight the wind was up to 60 knots and had veered, thus heading the trimaran. The seas were atrocious. At 03.30 on Tuesday the monohull *Pepsi* saw a red hand flare close by. She was unable to help as she had lost her rudder and was lying ahull. At 08.00 she saw a capsized yellow trimaran. With nothing else in sight the flare was assumed to have come from *Bucks Fizz* or her liferaft. Twenty-four hours later a Sea King helicopter sighted the upturned hull and lowered a diver to search the craft. He reported the hull sound, no sails set, the mast undamaged, the centreboard in the lowered position and the rudder missing. The bodies of all the crew were found and recovered (see also Chapter 16).

It is reasonable to conclude from these facts, and from the relative positions of the sightings, that she capsized while lying ahull. Possibly, her rudder was lost before the capsize which cancelled out the option of running off as a safety tactic. With her centreboard down she may have failed to sideslip to a steep wave, submerged her lee float and rolled over. This conclusion was reached by a committee of inquiry set up by the British Multihull Offshore Cruising and Racing Association.

*Azulao. Azulao* was a 31ft Kelsall trimaran with very low buoyancy floats (65 per cent). Nick Clifton was sailing from Martha's Vineyard to Bermuda in early April when he encountered winds of up to force 9. When the wind was force 7 he lay ahull, reluctant to cross the Gulf Stream until the wind had dropped. As the wind increased in the next 24 hours Clifton considered running off, but, as in so many other cases, he felt he was all right for the moment. The capsize was caused by a wave of over 20ft breaking under the float, and the whole rotation took only five seconds.

Clifton feels that had he turned around and run off there would have been no capsize. He also reckons that a drogue or sea anchor trailed from the windward float may have prevented the lee float digging in and stopped the capsize before it started. As it was he spent two days in a liferaft before being picked up.

There are several more cases of trimarans capsizing while lying ahull. In nearly every case the skipper felt 'we were riding quite comfortably and with no cause for concern' when the capsize came.

The theory of trailing a weighted sea anchor from the windward float ahull in order to hold it down has not been proved to work.

## By wave action while running

While it is my belief that running off is the safest storm tactic, there have been instances of capsize when a multihull was sailing with the wind aft. These documented cases are of vessels running with sail up, not under bare poles and not in survival conditions. The dangers are broaching (more likely with the sail set) and pitch-poling. Here are three examples.

*Gulf Streamer.* Phil Weld, one of the world's most experienced and safety-conscious multihull sailors was bringing his large Newick-designed trimaran across the Atlantic to England for the 1976 OSTAR. He had with him one crew. April 26th found them running under staysail only in a fresh south-westerly making an average of 9 knots. The next day at 38°N and 64°W the wind veered to just north of west and the sea subsided. The sailing conditions were ideal, the gale had gone and *Gulf Streamer* was sailing along happily – in fact a little under-canvassed, at about 8 knots. Then, without warning a large wave caused the boat to broach and she capsized.

Phil Weld is sure that he has sailed harder with more sail and in larger waves, quite safely. There is no doubt from his description that he was sailing in a perfectly seamanlike way. Yet a wave large enough to do what it did, caused no doubt by the wind shift and an eddy in the Gulf Stream, reared its head from nowhere and caught them out.

In this case it seems there was no way, besides staying ashore, in which the wave could have been avoided. Whether it would have been possible to have steered *Gulf Streamer* straight down the wave and have avoided a broach is purely academic. The crew were rescued after living in the upturned boat for several days.

*Gazelle. Gazelle* was a 28ft trimaran designed by Kelsall and sailed by Charles Denis. She was capsized in the same storm which hit *Bucks Fizz* and decimated the 1979 Fastnet fleet.

Denis was beating into a southerly force 8, bound for Sandwich in Kent. He was sailing alone in order to qualify for the 1980 OSTAR. On the morning of the 14 August *Gazelle* was down to a trisail and reefed staysail and as she was still over-pressed Denis decided to run off. He turned the trimaran on to a course that put the wind and waves 45 degrees on the quarter. It was obviously impossible for the lone helmsman to steer throughout the storm so he eventually lowered the staysail and continued with the trisail and lashed helm, still holding the off wind course. At 16.00 on the 14th the yacht was struck on the windward quarter by a large wave which heeled her over to almost 90 degrees. Denis afterwards recalled that the boat seemed to pause in that position and then turned stern over bow to complete the capsize when hit by a second wave.

The committee of inquiry concluded that the amount of sail set did not contribute materially to the capsize. Neither in their opinion did the half-lowered centreboard. It is conceivable, however, that a trisail set alone, with the wind and waves on the quarter, will provide a considerable broaching moment. This, combined with the centreboard, may have caused *Gazelle*'s initial steep heel. Had it been possible to have kept the trimaran pointing dead downwind the accident may have been avoided.

Denis now firmly believes he would not have gone over had he streamed warps to hold his boat on a dead downwind course.

*Kawasaki*. *Kawasaki* was a near sister ship to *Great Britain IV*. Her overall length of 54ft was the same. Her major difference was the addition of hydrofoils under the bow and stern to induce lift at speed. This, in normal circumstances, would keep her bows high. *Kawaski* was attempting to beat the West/East Transatlantic sailing record in 1980 under the command of Eugene Riguidel. They had not gone many miles from New York when they pitch-poled. They were running dead downwind under spinnaker and it appeared thier bow foil developed a negative angle of attack as she tore down a wave, thus immediately tripping her stern over bow. This rare accident actually happened in sight of a cargo ship which subsequently rescued them. The trimaran was later recovered intact.

*Twiggy/Rennie*. This 31ft trimaran has the distinction of pitchpoling twice. The first time was when running under spinnaker in the 1982 Round Britain Race, and the second time (despite the addition of considerable bouyancy forward) was in the 1982 Route du Rhum. On the first occasion crew and yacht were rescued – on the second only the crew. There can be no doubt that this design was not suitable for pushing downwind.

These cases all result from sailing downwind and do not discredit, in my opinion, the idea of running off as a safety measure – provided speed is kept down.

## By wave action while beating

Capsizing while sailing to windward can happen in two ways. A multihull sailing hard on the wind can be turned over by a combination of wind and wave action. If too much sail is being carried so that the vessel is continually overpressed it will only need the help of a large wave under the windward bow to set the boat rotating to leeward. The wind will do the rest. The other possibility is of a multihull sailing too close to the wind. When a large wave is encountered the vessel may not have sufficient momentum to clear the crest, causing her to fall off on to her leeward quarter or side. This, in itself, is not disastrous, but if the vessel is lacking in diagonal stability, (i.e. it has short floats), it could trip windward-bow over lee-quarter. The most likely cause of such a situation arising would be sailing to windward with too much canvas set in gale conditions, so that the helmsman was required to feather all the time to depower the rig.

*RTL Timex*. Nick Keig built this 53ft Kelsall design for the 1978 Round Britain Race. Under the name *Three Legs of Mann II* she came second in that event and was then bought by the

*Twiggy, 31ft, that pitchpoled when running under full sail in force 6/7 north of Scotland during the 1982 Round Britain Race.*

Frenchman, Alain Glicksman. Glicksman entered her as *Sieko* in the 1978 Route du Rhum (single-handed from St Malo to the West Indies) but was forced to retire after storms in the Bay of Biscay. After calling into the Azores for repairs she continued on with a full crew to Guadaloupe and refitted over the winter months.

Renamed (yet again) *RTL Timex*, Glicksman set out for New York, intending to launch an Atlantic record attempt from there. He and his three crew stopped at Bermuda to pick up a journalist and set off again for the last few days to New York. After a short time they encountered very strong and persistent headwinds with rough seas. For four days they struggled to make progress. Glicksman alternated between two rigs – a reefed main and staysail, and just a storm jib. Although the former gave more control the crew were concerned about the terrible hammering the boat was receiving as it powered over the waves. Changing down, though, meant losing speed and making little headway. Also contributing to their problems was a leak in the leeward (starboard) float. Sailing with just the storm jib to reduce the strain on the hull they failed to make it over the top of a wave, fell back on the leeward quarter, which tripped them over and a capsize followed in a diagonal direction. The crew were rescued nine days later.

Here is an example of a man determined to keep sailing but having to choose between two unpalatable alternatives. Either he should have kept up more speed or he should have run off.

*Bonifacio.* The 44ft *Bonifacio* was a Newick design built for the 1981 Two-handed Transatlantic Race. She was skippered by Phil Steggall, an experienced yachtsman and multihull enthusiast. He came third in the 1980 OSTAR sailing a Walter Green-designed 38 footer.

The start of the 1981 race was a beat into a force 6 with a nasty sea. Photographs of *Bonifacio* taken at the time indicate that Steggall was determined to win his class – he was pressing the boat very hard. They were beating hard into steep seas when *Bonifacio* simply sailed over. Steggall felt they were not pushing too hard and he was surprised by the accident. *Bonifacio* was well up with the leaders of the race and was several hundred miles west of Land's End. The worst of the first gale was over, but the waves were still large. The trimaran sailed into a steep wave, slowly heeling as it climbed the wall of water. Before the crest was passed, the boat continued to heel and slowly turned upside down. Steggall and his crew were picked up by the Royal Navy.

*Apache Sundancer.* This capsize occurred in an almost identical way to that of *RTL Timex.* *Apache* was a 40ft MacAlpine-Downie design cruiser/racer catamaran. She was well placed in the 1970 Round Britain Race and was attempting to beat against a force 8 and heavy seas on the last leg back to Plymouth. Her progress was very slow and on one wave she stalled, losing all way. That wave passed but a second picked up the stationary boat and pushed her backwards and sideways down its face, gently rolling her over in the process. As she was sailing at the time her centreboards were down which probably contributed to the roll over.

## Loss through structural damage

The failure of the structure of a multihull can lead to capsize. There is, of course, nothing to learn about capsizing from this type of loss, rather it concerns the structural engineering of the vessel to begin with. However, there are a few interesting cases worth looking at.

*Great Britain III.* This 80ft Kelsall-designed trimaran was the first multihull I sailed. She really was enormous, and when she was launched in 1975 she was the largest sailing multihull in the world.

Her sad moment occurred in 1976 when Chay Blyth was sailing her single-handed to qualify for the 1976 OSTAR. He had managed to handle the monster for 700 miles and was approaching his home port of Dartmouth, no doubt relieved to have completed the voyage and proved that *GB III*, despite her large rig, could be handled by one man. Nearing Start Point *GB III* closed with a coaster. Thinking it would clear him easily Chay went below to prepare the anchor for bringing on deck. It seems the coaster misjudged the speed of the yacht and a collision occurred. The force of the blow broke off the front part of the starboard float, aft of its watertight bulkhead. The coaster didn't stop (but fortunately was identified) and Chay immediately put the damaged float to windward. He was then faced with the difficult choice of sailing south, with the damaged float in the air but with no idea how he would get into any port on the French coast, or north to Salcombe. He chose the latter which involved putting the damaged float to leeward for about two miles. But no sooner had he done this than the float started to fill rapidly and a slow capsize resulted. Chay ended up in the water.

Fortunately the accident occurred within sight of the coastguard and a fishing vessel was on the scene half an hour later, during which time Chay was constantly being submerged and was suffering the severe cold of a freezing January sea. The fishing boat picked him up and then sent down a diver who tied a line on to a deck fitting, and the long tow to Plymouth began. In port the trimaran, now ex mast, was lifted ashore.

*GB III* was soon rebuilt using the original float bow which was fished up in a trawlers net! Unfortunately insurance problems put her out of the OSTAR and in fact she never raced again.

*Kriter III. Kriter III* was the MacAlpine-Downie design, originally called *British Oxygen*. This 70ft racing catamaran was sailed in the 1976 OSTAR by the Frenchman Jean-Yves Terlain.

Her break-up started in mid-ocean during one of the severe gales that hit the majority of the fleet. Terlain was rescued before the catamaran finally fell apart or turned over so nothing is known of her last moments. One of the hulls was later reported washed ashore on the south-west coast of England.

These examples illustrate the various dangers lying in the path of the intrepid multihull sailor. My advice on how to minimize the risks has already been set out in Chapter 14. But one must be realistic: as long as there are offshore races, there will always be someone who pushes too hard, someone unlucky enough to encounter a rogue wave, someone who refuses to stop racing when maybe he should run off – in fact there will always be capsizes.

# 16

## Capsize: How to Live Through It

Fortunately a very high percentage of capsized crew are rescued. This is especially true now, with air and sea rescue a fine art. Also, the equipment available to pin point a yacht in distress has improved enormously in accuracy and reliability. In many offshore races the ARGOS system is used to track vessels, a system which has revolutionized safety procedures.

Half the secret of surviving a capsize is to have prepared for it beforehand. This means carrying the right equipment and fitting out the multihull correctly.

### Capsize survival equipment

Modern race rules insist on a minimum level of equipment being carried; this should be extended to cover further gear. Below are the important items.

*Argos. Argos* is not available to all multihull sailors yet. Perhaps one day it will be but at present it is a system lent to competitors in most of today's trans-ocean races.

The system consists of a self-contained unit which can be mounted on deck as it is fully waterproof. In size it is no larger than a briefcase. The system has its own batteries with a life of over three months, in fact, under normal conditions the sailor can simply fit it and forget it. Inside the case is a sensor continually monitoring air temperature and pressure, which information is automatically transmitted to tracking satellites. In the context of a yacht's safety it is not the contents of the message that is important but the position of the transmitter.

The receiving satellite is moving in a known orbit and as it monitors the signal from the onboard unit, it records the frequency change as it passes. This frequency change gives, on the Dopler shift principle, the position of the transmitter and hence the yacht. Thus, computers can receive information from the satellites which allows them to keep an accurate track of the vessels.

If the yacht capsizes the signal will stop as the aerial is transmitting only downwards; alternatively, if the yachtsman manages to recover the unit and requires immediate assistance, there is a panic button on the case. Either way the computer recognizes an anomaly and prints out a warning giving, of course, all the details of the known position of the yacht.

So this is the most important survival aid to date as it indicates the two most vital factors in any accident: first, that the worst has happened and, second, where it has happened.

*EPIRB and marine distress beacons.* The emergency position-indicating radio beacon is an emergency radio transmitting on 121.5 megacycles, the aircraft distress frequency. This unit, which has been responsible for several rescue operations, is most useful in the North Atlantic owing to the density of the air routes. Most units are self-contained and require only the erection or streaming of an aerial and a push on the 'go' button.

The marine beacon is a similar unit but transmits on the marine distress frequency, 2182 megacycles. The signal from such a unit will trigger an automatic alarm on all merchant vessels. The problem is that it has only a limited range, which means that unless a ship is within a radius of about 20 miles – a rare occurrence in mid-ocean – no one will receive the distress call.

*Liferaft.* An absolutely essential piece of equipment. There are several standards of liferaft available. One should specify a raft with two air-chambers, a double floor and the offshore emergency pack (referred to as an E-pack in the UK). This specification is more expensive and heavier than the inshore equipment, but the race rules for most offshore races now require, quite rightly, that an E-pack be carried.

The raft should be stowed where it can be reached when the multihull is upside down. Probably the best place is on the aft face of the aft crossbeam close to the centre of the vessel. It is out of the way of waves and can still be reached if the boat is the right way up.

When *Boatfile* capsized (see previous chapter) it was one of those rare occasions when the inverted multihull started to break and sink, so the liferaft, as the last resort, was inflated. Unfortunately one of the lashings caught round the raft, preventing it from inflating fully. In a case like this the reserve $CO_2$ pressure simpy blows out of the release valve leaving a soft raft. The raft then began to break up from the onslaught of the waves before the crew could pump it up. Luckily their EPIRB had alerted a commercial aircraft and an RAF Nimrod was soon on the scene to drop a new liferaft.

*Flares.* An obvious requirement. I suggest at least 12 parachute flares and 12 hand-held flares, plus six orange smoke flares for daylight.

*Survival suit.* As will be seen shortly it may be necessary to live in a very wet environment inside the upturned vessel. Certainly one will be underwater a good deal of the time and so a survival suit is essential. The suit is designed to be completely air- and watertight, usually encloses the feet with seals at the wrists and neck or face. Even if put on over wet clothing the suit will maintain the body at a reasonable temperature as evaporation and wind chill are prevented.

*Cut-out kit.* Of prime necessity is some method of entering and leaving the capsized vessel safely. With cruising and older racing multihulls this can be achieved via a hatch fitted underneath the bridge deck (see fig. 83). Today's modern offshore multihulls will have no convenient place to mount such a hatch. The opening has to be as low in the boat as possible so that it is clear of the water when upside down, and yet a hatch obviously

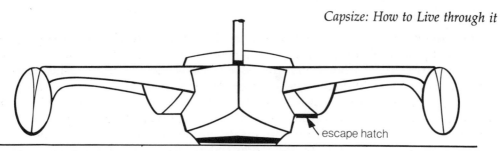

escape hatch

**Fig 83** *Escape hatch arrangement on older trimarans or cruising catamarans*

cannot be fitted below the water-line for normal sailing. For this reason I favour an efficient cut-out kit with which to attack the bilge. The traditional axe may still be suitable for a wooden vessel but a drill and saw are better for composite or alloy boats. At least two kits (one inside and one outside for cutting composites. Two kits should be carried, one inside and one outside the hull, both stowed in accessible places. (One cannot rely for access and egress on the main hatch. It will be underwater and those who have dived in and out report it as frightening and dangerous.)

*Harnesses.* Conventional safety equipment for any yacht and with two particularly important aspects for fast multihulls. The safety lines for the harness hook must be positioned in a way that prevents a man going into the water should he fall. (Care must be taken in choosing the length of the actual harness line as well). Also vitally important in the context of a capsize is the need for the harness to attach a crewman to the smooth, slippery surface of the underneath of a multihull. Towards this end there should be sufficient attachment points under the bridge deck (if one exists) or under the crossbeams.

Several capsize survivors have complained of the difficulty of hanging on to an upturned vessel.

*A torch.* After a capsize the lights will probably go out so keep a torch handy.

*Radar reflector and bright paint.* An upside down vessel is very difficult to see as it is low in the water and almost wave shaped. If a radar reflector can be rigged on the bottom of the hull, preferably held aloft on a boat hook or some other item of equipment, the situation will be enormously improved.

For the same reason, a brightly painted underside – not white – will help to make the yacht visible in the waves.

One cannot emphasize enough the importance of tying all the safety equipment down securely; survivors have lost vital gear which has fallen from the boat on capsize, washed out of the upturned hulls or carried away by the considerable surge of water that builds up. Also all gear that needs to be kept dry during a capsize should be stowed low in the boat and secured so it will not fall in the water when upside down. This is vital.

## Post capsize action

*Trimarans.* Immediately after a capsize the crew will be either inside or outside the main hull. If outside they will, hopefully, be hooked on – and here a harness with a hook at the body end obviously becomes essential. The danger of being trapped under the main hull,

267

in the cockpit or under the netting and being unable to reach the harness-to-yacht attachment point is obviously very high. In general one is safer below during a capsize. Chay Blyth was on deck when *GB 111* turned over and he momentarily considered leaping below, but decided he'd prefer to be on deck. The result was nearly an hour in freezing water unable to cling on properly to the bottom of the hull – rescue was close at hand in his case but in mid-ocean down below would be a better place from which to begin the survival exercise. Therefore, if caught outside, it must be possible to get into the hull either via the escape hatch or by the more modern idea of cut-out (or in this case the second 'cut-in') tools.

If down below the crew will find that the hulls settle down quickly as the main hull fills with water. The final stable position will depend on the position and buoyancy of the crossbeams and floats. In a trimaran with standing headroom in the main hull the inverted water-line will settle at a point between thigh and waist level depending on design. At this moment the floats and crossbeams will be supporting the whole weight of the vessel, and there is no danger in removing a skin fitting (log, echo sounder, sink drain etc) from the main hull. One may initially feel that this might release a supporting build up of air in the main hull. This is not so. At any rate, it is a good idea to improve the fresh air situation below. (Any water coming in via this source would not continue to fill the boat up, the same level will be maintained provided that the main hatch is open. On the other hand, if the main hatch could be closed and made sufficiently watertight, water could be pumped out; but most main hatches will not serve this purpose.)

At this juncture, gear will be floating and banging about everywhere; every attempt must be made to secure safety items and any other equipment that may cause a hazard. If the batteries are immersed and they are not of the sealed variety it is as well to dump them as soon as possible.

Having located and saved all equipment which can be stowed in the high spots (under the bunks and chart table, for instance), the next move is to don a survival suit. While the cold may force one to get into the survival suit immediately on immersion, it is obviously better, if one can bear it, to consolidate one's position, and in particular to save gear.

The EPIRB can be activated with the antenna up through a skin fitting aperture in the roof. Once that is bleeping it is time to tackle the task of cutting a hatch in the bilge of the hull. The best place to cut should have been marked previously after discussion with the designer. This would simply make the decision of where to attack so much easier. A hole 18ins by 12ins should be made first by drilling and then sawing. The cut-out kit will, of course, have been stowed low down in the yacht so it is now high up and ready to hand. The drill should have been stowed already fitted with the correct drill. The saw will need to be tungsten bladed to cope with a modern composite construction; such saws are readily available in hardware stores.

Once the hole has been cut in the hull it will be possible to keep a look out and go about the business of preparing the vessel below so that a more or less normal existence on board can be conducted.

Here two facts are worth mentioning:

(i) *Do not get into the liferaft.* As long as the wreck stays afloat it will afford much better shelter – and chance of visual discovery – than a raft. It is very unlikely that the vessel will sink. Having said that, it must be noted that a water-logged multihull upside down will experience far greater structural strains than when sailing normally. If the weather continues to be extreme the vessel could break up. Of course, in this case, the liferaft – and as much safety gear, food and water as possible – are the last resort. But the rule is 'Never get into the raft until you are sure the vessel is sinking'. Employing the raft and tying it to the hulls just in case is a bad idea as it will most likely be washed away, with or without you on board, by the first big wave.

(ii) *You will not be able to right your boat.* Despite all sorts of experiments in ideal conditions – some successful, some not – no one has yet righted a racing multihull after a capsize in anger and it is my view that no one ever will. I have seen all sorts of arguments and formulae that prove it is possible but ask anyone who races offshore and has seen a gale and the seas it leaves behind and the answer is *impossible*! The only conceivable exception is a cruising multihull designed not for racing but for self-righting. So, forget it, settle down, organize life down below, keep a good lookout and your spirits up.

To organize life down below it is essential to make a living area above water. This should be prepared for in advance. The way we went about it on *Colt Cars GB* is as follows.

Two shelves are fitted low down in the bunk area. On top of these one can stow everyday gear in normal circumstances. Underneath the shelves we lashed the cut-out kit and some safety gear so that, in the event of a capsize; it would not even get wet. The tube and canvas bunks have two positions: the conventional and a second attachment point so that they are high up after a capsize. (See fig. 84.) The escape cut-out would be aft of the bunk area and I would do what Phil Weld did when *Gulf Streamer* went over; fix a catwalk by which I could get off the new bunk position to the hatch without getting wet.

Once organized it is necessary to sit back and wait. The EPIRB will, hopefully, be attracting aircraft and the marine distress beacon can be activated as well. The former will have the greater chance of success especially if you are out of shipping lanes but every attempt must be made to attract a stray ship as well. Towards this end it is necessary to

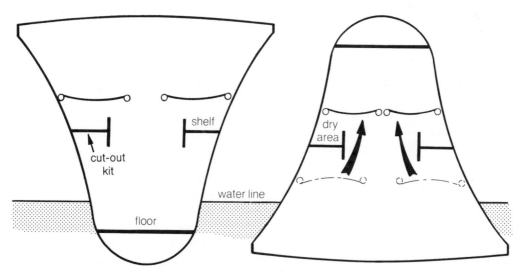

**Fig 84** *A way of keeping dry after a capsize*

keep a lookout so that flares may be deployed at any time. From previous experience gained by those unfortunate enough to have been turned over several facts emerge.

1. Don't expect to be spotted by the first ship you see – the ninth ship is the record worst.
2. Flares will not be seen easily during the day – use smoke signals.
3. When a ship passes at night it always appears to slow down and alter course. It may not actually be doing so.
4. A watch keeper on a merchant ship is quite likely to be looking at a chart, making tea or reading a book at the second your flare goes up – another possible disappointment.
5. Anyone on the deck of a ship will always lean over the lee rail, hence a ship passing you to windward has a better chance of seeing a flare than one passing to leeward.
6. Although a ship in mid-ocean will not be using its radar it *will* be switched on if the watch keeper thinks he sees a flare. So mount your radar reflecter outside the hulls somehow.
7. All radio officers on large ships keep an automatic alarm watch on 2182m htz. Bearing in mind that the range of 2182 emergency beacons is small, it may pay to save transmission until a ship is seen.

*Catamarans.* Many of the previous points also apply to catamarans. They however, do have a special problem in that the only reserve of buoyancy is in the crossbeams. What buoyancy there is may not be sufficient to support the weight of the craft unless the construction material itself has buoyant properties.

Very little information is to hand on catamarans – other than the cruising type which are more similar, with regard to inverted buoyancy characteristics, to trimarans. The racer, with accomodation in each hull and no bridge deck, will only be tenable upside down if each float has watertight compartments at bow and stern. Even so the vessel will probably float lower than a trimaran, but providing it does float, the previous arguments apply.

# 17

## Self-Steering

The majority of races in which multihulls take part are for single-handed and two-handed entries; hence the importance of a good self-steering gear is paramount. Single-handed races have been won in vessels without self-steering but never in multihulls without self-steering. It is very difficult, if not impossible, to get a modern multihull to sail with no steering aid whatsoever. Even to windward, I have found that the only way to balance the boat so that the helm can be left to itself is to reduce sail severely. This will not do in a race. There are two reliable self-steering systems: a windvane and an electric autopilot.

*Windvanes.* All early self-steering systems were wind powered and they are still common today. This type of gear is totally self-sufficient. They get their power from the motion of the yacht through the water. There are numerous designs afloat, a lot home made, which fall mainly into the following categories:
1. A windvane connected straight to the yacht's tiller.
2. A windvane connected to a trim tab on the aft edge of the rudder.
3. A windvane and servo oar influencing the yacht's rudder.
4. A windvane and servo oar influencing the rudder of the self-steering gear.
Unfortunately, this sort of arrangement does not work very effectively on a fast multihull. The one advantage the windvane possesses – the ability to keep the yacht at a constant angle to the apparent wind – is its Achilles' heel on a very fast boat, as can be illustrated by an example.

A multihull is sailing at a speed of 10 knots, 45 degrees to the true wind. The apparent wind speed is 23 knots and the apparent wind angle is 27.25 degrees. The windvane is set up in line with the apparent wind and the self-steering gear activated. Then a wave knocks the bow so that the yacht is sailing 60 degrees to the true wind and immediately it picks up speed. Very soon it is sailing at 14 knots and the apparent wind has barely changed – it's now reading 31 degrees. So the boat is now 15 degrees off course, yet the apparent wind has only altered 3.75 degrees, not enough to move the windvane sufficiently for it to restore the vessel to the correct course. (These figures are taken from Table 12.)

Wind vanes have not been in use on multihulls since about 1976 when smaller, lighter, and power-efficient autopilots were developed as a better alternative.

## Autopilots

An electric autopilot steers a yacht on a steady compass course regardless of wind direction. The pilot consists of a compass and a motor drive unit. Either the course to be steered is set at the dial on the compass unit or it is automatically taken as the course the yacht was on when the pilot was switched on. Any alteration to the yachts heading is picked up electronically and the signal given to the motor drive to act on the main tiller or wheel to restore course. Thus a steady compass course is maintained while the crew trim sails to match any change in wind direction.

Sailing to windward effectively is achieved by setting the compass course on the autopilot so that the angle to the apparent wind is correct. Any change in wind direction must be compensated for by making hand alterations to the autopilot control.

Autopilots are now so small and light and use so little electric power that they are the ideal solution for modern multihulls. There are several systems to choose from.

*Autopilot to tiller direct.* This is the simplest arrangement. The compass control unit asks for power to be supplied to the main steering by way of a linear motor, driving a push/pull arm attached directly to the tiller. Fig. 85 shows a typical arrangement. Power consumption could be as little as $\frac{1}{2}$ amp at 12 volts for a small unit (multis up to 50ft), up to 2 amps at 12 volts for larger craft.

*Autopilot to wheel.* In this case the motor drive rotates and, by way of a belt linkage, turns the wheel. The control will be much the same as the one above (see fig. 86). Again, for multihulls under 50ft a small unit with low power consumption can be employed. However, if the steering is too heavy, difficulty may be encountered with the belt drive system. In this case a more substantial unit using a chain drive to a cog attached to the steering linkage can be employed, but with consequent power penalty.

*Autopilot to trim tab.* A clever way to steer a large multihull with a low-power autopilot is to use the pilot so that it activates a trim tab on the back of the rudder. The trim tab in turn

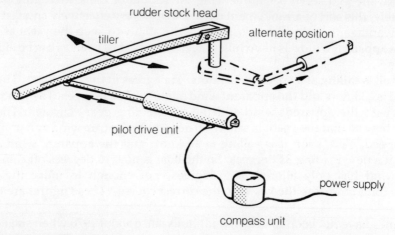

**Fig 85** *An autopilot to tiller system*

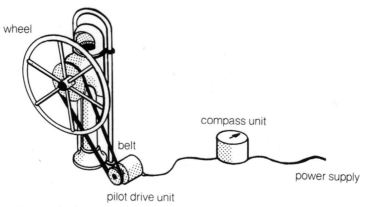

wheel

compass unit

belt

power supply

pilot drive unit

**Fig 86** *An autopliot to wheel system*

works the rudder. The ingenious part of this system – designed by John Shuttleworth for *Brittany Ferries GB* – is in the way the trim tab, and the yachts motion through the water, provide a servo effect. The faster the yacht travels, the greater the servo, which nicely matches the extra steering power required. The system has been described in an earlier chapter (fig.10). It was very effective at all speeds and the only criticism against it can be its vulnerability to sternway. *Brittany Ferries* damaged her tab linkage when she was knocked backwards by a wave. She had been caught in irons when put about by an unlit yacht off Ushant on the first night of the 1982 Route du Rhum. The damage caused by the lack of a stop on the tab put Chay Blyth out of the race.

It is very important for a multihull sailor to get used to using an autopilot. The unit maintains a steady compass course so the heading never has to be checked; instead, the trim of the sails must be constantly monitored. When close-hauled, trim the sails for effective beating and then fine tune the autopilot, freeing off a couple of degrees when the sails lift and squeezing up if the speed increases too much. After a while the yacht can be made to go to windward very well just by constant and very fine adjustments at the control unit.

# 18

## Future Trends

The modern multihull has reached a plateau of design in both hull shape and rig. There are, of course, small improvements to be made in both areas; for instance, *Colt Cars GB* gained through having a finer than normal bow section and a really up-to-date but conventional rig. Still, it seems now there are no major leaps forward to be made while following traditional lines. The two areas in which possible gains are to be made are certainly not traditional. One is wing masts and the other hydrofoils.

### Wing masts

As there are no rules governing a multihull rig, anything goes in an attempt to get more lift for less drag. There must be a more efficient mechanism for drive than soft sails. After all, aeroplanes gave up cloth wings years ago. The answer is solid sails: either a symmetrical wing with a soft trailing edge (fig. 87) or a completely solid articulating wing. Both systems have been tried with varying degrees of success on small mulithulls. In general, the results have been favourable, so how could the ideas be applied to larger yachts?

The completely solid articulating wing is so obviously impractical that in the foreseeable future it need not be considered. It could not be reefed or even lowered, in a gale or in port, which could create some intriguing problems! Apart from that, the weight of the rig would be prohibitive, even given today's sophisticated construction materials.

The part wing, part soft sail is altogether a more realistic option. This type of rig has been tried on Phil Weld's *Rogue Wave*, Mark Pajot's *Elf Aquitaine* and Eric Tabarly's *Paul Ricard*.

The mast tried on *Rogue Wave* was built from wood and epoxy and early reports indicate a knot or more speed than before when she was 'in-the-groove'. However, 'out-of-the-groove' the speed loss was as much as 4 knots. The difficulty lies in keeping the mast at the perfect angle to the wind for maximum efficiency. These problems are compounded by the yacht's inevitable pitching, continually causing small alterations in apparent wind angle.

Pajot's wing mast is carbon fibre and about 2ft fore and aft and is 8ins thick – more like an aerodynamic normal mast than a full wing. This option which has proved successful is

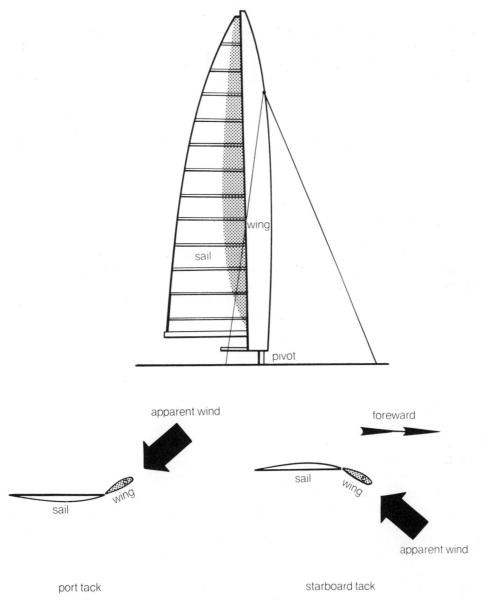

**Fig 87** *A wing and sail*

easier to keep at the correct trim and at full power, and is probably the stepping-stone required to larger wings.

In my view the biggest disadvantage in a wing mast is its complete lack of twist. Perhaps the most sensible way to employ a wing rig would be to incorporate a jib for light airs, then go straight to wing and main alone as the wind increases. Both with or without the jib the main should twist to allow for the varying angle of apparent wind. With a small wing the soft sail can be twisted off behind it; with a larger wing one is stuck with a straight, or parallel leading edge.

I believe that the next move to precipitate the 'day of the wing rig' will only come when a wing mast is designed in such a way that twisting off to leeward at the head can be induced on both tacks.

A wing rig was designed for *Colt Cars GB* by Adrian Thompson (fig. 88). This rig is higher, stiffer, has a greater compressive strength, a lower centre of gravity and is a more efficient shape than the rig it will replace. At the same time the effective sail area is increased.

## Hydrofoils

While the development of wing masts will be pursued in the hope of achieving more lift for less drag aloft, a similar movement will be afoot underwater, with hydrofoils.

In the multihull concept there are two ways of looking at foil assistance: as an aid to stability in trimarans (i.e. to double up the job of the outrigger); and as a total lifting device to project the whole vessel clear of the water.

Considerable work has been done already on the former idea. Eric Tabarly produced *Pen Duick VII* in 1979; she was a 56ft trimaran with a wing mast, small floats and fixed,

*A well-developed conventional multihull which will benefit from the addition of hydrofoils fitted in line with the forward beam and outside the float.*

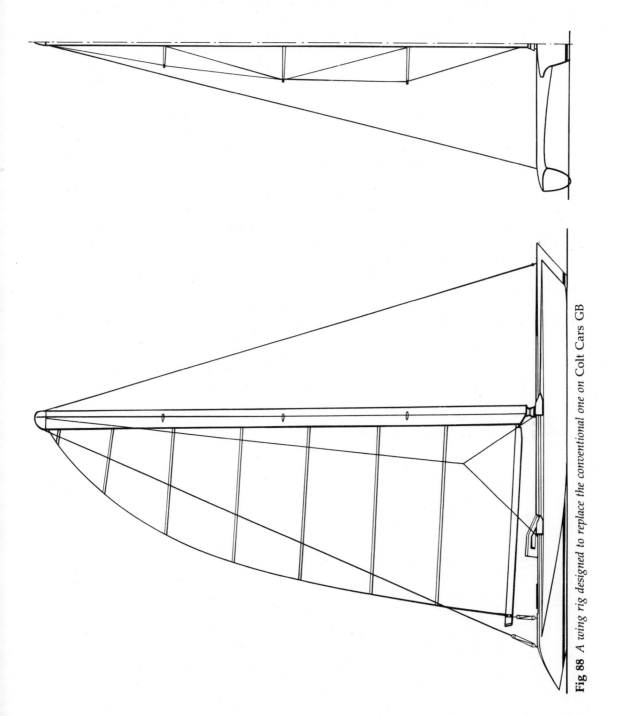

Fig 88 *A wing rig designed to replace the conventional one on* Colt Cars GB

straight foils, inclined at a 45 degree angle inwards under each float. In most people's hands she would have been a liability; her floats were so small that she had very little stability in a static condition, making survival in heavy weather a matter of keeping up speed and hence hydrofoil lift. Stopping in a gale would have been disastrous. She took part in the 1979 Round Bermuda Race and proved to be quite a lot slower than the conventional trimaran that beat her. Her wing mast was then removed but the foils remained. Other than setting up an Atlantic record – since beaten by *Elf Aquitaine* – she has not really shone. Her problem is probably one of overweight; initially she relied on her foils for lateral resistance but as this didn't work too well, two asymmetrical centreboards – and a lot more weight – were added.

Apart from *Pen Duick* there were several other foil-assisted vessels in the 1981 Atlantic race. None managed to complete the course so nothing new was learnt about their performances. It was noticeable, though, during the windy, first day of the race, how much less the foilers pitched . . . interesting.

There are several ways of arranging foil stabilization. Fig. 89 illustrates the following:

(i) *Straight fixed*. As in *Pen Duick VII*. This foil is relatively light as it requires no mechanism. However, the leeward foil is always down, even in light airs when it can only be a drag, and the windward one creates windage.

(ii) *Inverted T fixed*. As in *Gautier 111*. This foil is at a more efficient angle than the above but suffers the same disadvantages.

(iii) *Straight pivoting*. As fitted to *Royale*. The advantage in this system is the ability to retract the foils in light airs and also to stow the windward one in such a way that its windage is reduced. The disadvantages are several: the foil is surface piercing, which creates a lot of wash and spray, and hence drag; and the high weight involved in the pivoting mechanism. This system could be improved by pivoting the foil over and down outside the float. This would lengthen the righting arm and hence a smaller foil could be used.

Completely foil-borne vessels do exist (Fig. 89(4)); but in terms offshore multihulls, their days of glory are still a long way off.

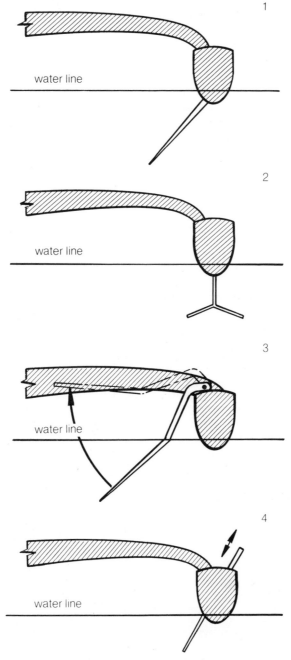

1

water line

2

water line

3

water line

4

water line

**Fig 89** *Foil stabilization on a trimaran*